BACKYARD BIRD GUIDES

PETERSON
FIELD GUIDES ™

BIRD WATCHER'S
DIGEST ®

Hummingbirds
and Butterflies

Hummingbirds
and Butterflies

Bill Thompson III
and Connie Toops

HOUGHTON MIFFLIN HARCOURT PUBLISHING COMPANY
BOSTON   NEW YORK   2011

Copyright © 2011 by *Bird Watcher's Digest*

For information about permission to reproduce selections from this book, write to Permissions, Houghton Mifflin Harcourt Publishing Company, 215 Park Avenue South, New York, New York 10003.

www.hmhbooks.com

Library of Congress Cataloging-in-Publication Data is available.

ISBN 978-0-618-90445-7

Book design by George Restrepo
Printed in China

SCP   10 9 8 7 6 5 4 3 2 1

The legacy of America's greatest naturalist and creator of the field guide series, Roger Tory Peterson, is kept alive through the dedicated work of the Roger Tory Peterson Institute of Natural History (RTPI). Established in 1985, RTPI is located in Peterson's hometown of Jamestown, New York, near the Chautauqua Institution in the southwestern part of the state.

Today, RTPI is a national center for nature education that maintains, shares, and interprets Peterson's extraordinary archive of writings, art, and photography. The institute, housed in a landmark building by the world-class architect Robert A. M. Stern, continues to transmit Peterson's zest for teaching about the natural world through leadership programs in teacher development, as well as outstanding exhibits of contemporary nature art, natural history, and the Peterson Collection.

Your participation as a steward of the Peterson Collection and supporter of the Peterson legacy is needed. Please consider joining RTPI at an introductory rate of 50 percent of the regular membership fee for the first year. Simply call RTPI's membership department at 800-758-6841 ext. 226, or e-mail membership@rtpi.org to take advantage of this special offer to purchasers of this book. For more information, please visit the Peterson Institute in person or virtually at www.rtpi.org.

For Bella, Adventure Joe, Buzz, and Rufus—four ruby-throated hummingbirds that lived in our home one summer and taught me so much about these amazing tiny creatures. And to Julie, who became their mom until they were ready to leave the "nest."
                                            —Bill Thompson III

To Pat, who keeps the flowers blooming and the home fires burning.
                                            —Connie Toops

Contents

Chapter 14: Butterfly Species Profiles

Acknowledgments

I AM GRATEFUL TO SO MANY PEOPLE who helped with not just this book but with every single bit of bird content I've ever produced. However, for brevity's sake, I'd better just stick with this book.

Foremost among the people to whom I owe a debt of gratitude is my coauthor Connie Toops. Connie is a true professional, a consummate writer and photographer, and a stickler for getting it right—something sometimes sorely lacking in me. Without her organizational skills, drive, and artfully applied energy, I'd still be sitting at my desk looking at a cursor blinking on a computer screen inside a document that said "Chapter 1" and nothing else.

Connie and I were assisted greatly in our content refinement in various ways by Pat Sutton, Julie Zickefoose, Geoff Heeter, and Melanie Singer. I am especially grateful to hummingbird maven Sheri Williamson for her input on the manuscript.

The photographers who supplied us with their fine images deserve a hearty helping of thanks: Robert McCaw, Charles W. Melton, Maslowski Wildlife Productions, Julie Zickefoose, Connie Toops, Dr. Hugh P. Smith, and Richard and Susan Day.

The peerless team at Houghton Mifflin Harcourt made this project possible and brought it to fruition, making us look even wiser and more articulate than is deserved. They are Lisa A. White, Beth Burleigh Fuller, Katrina Kruse, Brian Moore, Tim Mudie, Elizabeth Pierson, and Taryn Roeder.

Keeping the lamps lit at *Bird Watcher's Digest* while I was off tapping at my computer was the special work of Jim Cirigliano, Claire Mullen, Andy Thompson, Ann Kerenyi, Laura Fulton, Chris Blondel, Katherine Koch, Susan Hill, Helen Neuberger, and Kimi Carroll.

To my unbelievably talented and knowledgeable wife, Julie Zickefoose, I owe much of my basic natural history know-how. Thanks, Zick! You are a wonder! To Phoebe and Liam, our children, thanks for being so willing to share me with these book projects. You two keep me grounded.

Finally, I'd like to thank you (and others like you) for buying and reading books (including mine). Without readers there would be no authors. I really like being an author—in fact, it was a dream of mine from long ago. Thank you for helping to make this dream come true again for me.

—BILL THOMPSON III
Whipple, Ohio
September 2010

MY PROFOUND THANKS GO TO BILL THOMPSON III for asking me to join this venture and for his cheerful outlook on life throughout the years we have shared birding and nature observations. Bill has the enviable ability to see birds, hear birds, photograph birds, and share birds' natural history highlights with those around him—always doing this with characteristic grace, wit, and charm. It's a joy to know Bill and witness the deep-seated love for birds he embodies. It's an honor to coauthor this book with him.

Thanks also to Pat Sutton—author, avid butterfly gardener, and environmental educator—who carefully reviewed sections of this book. Pat contributed a wealth of knowledge and enthusiasm to this project. I gratefully acknowledge the contributions of Jeff Caldwell, horticulturalist and butterfly expert from Santa Clara Valley, California, and Denise Gibbs of Gaithersburg, Maryland, a naturalist, former native plant nursery owner, and dedicated butterfly watcher for more than three decades.

To Richard and Susan Day, Fred and Sandy Dayhoff, and Hugh and Sue Smith, thank you more than words can express for your lifelong advocacy for wildlife and for the wonderful conversations about nature and life we have shared over the years. Knowing each of you is a great pleasure!

Two decades ago, Curt and Anna Reemsnyder invited me to observe and photograph in their yard as openly as they welcomed hummingbirds and butterflies. I am awed by their dedication in turning "secondhand land" into a wildlife haven and grateful for their continuing friendship. Tom Pawlesh has likewise shared interests in photography, hummingbirds, and butterflies for years. Thanks to Tom and his wife, Marina, for hosting me at their home and recounting their wildlife experiences.

I also appreciate the input of butterfly enthusiasts Jim and Dotti Becker, Goodwin Creek Gardens, Williams, Oregon; David and Jan Dauphin of Mission, Texas; and Kazz Workizer, Kazzam Nature Center, Patagonia, Arizona.

To friends Ken and Linda Kerr, Bob and Pat Momich, Nancy Scholl, and Bill and Barbara Weber, for whom the wonders of nature have always been an inspiration, thanks for your help and encouragement! And to Karol Kavaya, thank you for helping me see butterflies from a new perspective and for laughter on winter days when the butterflies weren't flying.

Kudos to all the volunteers who have contributed to the very help-ful North American Butterfly Association (NABA) website, and to Ann Ryan and the talented team at Monarch Watch. Their websites provide a wealth of information and their educational program is su-perb. Thanks also to the good folks at the Madison County Library, Marshall, North Carolina, for always having a computer with a broad-band connection when I needed it.

Last and most significantly, to my life partner, Pat Toops: You made this possible. Now let's go watch some wildlife together!

— Connie Toops
Marshall, North Carolina
September 2010

Introduction

WELCOME TO THE BUZZING and beautiful world of hummingbirds and butterflies. These two types of creatures may not be related taxonomically; after all, hummingbirds are birds, and butterflies are insects. But to those of us who love them, they are related in several ways. Hummingbirds and butterflies are experts at flying, they can be quite colorful in appearance, and they are easily attracted to our yards, gardens, and even our patios and windowsills.

This book will help you enhance your enjoyment of hummingbirds and butterflies, no matter where you live in North America. We will guide you along the path to attracting more of these delightful creatures and to identifying them when you see them.

My coauthor for this book is Connie Toops, a lifelong naturalist, knowledgeable gardener, talented photographer, and the author of many books and articles on natural history topics. Connie has a special interest in gardening for wildlife, so she was the perfect coauthor for this project. Connie wrote the text for all of the butterfly chapters, as well as the chapters "Plants for Hummingbirds" and "A Hummer Garden Plan." She also contributed many of the photographs in the book.

I wrote all of the hummingbird chapters as well as some of the front and back matter of the book.

We hope you'll enjoy *Hummingbirds and Butterflies,* which we're proud to contribute as a volume in the legendary Peterson Field Guide series.

—BILL THOMPSON III

Hummingbirds

Chapter 1: What Is a Hummingbird?

A MALE ruby-throated hummingbird visiting a hibiscus flower for nectar.

HUMMINGBIRD. Even the name hints at the mystery of this amazing feathered creature. The name "hummingbird" was inspired by the humming sound the wings make, flapping as they do at speeds as fast as 80 to 100 beats per second. Think of that! In the time it takes you to blink your eyes, a hummingbird's wings go down and up as many as 100 times. A medium-sized hummingbird flying under normal conditions probably beats its wings about 50 beats per second. Even the largest, heaviest hummingbirds beat their wings about 10 beats per second—still a remarkable speed record. It's no wonder the wings emit a hum as they slice through the air.

This high rate of wing beating permits hummingbirds to defy gravity in some unique and incredible ways. They can zip along at a high rate of speed and stop on a dime, they can hover in place, they can perform incredible loops and spirals, and most amazing of all, they can fly backward. They are the only creatures in the entire class of birds that can do this.

Hummingbirds are unique to the New World, that is, the Western

MALE HUMMINGBIRDS *can flash their gorget feathers when the sunlight catches them at exactly the right angle. This is a male Anna's hummingbird.*

Hemisphere of the globe. Those of us who live in North, Central, and South America can thumb our noses at our unlucky friends in Europe, Asia, and Africa: we have *all* of the 330-plus species of hummingbirds in the world. They have none. Before we get too proud of ourselves here in North America (at least in those parts north of the U.S.-Mexico border), we should remember that we have only about 19 regularly occurring hummer species in the U.S. and Canada, and of these only about 8 species are widespread breeding birds. To get into the big numbers of hummer diversity, you need to be near the equator. The true bragging rights for most hummingbirds go to Ecuador and Brazil, each of which has about half the total number of hummingbird species breeding within its borders.

"Small," "colorful," "insectlike," "pugnacious," "built for speed," and "hyperactive" are all terms that can be used to describe hummingbirds. Here are some reasons why these words apply. The very smallest bird in the world is the bee hummingbird of Cuba, which measures a diminutive 2 inches from bill tip to tail tip. The largest hummingbird in the world, the appropriately named giant hummingbird, is just 8¼ inches long. To put this "giant" in perspective, an American robin is 10 inches long.

There are not too many birds that can blow your mind with a blast of color the way many adult male hummingbirds can. Their throat patches, or gorgets, are covered in iridescent feathers, which when struck by direct sunlight can look like sparkling jewels. The males use these flashy feathers to communicate with females and rival males.

When hummingbirds zip from flower to flower, hover briefly, then zip off with a buzz of wings, it's easy to see why so many people confuse hummingbirds with insects. In fact, there are several species of large nectar-drinking moths that look so similar to hummingbirds that they are called hummingbird moths. In Chapter 2 I'll tell you how to tell the hummers apart from the moths, but here's a hint to get you started: hummingbirds don't have antennae.

Why do I say that hummingbirds are pugnacious and hyperactive? Watch hummingbirds interact at a busy feeding station, and you

might be surprised at the level of aggression they exhibit. Antagonists fly at one another, chattering and buzzing, sometimes even colliding with such force that you can hear their bodies smack together. All this aggression and energy is fueled by their diet, which is primarily sugar-rich plant nectar and protein-rich insects. On a normal day of feeding, a hummingbird will consume food equaling more than its body weight. By contrast, we humans consume less than 1 percent of our weight each day. Hummers have a metabolism that rapidly turns food into energy, and they burn that energy up in foraging, flying, and surviving.

THESE RUFOUS hummingbirds are fighting for access to nectar at a feeder port.

But this is merely scratching the surface of what a hummingbird is. Let's take a closer look at the natural history of our North American hummingbirds.

Hummingbird Life History

Inside an egg that is no larger than the eraser on a number 2 pencil, the beginnings of a new life are coalescing. In two weeks, during which the egg is incubated by the female that laid it, an embryo is changing into a tiny, curled-up hummingbird. Hatching from its shell with a stub of a bill and sparsely covered in thin black or gray down, the nestling hummingbird is a tiny, helpless thing. Its eyes are closed, and

THIS BROAD-TAILED hummingbird nest has two eggs in it, one of which has hatched.

it will rely on its female parent alone for food, shelter, and warmth as it grows.

The adult female leaves the nest throughout the day to forage for herself and her offspring, returning with a crop (a storage compartment in the esophogus) full of tiny protein-rich insects. She inserts her bill into that of a nestling and pumps the food into the youngster. This feeding and care continues for about three weeks, when the nestlings are feathered and ready to leave the nest. Once fledged, a young hummingbird continues to rely on its mother for supplemental feeding for a week or more.

As it grows, the young hummingbird, whether male or female, takes on the appearance of an adult female of its species. Young males will molt into their more colorful adult plumage by the following spring, though some may not complete this molt until early that summer.

Over the days and weeks after leaving the nest, a fledgling constantly makes short flights, gaining strength and improving its flying abilities. It also gains knowledge about foraging through trial and error, poking its bill into anything brightly colored and being rewarded with nectar when it finds the right blooming flower. By this time the young bird's mother may already be well into a second nesting cycle. Or if the young bird hatched in late summer, its mother may already have migrated. This is a crucial time in the life of all young birds, including hummingbirds. The period of adult care and supplemental feeding is over; it's time for the youngster to learn all the skills needed to survive on its own.

If it survives long enough to migrate, lives through the rigors of migration, avoids being eaten by a predator, and returns the following spring to the place where it was born, a hummingbird may be rewarded with a chance to find a mate and reproduce, passing its genes on to a new generation.

Fewer than 35 percent of all hummingbirds born in a breeding season will survive until the following breeding season (and some studies show even lower survival rates). Those that make it back home to breed are both lucky and smart—and the very lucky and smart birds may live as long as four or five years. Longevity records for wild hummingbirds are up to 10 to 12 years old for some species, but these are the exceptions.

The leading cause of hummingbird mortality is probably migration. Unlike other bird species that migrate in flocks or family groups,

THESE RUBY-THROATED hummingbird nestlings will leave the nest (fledge) about three weeks after hatching.

hummingbirds go it alone. A young hummer born in June in Ohio has a few months or less to figure out life before it must embark on the longest trip of its life, without guidance, without a map, all alone.

HUMMINGBIRD MIGRATION

Migration is about food and survival. Nearly all of our North American hummingbird species migrate seasonally, and for many this means the traditional migration patterns: north in the spring, south in the fall. But a closer look reveals a more complex reality. The Anna's hummingbird is resident year-round in much of its range along the Pacific Coast, but after breeding, this species may move up to higher-elevation mountain meadows to take advantage of bountiful feeding on blooming flowers. In fall, when the mountain flowers are slowing down, the Anna's heads back to the coast to begin breeding again.

The Costa's hummingbird breeds in the desert washes of Arizona, California, and Nevada from January to May, then many Costa's head off to the north, south, or east once breeding is done. Buff-bellied hummingbirds nest in south Texas, and while most go south to Mexico in winter, some move up along the Texas coast and around the Gulf to spend the winter as far east as Florida.

Our other common hummer species depart from their breeding ranges in mid- to late summer and head to greener pastures for the winter. For most of them, this involves mitigrating south to Mexico or Central America. Many of these species' migrations describe a circular or oval route. Among our western hummingbirds, many rufous, Calliope, and some Allen's move north along the Pacific coastal lowlands and move south through the intermountain flyway.

HOW DO THEY KNOW WHEN TO GO?

When you take a bit of time to dig into the latest research about birds, you find that, really, we know so little about what makes them do what they do that it's almost funny. At one point the following things were generally accepted as facts:

- Hummingbirds (and their relatives the swifts) lack feet or have such weak feet that they cannot perch and thus are doomed to spend their entire lives on the wing, unable to land.

- Swallows burrow into the mud for the winter and emerge in the spring.

- If you don't take your feeders down in the fall, the hummingbirds won't know when to migrate.

A MALE ruby-throated hummingbird laps up nectar from a feeder.

All of these statements are false, but the last one has lingered on in bird-feeding lore for more than a century.

We do know that hummingbirds migrate when an inner urge prompts them to do so. It is thought (by ornithologists, who—thank heavens—are willing to study such things) that this inner urge is driven by changes in the intensity of daylight. As the summer begins to wane, subtle changes in the ratio of daylight and darkness occur, and these are perceived instinctively by hummingbirds (and other migrant birds too). This in turn triggers an increase in the hummers' appetites, which helps them put on fat reserves for the arduous migration ahead.

So it's not the weather turning colder, nor is it the leaves turning brown, or the start of the football season that makes hummingbirds want to migrate. It's instinct resulting from millions of years of evolution. No amount of sweet, fresh nectar in your feeders or gorgeous blooming flowers in your garden will keep a migrant hummingbird from leaving.

COURTSHIP

Hummingbird courtship can be an elaborate thing. Because no male hummingbirds have anything to do with nest building, incubation, or raising of young, they can put all of their energy and time into courting females. And they do it very well.

U-Shaped Courtship Display—

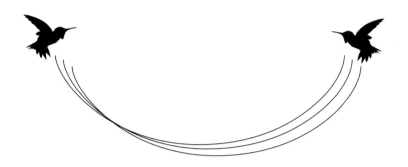

J-Shaped Courtship Display—

Oval Courtship Display—

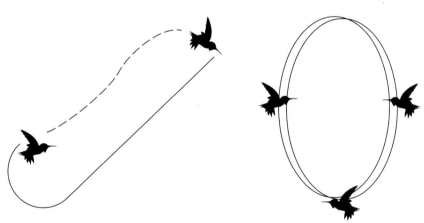

Shuttle Courtship Display—

DIAGRAMS OF *the four typical courtship flight patterns of male hummingbirds of North America: the U-shaped display, the J-shaped display, the oval display, and the back-and-forth shuttle display.*

Zipping high into the sky, a male will dive down in a long speedy arc, swooping past a perched female and flashing his gorget at her. If this is not enough, he may fly immediately in front of her in a series of short U-shaped swoops, chittering all the while and doing the requisite gorget flashing. Spooking a female into flight, a randy male will pursue her, trying his best to impress her as they zoom about at speeds of 25 to 30 miles per hour.

Once she acquiesces, she perches—often near her nest site. Their copulation is brief, lasting about two seconds. This completes the male's parental involvement. The female goes back to her nest site, perhaps to finish building the nest. She is the ultimate single parent.

NESTING

Adult females begin the nesting season by selecting a nest site and building the nest. Nest sites can vary widely. Many species choose a fork in a tree branch on which to anchor the nest. Most of the ruby-throated hummingbird nests I have found have been located in the crotch of a branch fork, with a large overhanging leaf that provides a kind of natural roof. Some western species seem to prefer to nest near human habitation, under eaves, on plant hooks, and even inside open outbuildings.

For building materials, female hummers use strands of spider web, fluffy plant fibers, and animal hair, which are layered together and formed into a tiny cup measuring about 2 inches across. The outside of the nest is usually camouflaged with bits of lichen, bark, leaves, or moss. To the unknowing eye, the nest looks like another bump or knot on a tree branch. I can't tell you how many times I have found a hummingbird nest, turned to alert a companion, and then found it nearly impossible to locate the nest again.

It's critical that the nest be concealed from the eyes of hungry predators, because as a single parent, the female will have to leave the nest regularly to forage for herself and her nestlings. For an interested bird watcher, a little patient observation is the best way to find a hummingbird nest. When you see a female hummingbird fly into the central part of a tree (as opposed to perching on an outer branch), watch closely. She may be returning to her nest. Watch where she goes inside the tree's leafy canopy and train your eyes (or better yet, your binoculars) on the spot where she seems to disappear. This disappearing act is a result of the female perching and ceasing to move or to beat her wings. This will be the nest site, and she will be settled down on top of the nest.

FEMALE HUMMINGBIRDS *get to do all of the nesting duties. This female black-chinned hummingbird is incubating eggs.*

Did You Know?

I could fill an entire book with "amazing facts" about hummingbirds because they are birds to which the adjective "amazing" very much applies. Here are just a few of the best ones.

MIGHTY MITES

Hummingbirds require proportionally more energy to live than any other warm-blooded animal. And they beat all other birds in these categories: the highest body temperature, the proportionally largest brain and heart, the fastest heart rate, and the fastest wingbeats.

SPEED

In normal direct flight, hummingbirds can fly as fast as 25 to 30 miles per hour. During the steep downward dives in a courtship flight, a male hummingbird may reach speeds of 60 miles per hour.

METABOLISM

Hummingbirds have such incredibly active metabolisms that they have to feed throughout the day in order to "keep their motors running."

FOOD INTAKE

It has been estimated that a hummingbird will visit as many as 1,000 individual flowers during a single day. In addition to consuming a lot of protein (i.e., insects), hummingbirds consume approximately 1.5 times their body weight in nectar daily. A human trying to match this rate of consumption would need to eat 60 times the amount of food we normally eat on a daily basis. We all get extra hungry from time to time, but could you handle 120 cheeseburgers in a day?

TORPOR

Hummingbirds have evolved the unusual ability to go into a hibernation-like state called torpor to help them survive cool temperatures and periods of inactivity, especially while sleeping at night. In torpor, a hummingbird's body temperature drops significantly, its heart rate slows, and its metabolism runs at a greatly reduced rate. This saves a hummingbird from burning up all of its energy and starving, because the metabolic rate of a torpid hummingbird is as little as 1/50th that of an active bird.

FEATHER COLOR

The brilliant iridescent colors on the heads and throats of many hummingbirds—especially males—are created structurally rather than by the color of the feathers themselves. The feathers contain tiny particles that reflect specific segments of the light spectrum. The colors we perceive when we look at these feathers are constantly changing along with the angle of the light striking them and being reflected to our eyes. The throat and crown of a male Anna's hummingbird can appear black, gray, or brilliant magenta depending on the angle of the light. Male hummingbirds benefit from this light-reflecting ability to send bright flashes of color out from their gorgets simply by flaring the throat feathers to catch the light at the perfect angle.

BEHAVIOR

Female hummingbirds hunting for nesting material will not only steal webbing from spider webs, they may also eat insects caught in the web and perhaps even eat the spider too! As if this weren't enough of a crime, females will steal nesting material from other nests being built nearby. I once watched a female blue-gray gnatcatcher building her nest out of material from a tent caterpillar web. A female ruby-throated hummingbird was also watching, and each time the gnatcatcher left her nest to get some more material, the female hummer would zip in and swipe a bill-full of nest material for her own nest about 70 feet away. The gnatcatcher never caught on, but she did seem to be annoyed that her nest was messier than she'd left it only seconds before.

HUMMINGBIRDS AND PLANTS

Hummingbirds and native plants have evolved together. Hummingbirds derive nectar from probing into plant blossoms, and in turn, plants have their pollen distributed by the hummingbirds. Botanists and evolutionary biologists have identified more than 150 native plants species that have evolved tube-shaped flowers that specifically accommodate the feeding methods of hummingbirds.

Myths Debunked

Myth: *Hummingbirds migrate on the backs of larger birds.*

Names

Among the more colorful names applied to some of the world's hummingbird species are azurecrown, blossomcrown, coquette, emerald, firecrown, helmetcrest, metaltail, plumeleteer, puffleg, rackettail, snowcap, spatuletail, starfrontlet, sunangel, sunbeam, sungem, sylph, topaz, trainbearer, velvetbreast, woodnymph, and woodstar. —BT

Reality: One of the most persistent myths in the world of birds is that hummingbirds migrate on the backs of larger, stronger birds. On the surface this might make sense, if one is willing to put one's brain in neutral and simply rely on one's natural ability to presume something is true. After all, hummingbirds are tiny little things. How could they possibly migrate over a long distance, overcoming enormous natural obstacles? Take the ruby-throated hummingbird, for example: It migrates south from the eastern United States and Canada, around the Gulf of Mexico, to spend the winter in the Neotropics. It's gotta have

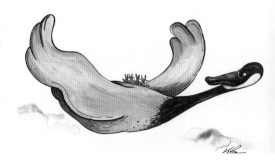

IT IS *a myth that hummingbirds hitch rides on geese or swans in order to survive migration.*

some kind of help, right? Poor little sprite. Well, that myth is so much horse hockey. Rubythroats make it on their own just fine by using some techniques that are not that different from those of other birds. They fatten up for the trip by eating large amounts over a period of days prior to migrating. They may also wait for favorable winds to help them along their route. But one thing they do not wait for is a friendly passing goose on which to hitch a ride.

Myth: *Hummingbirds feed only on red flowers.*
Reality: While it seems to be true that brightly colored flowers are more easily noticed by hummingbirds because their vision skews to the red, or "warm," part of the light spectrum, hummers will feed on flowers of any color as long as the blossoms contain nectar. In our garden, the rubythroats regularly feed on purple, pale blue, and yellow flowers. Bright red and orange, however, do seem to be the colors that most readily catch a passing hummingbird's eye.

Myth: *Nectar in feeders must include red dye to attract hummingbirds.*
Reality: Red dye in nectar in feeders is totally unnecessary. Most feeders have bright red parts, which will attract a curious, hungry hummer. If your feeder lacks red parts, hang a bright red artificial flower on the feeder, or a short piece of pink surveyor's tape, or a red bandana. Red dye is an unnecessary additive, and it may pose a health risk for hummingbirds that ingest a lot of it. My advice: say bye-bye to red dye.

WHILE RED and orange flowers seem to be most attractive, hummingbirds will visit nectar-producing flowers of any color. This male Costa's hummingbird is visiting the yellow flowers of bladderpod.

THERE IS absolutely no reason to use or make nectar with red food coloring in it. Most feeders have enough red parts to attract a hummingbird's attention.

Myth: *Hummingbirds must migrate to survive.*
Reality: This is true for many of our North American hummer species—they must migrate to habitats that have blooming flowers and active insects. But not all hummers migrate. Many Anna's hummingbirds are year-round residents along the Pacific Coast as far north as southwest Canada.

Myth: *Feeders have to be removed in fall to encourage hummers to migrate.*
Reality: Field studies and testing have shown that hummers migrate when an instinctive inner urge tells them to move. When this happens, nothing short of injury or illness will keep a hummingbird from migrating. But leaving your feeders up and filled in fall may help late migrants (often birds hatched that summer) refuel on their way south. Hummers that hang around feeders late into the fall are likely individuals that are sick or injured. Your feeders may help them survive and recover.

Myth: *Hummingbirds have no feet and can't perch.*
Reality: Do I really need to refute this one? Hummers have tiny feet and they do not walk well, but these feet work great for perching, and hummingbirds do a lot of perching while resting and digesting their food.

Myth: *Hummingbirds sip nectar through a strawlike tongue.*
Reality: Very few of us will ever get a close-up look at a hummingbird tongue, but you can take my word for it (and the word of scientists who study such things). Hummer tongues are shaped like a W with twin canals. The tip is forked with tiny featherlike edges, which work to lap up the nectar, which then moves up the grooves in the tongue toward the throat. Once the nectar is partway up the tongue, the bird pulls its tongue into its bill and moves the nectar into its throat with a licking motion.

Myth: *Nectar at feeders is better for hummers than nectar from plants.*
Reality: Naturally occurring flower nectar from native plants (along with small insects) is the mainstay of a healthy hummer diet. Nectar at feeders is an approximation of natural flower

nectar, just as fast-food burgers are an approximation of a home-cooked meal. We owe it to our hummingbirds to offer the nectar in the proper ratio (four parts water to one part sugar) and to keep our feeders clean. Even so, what we offer in our feeders is not a complete diet.

Myth: *Hummingbirds mate for life.*
Reality: Hummingbirds don't even mate for a minute. The male impresses a female sufficiently to earn a few seconds of copulation so he can fertilize her eggs, and that's it. We humans love to impose our views of "family values" onto creatures in nature, but things rarely work that way. And with hummers, the dads are all deadbeats and the moms are all single parents struggling to raise the family.

Myth: *Males have brightly colored feathers on the throat (gorget) and head.*
Reality: In reality, the feathers on a male hummingbird's throat, or gorget, are not brightly colored. Rather, they contain tiny light-reflecting particles in the structure of the feather. These particles catch light, absorbing some of it and reflecting other portions of the color spectrum. This reflection of light produces the brilliant colors we often see on the throats and heads of male hummingbirds.

Myth: *I have a family of hummingbirds visiting my feeders.*
Reality: This statement has a couple of problems. First of all, family units don't exist for long among hummingbirds, and they never include adult males, as we've learned. Females may supplement fledglings for a time, but it's not thought that they move around in a family unit, visiting feeders together.

Second, telling individual hummingbirds apart is nearly impossible for most of us. So how would we know how many and which individual hummers are visiting our feeders?

Hummingbird researchers working at busy feeding stations tell stories of catching individual hummingbirds in special (and very safe) cages for the purpose of banding, measuring, sexing, aging, and weighing them. They report catching birds all day long without any recaptures, or with just one or two recaptures. There are far more hummingbirds visiting a single garden or feeder than we perceive. Over the years of doing such work, these experts have arrived at a way to calculate the actual numbers visiting. They suggest counting the number of hummingbirds you can see at your feeders at one time, during the busiest time of day. Then multiply that number by six to arrive at the estimation of your total number of visitors.

At our feeders here in southeastern Ohio, we can see about 24 hummers at once on a busy July afternoon. Multiplying this number by 6, we estimate our total number of feeder visitors to be about 144!

A FEMALE broad-tailed hummer ready for release at a banding station.

Chapter 2: Watching Hummingbirds

WATCHING HUMMINGBIRDS can be endlessly fascinating. Their flying ability alone is enough to catch and keep the attention of even the most technology-addled brain. Add in their pugnacious behavior, humming and twittering sounds, flashes of color, and willingness to visit flowers or feeders practically within touching distance of us, and you've got a veritable magic show to enjoy.

Where you live in North America has a bearing on how many hummingbird species you can expect to see regularly. Here in the East, we have just one species that spends its summers with us: the ruby-throated hummingbird. Check the range maps that accompany each of the species profiles in Chapter 7.

Nearly any garden, backyard, or deck with flowering hanging baskets in North America may be host to at least one hummingbird species. However, these tiny flying jewels are not evenly distributed across our fine continent. There are places in the deep woods, in the far North, and in the Great Plains where it can be difficult to find hummingbirds on a regular basis. In the desert Southwest, there are hummer hotspots where one might see 10 or more species visiting a single feeder and as many as 15 species in a day or two of serious hummingbird watching.

Most of us enjoy watching the hummingbirds that come to our gardens and hummer feeders. There is a world of hummingbird watching (and 330-plus species!) awaiting you if you are willing to travel to one of the hummer hotspots in North America, or farther south, in the Neotropics.

THESE ANNA'S hummingbirds (mostly males) are occupying every feeding port of this feeder.

Finding Hummingbirds

In order to watch and identify hummingbirds, you first have to spot them. This can be tricky. An adult hummingbird is about the size of your thumb, and it may be zipping across your yard at 30 miles per hour. If it stops to perch, it may seem to disappear against the backdrop of vegetation. You are likely to hear a hummingbird before you see it. The buzz or even whistle of the wings in flight, or the chittering-chattering call notes may be what catches your attention. And you'll have to look quickly—flying hummingbirds don't normally stay in one place very long.

Even when they perch on an exposed twig or along a wire clothesline, their small size makes them inconspicuous. But perched hummingbirds offer us the very best chance to get a really good look at these tiny creatures.

How do you know where to find a perched hummingbird? Talk about finding a needle in a haystack!

Studies of the daily activity of hummingbirds shows that they spend about 15 percent of their waking hours feeding and about 75 percent of their time perched to rest, digest their food, preen, and watch for predators or interlopers. This makes sense from a biological standpoint, considering the super-high rate at which a hummingbird's metabolism burns. They are like drag racers that burn high-octane fuel attaining extreme speeds for a very few seconds. What precedes and follows a dragster's racing is hours and days of preparation, fine-tuning, and repair.

WHEN RESTING, hummingbirds may seek the protection of a perch in deep cover. This is a male Costa's hummingbird.

Watching the ruby-throated hummingbirds on my farm in southeastern Ohio, I notice that individual birds seem to have favorite perching sites. The males that try their best to dominate the flowers and feeders near our front stoop nearly always perch on the leafless branches on the crown of our Japanese maple tree 50 feet from our front door. From here they can see in all directions. They can warm themselves in the direct sunlight or flash their gorget at other hummers. They can sally forth to nab a passing insect or to intercept and chase a trespasser. Knowing that this is a preferred perch, I can sit opposite it and watch the hummingbirds using it. Our kids love it when we train the spotting scope on a perched adult male. When he turns toward us and the sunlight catches his gorget, the flash of brilliant magenta often causes the scope user to jump back in surprise.

In my travels to other hummingbird-rich areas, I've noticed that most hummingbirds are creatures of habit. Not only do they have favorite perches, they also have favorite flowers to visit, favorite feeders, and even regular paths coming and going to these attractants. It's possible, therefore, to learn their patterns of behavior and to position yourself ideally to observe them. I've put this knowledge to good use in Brazil and Panama while trying to photograph hummingbirds, and in southeast Arizona while on the hunt for some of our rarer hummingbird visitors. In all cases, watching for repeated patterns of behavior and perching helped me see (and photograph) the hummingbirds I was seeking.

Watch the hummingbirds in your garden and at your feeders to see if you can follow them to their favorite perches and note some of their patterns of behavior.

A Word about Optics

If you are already a bird watcher, you're aware of the value of binoculars in enhancing your view of distant birds. If you are not a bird watcher or do not own binoculars, I suggest you buy some. You can purchase reasonably good binoculars for $100 to $250. Find a model that is easy and comfortable for you to use. They should fit well in your hands, and you should feel no eye strain when using them. I've been advising people on optics purchasing for more than two decades, and I always say "Buy the best you can afford."

If you have some extra money lying around (and if you do, please call me!) and you really want to experience the amazing beauty of hummingbirds, purchase a small spotting scope and tripod. Then you can train your scope on a favorite hummer perch and experience that moment of "Wow!" when a blast of bright color reaches your eyes. —BT

SOME HUMMINGBIRDS, like this male violet-crowned, show an obviously two-toned bill.

Hummingbird Anatomy

If we were ornithologists, this is where the terminology would start to get complicated—naming all the parts of a hummingbird's anatomy. Lucky for us, we're just people who love to watch hummingbirds, so we can boil the terminology down to the basic parts we need for identification.

Not all parts of a hummingbird will be visible at all times. For example, flying hummingbirds may pull their feet into their belly feathers, making them look footless. Sides and rumps may be covered by flight feathers on perched birds.

Identifying Hummingbirds

While the art of hummingbird identification is not as easy as, say, bluebird identification, there are some general rules that are helpful to follow.

Crown

Upper Mandible

Lower Mandible

Gorget (throat)

Rump

Belly

Flank

Tail

Undertail

PARTS OF a hummingbird.

1. START AT THE TOP. Identifying a hummingbird follows the same basic steps as identifying any other wild bird: start at the top of the head and work your way down and back toward the tail, noting important field marks along the way. For most of our hummingbird species, the field marks are on the head, throat, bill, and tail. For example, several of our hummer species have a noticeably two-toned bill, often with some orange or red on it. Flip through the species profiles in this book or the hummingbird accounts in a field guide, and you'll immediately notice that many of the adult males are nearly unmistakable. Other field marks to look for: gorget color, the presence of an

Crown

Eye spot

Chin

Cheek

Nape

Back

Breast

Rump

Belly

Flank

Undertail

Wing Primaries

Tail

PARTS OF a hummingbird.

eye line, and patches of contrasting color on the wings, breast, belly, or tail spots. Any one of these field marks can be useful in narrowing down the identity of a mystery hummingbird.

2. CHECK THE BIRD'S SIZE. Is the hummingbird noticeably larger or smaller than other birds around it? If possible, compare it with other hummingbirds. If it is alone, compare it with the size of other birds nearby. Most of our common hummer species are between 3½ and 4 inches long from bill tip to tail tip. A very large or very small hummingbird could be something unusual.

3. NOTICE THE BIRD'S COLOR. If you see color on a hummingbird, it's as important to note *where* the color is as *what* the color is. A large dark gorget on a male is a good field mark—not all males have a large dark gorget. But there are some caveats about color. . . .

4. BE AWARE OF TRICKS OF LIGHT. As we discussed in Chapter 1, the iridescent colors we see on hummingbirds are produced by the reflection or absorption of light in the structure of the feathers. This means that as the intensity and direction of the light change, so does the color our eyes perceive. A full adult male Anna's hummingbird is a striking beast with its magenta crown and gorget. But on a cloudy day in indirect light, these areas will look dark to our eyes or they may appear cherry red, orange, or even yellow from different angles as the bird changes head positions. Bear this in mind as you are looking at hummer colors.

5. LOOK OUT FOR COLOR ANOMALIES. I'll never forget how my eyes popped out of my head when I saw her for the first time. She was a gorgeous thing, all lime green and white, flitting from cardinal flower to cardinal flower, but her head was vivid yellow-orange. I was *sure* I had made the rare hummingbird find of the century. That is, until she perched to preen and I saw the yellow-orange color come off her head in bits of powdery pollen falling to earth. As they probe for nectar, hummers can get covered in flower pollen, and it can really alter their appearance. My bird was a female rubythroat that had clearly spent some time with the tiger lilies along the edge of our garden.

WHILE FEEDING at flowers, hummingbirds may pick up a bit of pollen, as this female Costa's hummingbird has on the top of her head.

6. IMMATURES AND FEMALES CAN BE IMPOSSIBLE. Even hummingbird experts cannot tell some female hummer species apart. Take the Allen's and rufous hummingbirds: the males are not easy to ID in the field, but the females and immature males are impossible. Most positive identification of the females and immature males of these species is done in the hand by licensed bird banders and researchers. Immature males of most species look exactly like females, at least until they attain their adult plumage in the months leading to what would be their first birthday. It's okay to let a mystery hummingbird go unidentified—it's not humanly possible to ID every hummer you see.

7. RANGE IS IMPORTANT. *Where* you are when seeing a hummingbird can be very useful in narrowing down the likely possibilities. For example, if you are in a garden in June in western New York (or anywhere east of the Rocky Mountains), the chances are better than 99 percent that the hummingbird you are seeing is a rubythroat. In the West, range can be helpful too, since some of our hummingbirds hug the coast whereas others prefer to be inland. After gathering the basic field marks, check the range maps.

MANY FEMALE and juvenile hummers have no obvious field marks. This is a female ruby-throated humming-bird.

8. LISTEN FOR SOUNDS. In most cases, our hummingbirds are not gifted singers, but this does not mean they don't make noise. Some of them make distinctive sounds, such as the harsh-sounding calls of the buff-bellied hummingbird. The male broad-tailed hummingbird's wings make a high-pitched trill when it flies. Many other male hummers make specific sounds during courtship flights. Sound is not a primary clue to a hummingbird's identity, but it can be helpful.

9. IT'S PROBABLY NOT A RARITY. When you encounter an unfamiliar hummingbird—or any unusual bird, for that matter—it's a good idea to remain calm while going though the identification process. If you jump to the conclusion that this is a mega-rarity and that you'll soon be on the cover of *National Geographic* for discovering it, your mind may start gathering only the evidence that supports such a discovery, however slim that possibility might be. "Rare birds are rare," my friend Ric used to tell me. "Don't get blind with excitement until you've eliminated all of the completely likely possibilities." Stay calm. Work through the field marks. Find your bird in the field guide. Having said that, I need to say this:

10. TAKE PHOTOS AND VIDEO! Just because rare birds are rare does not mean you don't have a first North American record of some vagrant hummingbird from El Pajarero Loco, Mexico, sitting on your feeder. Grab the camera (digital or video) and record the evidence of the bird's visit. It probably is only a weird individual of a common species, but if it's not, you'll have something to show your friends, the birding experts who ID such vagrant birds, and the editors of *National Geographic*.

IMPOSTERS

One additional ID tip that should go without saying, but I'm saying it just in case, is this: make sure you are looking at a hummingbird. There are several species of flying insects that visit the same nectar sources as hummingbirds. Commonly known as hummingbird moths, hawk moths, or sphinx moths, these species can be seen both day and night hovering at flowers to drink nectar. A few clues to help separate them from hummingbirds: these moths are always smaller than the smallest hummingbird, they may have obvious antennae (which hummers lack), and their wings and back are boldly patterned. Beware the imposters in your garden!

THE SPHINX, or hummingbird moth looks similar to a hummingbird. But note the two antennae coming from the moth's head. Hummers lack antennae.

Hummingbird Behavior

It can be a rude awakening for a new hummingbird fan to discover just how obnoxious, territorial, and feisty these tiny critters can be to one another. A half-dozen times each summer, we pick up a worn-out and possibly bruised hummingbird—often a recent fledgling—that has wound up on the losing end of a fight. We hold the bird gently or place it on a branch out of harm's way until it recovers its senses and flies off. Only rarely do these skirmishes prove fatal.

TERRITORIALITY

Why are hummingbirds so seemingly nasty? It has to do with turf and access to food. Hummingbirds have to feed many times throughout the day in order to maintain their metabolism. But they cannot do all that eating in one big session—they'd become too heavy to fly. Instead, they eat dozens of small meals throughout the day. This requires visiting many flower blossoms, since each one yields only a tiny slurp of nectar, and some may yield none at all.

One field study estimated that a single Anna's hummingbird needed to probe 1,022 blossoms in a single day to find sufficient nectar. That's a lot of flying around in search of a meal! But the less flying a hummingbird has to do to find its food, the better it will be able to survive and to pass along its genes to the next generation of tiny combatants. This is why hummingbirds try to defend their food sources against all trespassers.

A large patch of flowering lupines in a Rocky Mountain meadow, a bed of cardinal flowers in North Carolina, and a large nectar feeder in an Arizona backyard—these are all reliable food sources that hummingbirds will defend. Often we see adult males as the main defenders of such resources, which makes sense since they have nothing

else to do besides feed themselves, drive off trespassers, and chase females. Certainly this is the norm through spring and summer. In late summer, however, when the adult males may have already begun migrating, we often see adult females becoming the bullies—but they seem to be less energetic about it than the males.

A defensive territorial male will perch at a good vantage point near his food source. A female flies in to feed. He flies at her chattering, and she may move to engage him in battle or she may turn and flee. If she flees, he may chase after her, hoping to convince her that he's the perfect dad for her offspring. And if she concurs, she'll perch and let him display to her, flying back and forth before her eyes, or perhaps performing feats of aerial mastery, swooping in giant arcs from high in the sky.

Of course, while he's gone, other hummingbirds may be sneaking into his territory, surreptitiously slurping nectar. If he returns to find this happening, he'll attack more viciously—especially rival males—flying at them with a whirr of wings and loud sputtering notes. If he can, he'll fly right into them with a smack, knocking them sideways and jabbing at them with his bill. In this way dominant males typically retain the best and most reliable food sources—whether natural flowers or hummingbird feeders.

If you think it's only hummingbird-on-hummingbird aggression that occurs in nature, you're wrong. Territorial hummingbirds defending food sources or nests and young will attack any creature they see as a threat. I've seen hummingbirds dive-bombing jays, crows, hawks, roosting owls, snakes, cats, and even humans who got too near to a nest. The hummingbird may be considered the Mighty Mouse of Nature when it comes to defending what's his (or hers).

COMMUNICATION

Watching the hummingbirds in your yard or garden, you'll be able to see the various ways in which they communicate using sounds and visual displays. The sounds come in three forms: calls, songs, and feather noise.

Hummingbirds use calls to communicate specific things, such as aggression, to other individuals. Males use calls to communicate to other males (saying things like "Get away from my feeder!" or "Now I'm gonna kick your tail!") and to females ("Hey, baby! Watch *this*!"). Females use calls to communicate to males, to other females, and to nestlings and fledglings waiting to be fed. Young hummers use begging and contact calls to let Mom know where they are.

Songs are used by male hummingbirds to advertise to females dur-

WHEN A *hummingbird is cold, sick, or injured, it may perch quietly with eyes closed and plumage puffed up. This is a female Costa's hummingbird.*

THIS MALE *rufous hummingbird is defending a feeder against all others trying to use it.*

Defeating a Bully Hummingbird

If you have a bully hummingbird knocking the tar out of all other visitors to your feeder, place another feeder a few feet away—better yet, place several additional feeders nearby. Your bully, male or female, will not be able to defend all of these feeders, and other, less dominant birds will be able to access the nectar.

Conventional wisdom used to be to place other feeders in other parts of your yard, out of sight of the original feeder and bully. This, however, may only serve to let other bullies set up their own kingdoms. Grouping the feeders, at least during the busiest times of the feeding season, seems to be a better solution to this natural problem.

ing the mating season and to notify rival males of territorial boundaries. These songs are delivered from a prominent perch within a male's territory. The song of the male Anna's hummingbird may be our most familiar example of singing in this family of birds. However, listening to a hummingbird's song, you might not be that impressed. Hummingbird songs are typically a high-pitched jumble of whistles, squeaks, chatters, and buzzes—nothing like the songs of our more vocally gifted songbirds, such as warblers and thrushes.

The nonvocal sounds of hummingbirds are perhaps more interesting than their vocal sounds. There are two types of nonvocal sounds made by hummingbirds: flight sounds and dive display sounds. Adult male broad-tailed, rufous, Allen's, and to a lesser extent ruby-throated and black-chinned hummingbirds produce an audible wing trill or buzz when in certain types of territorial flight. This audible wing sound is thought to be a replacement for territorial singing since these species do not typically sing. The trilling or buzzing of a territorial male's wings may serve the same purpose as the beautiful song of a warbler or thrush: warning other birds that this territory is already occupied.

Dive-display sounds are produced only at high flight speeds, at the bottom of a diving or swooping courtship flight by adult males. The short, high-pitched whistle or squealing sound is produced as air rushes over their tail feathers. Adult male Anna's, black-chinned, ruby-throated, broad-tailed, rufous, Allen's, Calliope, and Lucifer hummingbirds produce these dive-display sounds.

It's wonderfully enriching to watch hummingbirds interacting with one another. Despite their small physical size, they do not seem to avoid conflict either with other hummingbirds or with other, much larger creatures.

Chapter 3: Attracting and Feeding Hummingbirds

HUMMINGBIRDS ARE NOT EVENLY DISTRIBUTED across North America. The greatest numbers of hummingbirds are found where the habitat is best suited to their needs.

Flowers versus Feeders

In my mind there is no debate about flowers versus feeders: flowers are better.

And the flowers of native-blooming plants are the very best food source for hummingbirds in the wild. Feeders are there for us more than for the birds—they bring these delightful creatures in close where we can see and enjoy them more fully. And that's something I hope you'll keep in mind as you enjoy bird feeding: when we feed the birds, they are our invited guests and so it's our responsibility to make sure our yards, feeding stations, birdbaths, and bird houses are places where birds can thrive and live healthy lives.

Nothing in the bird world makes me more upset than seeing a hummingbird feeder that's black with mold. Okay, that's a bit of an exaggeration. A free-roaming housecat with a freshly killed songbird in its mouth probably makes me angrier than an ignored hummer feeder, but that's an ax to grind another time.

Feeders filled with sugar water and

HANG YOUR hummingbird feeder where it will be easily noticed by passing birds and easily viewed by you.

exposed to sunlight will inevitably begin to form mold as the solution ferments and natural bacteria find this perfect growing spot. This moldy growth is easily prevented with a minimal amount of maintenance. Hummingbird feeders should be washed with warm soapy water as often as possible. In the summer on our farm, when the feeders need to be refilled, we bring them in to the kitchen sink, dump out the remaining old solution and any insects that have crawled inside the feeder, and plop the feeders into a sink full of hot, soapy water for a quick soak.

Hummer in the House!

AN INJURED *hummingbird should be picked up and put in a safe place where it can recover away from the dangers of predators and pets.*

Occasionally, when the action is really hot at the feeders, a hummer will follow the feeders inside as we carry them in to clean them. What ensues is a crazy game of trying to keep the hummer's attention on the feeders as we take them back outside. When panicked, a hummingbird will do what it naturally does to escape danger: fly straight up. When this happens inside our house, where several rooms have very high ceilings, we have to fetch the extension ladder from the garage. We wait and watch the hummingbird, letting it tire a bit. Sometimes it will settle on a high window ledge and we can quietly climb to retrieve it. Other times a worn-out bird will slowly drift to the floor where we can gently grab it for transport outside.

Holding a hummingbird is one of birding's richest experiences. They weigh nothing at all, and you can feel the warm life coursing through them as they lie still, perhaps panting from exertion. We hold them in clean, cupped hands until we get them outside, then we open our hands to let the bird fly away when it's ready to go. We find we must watch closely, because they are there one moment and gone the next in a hum of whirring wings. —*BT*

After 10 minutes or so, we thoroughly rinse the feeders in clean water from the tap and check them for any remaining scum, which we go after with bristle brushes, toothpicks, and pipe cleaners. Then we rinse them once more to remove any dislodged debris, refill them, and hang them up outside.

Flowers never have the problem of spoiled nectar. Each blossom produces a small amount, and a single visit by a hummingbird may remove all of it.

Over millions of years, hummingbirds and flowers have evolved in parallel, developing a very special relationship. All across the Neotropics, wherever nectar-producing flowers bloom, there are hummingbirds with bills ideally suited to gain access to that nectar. While most of our North American hummingbirds have straight or slightly decurved bills of medium length, there are species with vastly more specialized bills. And their names reveal these special schnozzes: swordbill, sicklebill, thornbill, avocetbill, and so on.

Hummingbirds get nectar and sometimes a few insects from flowering plants. While feeding at blossoms, a hummer's tongue, bill, face, head, and perhaps even wings come into contact with the pollen-bearing parts of the flowers. Small amounts of pollen hitch a ride on the bird as it goes from flower to flower, plant to plant, and thus the plants' benefit is better pollination with a variety of distant members of its species. In this way, hummingbirds contribute greatly to healthy populations of wildflowers and flowering plants in general.

Some people believe that all bird feeding, including hummingbird feeding, is bad because it takes away from birds performing their roles in nature. Birds eating seeds at a feeder may not eat the seeds of wild plants and distribute them (when the seeds come out the other end) across a habitat. Or the birds may not eat as many naturally occurring insects, which could then explode in population, creating an imbalance. The same is said of hummingbird feeders—that they lure hummers away from pollinating flowers and eating insects.

While I can understand this concern, I've also observed that the hundreds of hummingbirds coming to our feeders each summer clearly show a natural preference for flowering plants. Why else would our feeders see few visitors on spring days when the honeysuckle is bursting with blossoms? In our yard, the birds hit the flowers first, then visit the feeder, then visit the flowers again.

So my advice to you is the same advice I've given to would-be hummer enthusiasts for three decades: flowers first, feeders second—and make sure the solution is the right mix and the feeders are kept clean.

WHEN THE solution in a feeder begins to go bad, it may appear milky. Really old solution gets moldy and turns black.

HUMMINGBIRD NECTAR is easy to make. Dissolve one part white table sugar in four parts boiling water. Let cool and serve. Extra nectar can be stored in the refrigerator.

Nectar Recipe

The recipe for making hummingbird nectar is easy. Here it is.

Mix four parts boiling water with one part white granulated (table) sugar. Stir until sugar is dissolved. Let solution cool. Refrigerate extra solution.

Some additional information and tips:

WATER: Use clean tap water. Boiling removes impurities and excess chlorine or chemicals. Some experts recommend adding slightly more water when weather is hot and dry (above 100°F) and slightly less during migration and winter.

SUGAR: Use only white granulated sugar. No molasses, no artificial sweeteners, no honey, no powdered or brown sugar. In summer we go through a 10-pound bag of sugar per month, and the refrigerator's top shelf has giant plastic jugs of nectar awaiting deployment.

STORAGE: We use large plastic orange juice bottles so we can pour the solution directly into the feeders when refilling.

REFILLING: It's wise to do your feeder emptying, cleaning, and refilling at a large sink where any spilled nectar can be rinsed away. If you try to refill the feeders where they hang, any solution you spill will attract insects, ants, and perhaps other sugar-seeking creatures. We have to be careful on our farm to keep the feeders out of reach of the many raccoons. They will knock down a feeder just to lap up the spilled solution— sometimes even carrying the feeder off into the woods. We usually don't find those stolen feeders until winter, when the thick underbrush loses its leaves and we can see the bright red feeder parts. —BT

Choosing a Feeder

The very first hummingbird feeders were small glass tubes filled with sugar water and ornamented with an artificial red flower to attract the hummingbirds' attention. It's a matter of debate where and when this occurred and who first had this brilliant idea, but most sources point to the pioneering work of self-taught ornithologist Althea R. Sherman in Iowa in the early 1900s. She was perhaps the first person to train hummingbirds to find nectar at a feeder.

WHEN HUMMINGBIRD numbers reach their peak, adding extra feeders can ensure that more birds get access to food.

Since Ms. Sherman's time, hummingbird feeding has become a hugely popular pastime. Walk down the aisle at any store selling products for the garden, and you're sure to encounter one or more hummingbird feeders being sold.

SAUCER VERSUS VACUUM

There are hundreds of varieties of hummingbird feeders, but all of them fall into one of two design categories: vacuum or saucer.

Vacuum feeders are basically inverted bottles with some sort of base and feeding port at the bottom. Nectar is held inside the feeder

SAUCER-STYLE FEEDERS (right) have feeder ports above the nectar reservoir. Vacuum-style feeders (left) have ports below the nectar reservoir, like an inverted bottle.

BEES AND wasps are often attracted to nectar at feeders, but you can discourage them by using a feeder with bee guards over the feeding ports. The guards prevent these insects from reaching the nectar.

by the pressure vacuum created by trapped air. As a hummingbird's bill and tongue probe the feeder port, small amounts of nectar are released, and the hummer uses its tongue to lap this up. The advantages of simple, wide-mouthed vacuum feeders are that they are easy to clean and refill, and when they work properly the nectar is doled out over time. The disadvantage is their tendency to leak when the vacuum is broken because of one or more factors. Leaking can occur when the seals around feeding ports are not snug, when low nectar levels reduce the pressure of the vacuum, when sunlight causes the feeder parts to expand, or when wind sloshes the feeders about. A leaky feeder will attract insects and other pests with which you and the hummingbirds will have to contend.

The second style of feeder is a saucer feeder. As you might guess, a saucer feeder is a bowl-like reservoir of nectar that hummingbirds access by probing downward into feeding ports. Unless disturbed by wind or marauding larger birds or mammals, a saucer feeder is unlikely to leak—a big advantage. Some designs, however, have the disadvantage of being difficult to clean. I know from experience that a hard-to-clean feeder gets cleaned less often, which isn't good for the birds. Everyone has a feeder style that they find easiest to use, and yours may be different from mine.

PORTS: FLOWERS VERSUS BEE GUARDS

The feeding ports on hummer feeders are very important to the success of your offerings. Ports that are too small will not allow nectar out and will be difficult for the birds to use, so they won't use them. Ports that are too large will let nectar leak out and may let insects get in, which will hasten the spoiling process of the solution. The right size feeding port is $\frac{1}{8}$ inch in diameter or smaller.

Many feeders come with plastic flowers that snap over the ports. These are meant only to help show the hummers where to probe. They do nothing to prevent access by bees, wasps, ants, and other insects. Bee guards do a better job of this. They, too, snap over ports, and they make it difficult for insects to reach the nectar with their probing mouthparts. Hummingbirds have no trouble getting past these guards, since a hummer's tongue can extend almost twice the length of the bill to reach nectar deep inside a flower or feeder.

Many hummingbird feeders come with bee guards, and I recommend using them if you have problems with large insects at your feeders.

MORE TIPS FOR FEEDER SELECTION

A few final considerations when choosing a hummingbird feeder:

1. Make sure your feeder suits the amount of feeding you'll be doing. Start with a small feeder, then add others or larger-capacity models as your number of feeder visitors grows throughout the season and years.

2. Look for feeders that are easy to clean thoroughly. Narrow-necked bottle feeders or saucers with small filling holes are a pain to clean. Ceramic feeders prevent you from seeing nectar levels and mold build-up. The best feeders come apart for complete ease of cleaning.

3. Avoid buying feeders because they are pretty. Go for function over form. Many of the best-looking models being sold today are impossible to clean and may even be awkward or impossible for hummers to use.

4. Perches on feeders are not necessary but may permit you to get better looks at the birds. Perches also allow larger, nonhovering birds (finches, woodpeckers, orioles, etc.) to use the feeders. If this is not something you want, use feeders without perches.

5. Ask your neighbors or fellow birders which feeders they prefer.

6. Watch which feeders the hummingbirds prefer. You'll soon know which ones are most popular.

PLACING YOUR hummingbird feeder near flowers will increase your chances of getting hummers to "tune in" to your feeder.

Feeder Placement

There are a few things to keep in mind when placing your feeders. First of all, the feeders need to be where the birds can find them—near flowering plants is an ideal starting point. Second, the feeders need to be where you can see them, enjoy them, and easily access them for filling and cleaning. Third, the feeders should be out of direct sunlight to slow the fermentation process. Once the birds are tuned into your feeders, you can move them in short steps to a more advantageous position.

Hummingbirds remember a reliable food source—even from year

to year. Ask any veteran hummer host and they will be happy to tell you how their male hummingbird returns every spring and hovers in the exact spot where the feeder was last summer.

Hummer Babies in Our House

My wife, Julie, has been a licensed bird rehabilitator for several years. One summer, after a bad rain- and windstorm, we found ourselves caretakers of two sets of ruby-throated hummingbird nestlings whose nests had been blown down in the storm. It was a miracle that they survived, so once they came into Julie's care, she was determined to raise them to a successful fledging. For weeks they lived in a special bird room we set up in Julie's studio, and she and our daughter, Phoebe, diligently fed the four nestlings every 20 minutes. As they grew, they prospered and soon were taking short flights to poke at flowering plants we'd brought inside and at a small feeder filled with a special protein-rich solution.

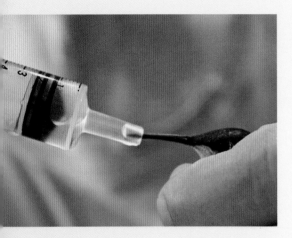

A SICK or injured hummer should be placed out of harm's way and given a chance to recover. If the bird is not better within an hour or so, contact a licensed bird rehabilitator in your area.

That August three of the birds—all males—fledged successfully (one was injured and never fully developed its flight muscles). For two additional weeks, the fledglings watched for us to walk out of our house with their special feeders, which we'd hold while they fed, whirring around us and one another to gain access to the single port. Soon they gained more strength and independence, and then they were gone, headed south (we hoped) on migration. We wondered if they would survive the winter in the Neotropics and the more than 1,000-mile journey down and back. Would they find our rural farm in southeastern Ohio?

In early April the following spring, I stepped outside into the sunshine with my coffee mug in hand. Immediately, I heard the familiar buzz of hummingbird wings— our first of the spring! But before I could turn to shout to Julie and the kids that the hummers were back, an adult male ruby-throat hovered before my mug-holding hand, probing between each pair of fingers looking for a taste of nectar. Then he flew up to my face, gave me a look, and buzzed away to a favorite perch on the Japanese maple.

As Julie said, "That was as close to a handshake as a hummingbird could get."

Two minutes later, the feeder was up and we had one, then two, then three male ruby-throats feeding together—and perching together—just feet from our kitchen window. Our boys were back! —BT

General Feeding Rules

I've covered most of the basic hummingbird feeding rules already in this chapter. Here is a bit of additional information.

CLEANING FEEDERS

How often should I clean my feeders? That's like asking "How often should I shower or brush my teeth?" The answer is as often as necessary. There's no such thing as cleaning your feeders too much. In areas with daily summer temperatures above about 75°F, feeders should be cleaned every two to three days. If your region has hotter ambient temperatures or your feeders get a lot of direct sunlight, clean them more frequently. Warm soapy water with a bit of gunk-scrubbing should do the trick. Some folks prefer to use white vinegar. Either way, be sure you rinse the feeders well before refilling them.

WHEN TO FEED

Some regions of North America host hummingbirds all year long, so residents there can put the feeder up now and never take it down—except to refill and clean it, of course! Some people may be concerned that leaving a feeder up will prevent hummingbirds from migrating in the fall. This is a myth. Hummingbirds (and all migratory birds) have an internal "clock" that tells them when to migrate. No healthy hummingbird would ever stick around just because you've left your feeder up in the fall. However, late migrants, young inexperienced birds of the year, and hummers that are not completely healthy may be helped by the presence of your feeder, especially in areas where blooming flowers are scarce in fall and early winter.

IN MIDSUMMER when recent fledglings increase hummingbird numbers, filling the feeders is a daily chore.

Ready for Arrival

Here in Ohio, we put our first hummer feeder up right around April 15 because our first male ruby-throated hummingbird usually shows up around this date each year. For hummingbirds, as with migratory songbird species, males return first each spring to establish territories and find reliable foraging spots. Having your feeder and plenty of blooming flowers already in place when the first males return will enhance your chances of hosting hummingbirds throughout the spring and summer. We use hanging baskets of flowering plants to attract the hummers in years when our spring gardens are not yet in bloom. —BT

HANGING BASKETS *are an excellent way to attract hum-mers in early spring when your flowers may not yet be blooming.*

WHEN PLANT *nectar is scarce or unavailable, hum-mingbirds may visit sap-sucker holes on trees both for sap and to consume the insects caught in the sap.*

HOW IMPORTANT ARE FEEDERS?

Hummingbird feeders are not vital to the survival of our native hummingbird species. At best they are an additional food source—after nectar-producing flowers —for hummingbirds. Nectar-producing flowering plants and flying insects are always going to be the most important food sources for hummingbirds. The two possible exceptions would be during periods of bad weather, when a late spring or early fall snow covers flowering plants and stops insect activity, and when a vagrant hummingbird shows up in winter at a nectar feeder. In such cases, a clean feeder filled with fresh nectar can make all the difference for a bird's survival.

As feeding and gardening for hummers have grown in popularity, more and more vagrant hummingbirds are being found in the East, Southeast, and Gulf Coast area. Each winter there are reports of western hummingbirds of several species spending the winter in places where they should not be. While you might be tempted to call these birds "lost," in fact they are merely players in nature's grand scheme of survival. If their internal compass directs them to migrate east in the fall instead of south, and they survive the winter in, say, Huntington, West Virginia, and return to breed the following spring in the West, their offspring may possess the same internal navigation differences. Over time, this is how species expand their range, through trial and error and survival of the fittest. There are hummingbird researchers who feel that the increasing numbers of overwintering rufous hummingbirds in the eastern half of the U.S. are a direct result of the increased presence of hummingbird feeders and hardy blooming plants in human-altered landscapes. It's an interesting phenomenon to ponder.

Ten Tips for Attracting Hummingbirds

Here are ten commonsense tips to help you attract more hummingbirds to your backyard.

1. ADD MORE FLOWERS AND FEEDERS. Flowers first, feeders second. But you knew I was going to say that, didn't you?

2. ADD A WATER FEATURE WITH A MISTER. Hummingbirds love to bathe, and a mister gives them just the kind of fine spray they prefer. If you cannot find a commercial source selling a birdbath mister, poking some tiny holes in a length of old hose (with a closed nozzle at one end) will work just fine. Place it near your birdbath so the mist is caught in the bath's basin.

3. PLACE TINY PERCHES AROUND THE YARD. We leave the bare dead branches in place at the crowns of our ornamental Japanese maples because the hummers *love* to perch on them. Think of how tiny hummingbird feet are, and find some small but sturdy branches to stick around your yard, garden, or deck. Once a hummer tunes in to a favorite perch, it will use it repeatedly.

4. GET YOUR FEEDERS UP EARLY AND LEAVE 'EM UP. Check the arrival dates map below to see when to expect returning male ruby-throated hummingbirds in the East. Put out the hanging baskets and feeders at least a week before the earliest arrival date.

FOR BATHING, *humming-birds seem to prefer flying through a mist of water, or rain bathing on wet leaves.*

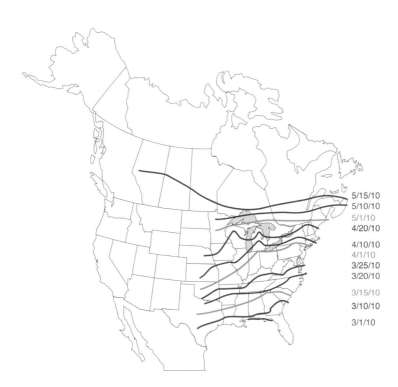

5/15/10
5/10/10
5/1/10
4/20/10

4/10/10
4/1/10
3/25/10
3/20/10

3/15/10
3/10/10

3/1/10

IN EARLY spring, use brightly colored objects to attract attention to your feeders. Some hummer hosts use red pieces of cloth, pink surveyor's tape, or even bright plastic flowers.

5. GET A HEAD START WITH HANGING BASKETS. This works great to attract hummingbirds before your gardens are blooming. Any garden center worth a nickel will have flower-filled hanging baskets for sale long before the local plants are blooming. I rarely buy more than one, but that's usually all it takes.

6. BE ORGANIC. With their incredibly high metabolism, hummingbirds are very susceptible to chemicals such as those used to control garden pests. If you want your hummingbirds to be healthy, avoid or limit the use of chemicals in your gardens, and never use chemicals of any kind on or near your hummingbird feeders.

7. VARY YOUR HABITAT. Hummingbirds need habitats other than flowering plants. They need trees in which to nest, shrubs in which to shelter, places to forage for insects, and access to water for drinking and bathing. Making your yard more bird-friendly will automatically make it more hummingbird-friendly too.

8. USE RED RIBBONS AND PLASTIC FLOWERS. If you are just starting to establish your yard or garden for hummingbirds, and you want to catch the eye of a passing hummer, a quick way to do it is to hang something bright red or bright pink. The vision of hummingbirds seems to be particularly acute for colors in the pink–red–orange parts of the color spectrum, which is why so many native flowers that have evolved to be visited by hummingbirds are these colors. If you can't get to the garden center for a hanging basket, hang out something red, such as a piece of surveyor's tape, an artificial flower, or even a handkerchief.

9. LEAVE SPIDER WEBS UP. Spider webs are among the materials that hummingbirds use to weave their nests. If you ever have a chance to look at a hummer nests closely, you'll see that the tiny fibers of spider webbing are what holds it together, what bonds it to its support, and what allows the nest to expand as the nestlings grow. Avoid the temptation to sweep away spider webs in spring and summer when hummers might use them as building materials. Hummers also visit spider webs to swipe and eat insects caught in the webbing—yet another reason to leave those webs alone.

10. PUT OUT ROTTEN FRUIT. This tip may be further than you'd like to go, but rotten fruit is very important to hummingbirds. Why? Rotten or rotting fruit attracts fruit flies and other insects, which are the perfect high-protein snacks for hummingbirds. Hummingbirds rely on insects as a major part of their diet. Don't believe me? Place a brown banana (or some other past-its-freshness-date fruit) out near your hummer feeder and leave it there until it begins to attract insects. Then watch to see if these insects don't in turn attract hungry hummingbirds. I've seen this in action in our vegetable garden, where rotten tomatoes buzzing with insects had two female rubythroats diving and snagging the flying bugs.

Chapter 4: Plants for Hummingbirds

HUMMINGBIRDS ARE AMONG the most fascinating guests you'll ever host. As they zoom from flower to flower, they flit forward, backward, sideways, and even hover like helicopters. On a typical day, a single hummingbird may visit 1,000 flower blossoms or more, lapping sugar-rich nectar with its long tongue. Although feeders stocked with fresh sugar water are a great supplement, the most reliable way to attract hummingbirds is to provide hospitable backyard habitat featuring a seasonal progression of colorful flowers. Rather than concentrating these plants in one location, distribute them throughout your yard so one dominant bird won't keep competing hummers away.

Planning Your Hummingbird Habitat

It's easy to design backyard habitats for hummingbirds, and as a bonus, many favorite plants also lure butterflies. Full sun is essential for most butterfly- and many hummer-attracting plants. If possible, select a place that receives at least six hours of daily sun, but don't despair if your yard lies beneath a tree canopy. Hummingbirds and a few butterflies regularly visit shade-loving plants. Plants that attract hummingbirds and butterflies are noted in Chapters 5 and 12, respectively.

A COLORFUL wildlife garden incorporating a path, borders, and accents. Arrange your garden with the tallest plants at the back, layering forward with shorter species, so hummingbirds have space to reach the flowers and nothing is blocked from your view.

Aesthetically pleasing gardens typically include a path that invites you to enter and one or more focal points, such as a natural-looking pool, a group of rocks whose crevices overflow with flowers, or a central bed whose blossoms radiate style and color. For a patio or deck, several containers of bright flowers might surround a hummingbird feeder hanging from a shepherd's crook. Any of these situations would be improved by adding a comfortable chair, garden bench, or similar quiet resting place to lure you into the habitat, where you can relax, enjoy the flowers, and watch your wild guests.

Informal borders divide spaces that encourage human activity from quieter places. Borders can be constructed of landscape timbers, rocks, or commercial edging, while paths are often marked by stepping stones, coarse mulch, or keeping a grassy swath mowed. Hummingbirds require maneuvering room when they fly, so they conveniently use the airspace over paths and borders to access the plants they seek. Read the tags that come in potted nursery stock or study catalog descriptions to determine how large plants will grow. Locate species with the greatest heights at the rear of beds, layering forward with sequentially shorter flowers. Allow ample room around plantings so hummers can whiz between the plants and hover without bumping their wings.

You can develop vertical levels to attract hummingbirds. Depending on available space, choose one or more trees that bear flowers in their canopy. Scattered around and accenting the major trees, plant a few shrubs that create color at eye level. Against this backdrop add lower-level perennials (species that come up every year from overwintering rootstock) such as beebalm, or annuals (species that must be replanted every year and grow only in the frost-free season) such as impatiens or petunias. Remember that edges—areas between forest and field, or woods and water—are extremely attractive to wildlife. Vines, including native honeysuckles and morning glories, are great choices for these ecological transition zones.

Backyard wildlife habitats supplement natural ecological communities near your home. If natural habitats have been destroyed, your backyard habitat and that of like-minded neighbors can help rebuild the native ecology of your region. Visit an established nature park near your home to learn what type of habitat (coastal swamp, hardwood forest, evergreen forest, prairie, desert, alpine mountaintop, etc.) would dominate if you did nothing to prevent native plants from growing for the next 100 years. If your goal is to have that kind

A MALE broad-tailed hummingbird nectaring at well-spaced flowers of autumn sage, which allow plenty of room for birds to maneuver.

NATIVE, NECTAR-RICH trumpet creeper flowers are irresistable to hummingbirds such as this male ruby-throat.

of habitat, simply plant native species and let them grow. If you wish to keep a sunny meadow with lots of wildflowers in a region where nature's plant succession eventually becomes a shady forest, you will need to do more maintenance, such as keeping shrubs and trees from eventually overtopping your sun-bathed meadow.

HABITAT CORNERSTONES

FOOD

All good wildlife habitats, whether completely natural or enhanced by humans, are built on four cornerstones: *food, water, shelter,* and protected *nesting sites.* The quickest way to provide food is to put up feeders, but they don't enhance the natural parts of your yard. If you don't fill feeders regularly, or if you fail to keep them clean, hummingbirds will leave. The best approach is to add magnet plants that lure the wild creatures you wish to attract. An example is including trumpet creeper in your landscape, because it bears bright, nectar-laden flowers that hummingbirds love.

WATER

Hummingbirds are so small that typical birdbaths will submerge them. But hummingbirds love to leaf-bathe, and on their miniaturized scale, a few raindrops on foliage probably equates to a robin splashing in a puddle. If you watch carefully, you'll see hummingbirds landing on dew- or rain-spattered leaves. They rub water drops onto their feathers, flutter to spread the moisture, and then groom to re-align their feathers.

Hummers also dart through fine spray from commercially available misting devices. The mister attaches to an outdoor faucet, and when the water is turned on, fine droplets fill the air. Attach the mister to a tree branch, where it can drench some leaves, or let it dribble into your birdbath. Hummers will repeatedly fly through the mist to get wet, then land on a favorite perch to preen. Many other birds—including doves, cardinals, robins, and even woodpeckers—will also luxuriate at your spa.

Hummingbirds also frequent shallow flowing water. If you don't live near a stream, you can achieve this effect by installing a recirculating pump that moves water from a pool through hidden tubing to the top of a textured rock. Make sure to plug the pump into a ground fault (GFCI) protected outlet, which prevents electrical shocks. The water flows by gravity over the face of the rock and back into the ba-

Hummers in the Mist

While my husband, Pat, worked for the National Park Service, we lived at Lava Beds National Monument in northern California. Located east of the Cascade Mountains, this sage-covered high desert was a summer hummingbird haven. Plentiful wildflowers offered food, but water was always in short supply. Average rainfall is less than 10 inches per year.

We lived in a small residential area for rangers' families. Each home had a tiny grass lawn where children could play without skinning their knees on the rough, angular lava. Although the surrounding native vegetation was well suited to drought, residents were asked to water the lawns occasionally so the grass would survive.

As soon as lawn sprinklers began spritzing, hummingbirds arrived to bathe. They seemed to delight in power-diving through the spray. I remember many occasions when I would stand perfectly still while using a garden hose, and the curious little birds would hover in the mist no more than a foot away. After their feathers were thoroughly wet, they flew to favorite twig perches in the mountain mahogany shrubs and preened their shimmering plumage. —CT

sin. Small units are perfect additions to deck or patio habitats. You can purchase components or complete systems at garden centers and bird specialty stores. Or you can install a backyard pond kit that works similarly but offers water on a much larger scale. Either way, remember that hummingbirds will need water no more than ¼ inch deep trickling over a gently sloping rock.

A MALE Costa's hummingbird bathing in a mister.

SHELTER

Well-rounded hummingbird habitats provide shelter from bad weather and protection from predators. Windbreaks created by a row of evergreen trees or clusters of densely branched shrubs reduce the intensity of hail- and thunderstorms. Evergreens and leafy shrubs also help buffer strong winds and insulate against cool nighttime temperatures, providing snug places for hummingbirds to sleep. These big, dense plants work well as accents along fences and create interesting design elements at the corners of your property.

GROOM YOUR garden so that you leave a few prominent perches for hummers like this female Anna's hummingbird, which typically rest on small twigs with a good view.

Hummingbirds pass the day by flying around for about five minutes at a time, gathering nectar and tiny insects from favorite patches of flowers. Once their crop (esophageal pouch) is full, they loaf on a perch for about 15 minutes to digest the meal. A hummingbird will return repeatedly to the same resting spot, especially if it affords a good view of its territory.

You can direct hummingbirds to perches that are easy to see from your favorite patio chair by selectively pruning the trees and shrubs in your hummingbird garden. Leave dead twigs that are 6 to 8 inches long and thin enough so tiny hummingbird feet can grip them. Male hummers typically select exposed perches at least 6 to 10 feet high. They need a wide view of their territory and a clear departure zone so they can fly away quickly. Female hummingbirds seek similar-sized but sheltered perches, often protected by a leafy bower overhead.

Large praying mantises sometimes capture and eat hummingbirds. Mantises are generally considered beneficial because of the many potentially damaging insects they consume. If you notice a mantis lurking at a hummingbird feeder or near a popular hummingbird perch, gently capture and relocate it.

NESTING SITES

The ultimate building block of wildlife habitat is a suitable place to nest. This is a specialized category of shelter that ensures available nest sites, abundant nest-building materials, and adequate conditions for feeding and protecting young while in the nest.

Female hummingbirds frequently position their nests on tree branches arching over a stream, trail, or open area, so the mother bird can dart up and into the nest quickly. Expectant mothers anchor their nests to knots and wyes on branches, where the uneven shape conceals the nest profile. Hummingbirds use spider webs and plant fibers to create soft, interwoven nests that stretch as the babies grow. Most North American hummingbirds decorate the outside of their nests with bits of lichen, camouflaging them to blend with supporting branches.

If your yard is situated near a creek, river, or grassy path, there is a good chance you may host nesting hummingbirds. About the time migrant warblers arrive in spring, watch for female hummers harvesting spider webs under your porch eaves or flying with tiny bits of lichen in their beaks. If you discover this tip-off behavior, watch for numerous back-and-forth trips. With patience, you may discover a walnut-sized nest under construction.

Since hummingbirds regularly dine on aphids, gnats, and tiny spiders, and feed them to their babies, avoid applying pesticides to plants in your hummingbird garden. Malathion and Sevin are common ingredients in broad-spectrum insect killers available for garden use. Diazinon is an especially potent insecticide that also kills birds. It has been banned for home use since 2004 but is still available for agricultural applications. All of these chemicals act indiscriminately, destroying more beneficial and benign insects than troublesome types. For the safety of your hummers and insect-eating songbirds, don't apply any of these substances near your wildlife habitat. If you must use insect controls, try eco-safe insecticidal soaps that are widely available at garden and hardware stores.

A FEMALE Anna's hummingbird in a nest made of spider webs and lichens built on a forking branch.

PLANNING YOUR REFUGE

Almost anywhere in the contiguous U.S. and southern Canada, you have a good chance of luring hummingbirds to your yard, deck, or patio with the right combination of plants. Before rushing to the nearest garden center, however, invest a few moments in the all-important planning process so your efforts will result in success. Using the suggestions below, assess your lifestyle needs and tailor your habitat to a manageable size. Quality habitat will attract birds throughout the yard, but to best enjoy your efforts, concentrate the action in places where you will readily see hummingbirds.

Although wild backyard habitats are much more common and widely accepted than they were a decade ago, check applicable community "weed laws" to make certain your plans aren't out of step with homeowner covenants. If you join a wildlife advocacy group, such as the National Wildlife Federation's Backyard Wildlife Habitat program or state natural resource efforts such as Texas Wildscapes or Maryland's Wild Acres, you can advertise your intentions using tasteful signs created by these wildlife affiliates. Or you can craft a clever sign of your own to proclaim that wildlife is welcome in your garden.

Be sensitive to neighbors' concerns about "wild" yards, which are perceived by some as an eyesore or source of weeds. Chances are, if you know your neighbors and share your plans to attract hummingbirds, they will be intrigued and may even join your efforts. If you don't know your neighbors, what better way to meet them and solicit their support than by inviting them to see what you are doing? Chil-

The Quiet Revolution

The way we think about gardening and landscaping is changing to include an increased awareness of the plant and animal life around us, as well as an awareness of our place within the web of life. —*Joanne Wolfe, editor, Better Homes and Gardens Special Interest Publications*

dren are especially curious and receptive to projects that involve wildlife. Be sure to include your own children or grandchildren in these activities, and if applicable, let neighbor children help as well.

INVENTORY YARD ASSETS

Nearly every yard offers some benefits for wildlife. Do any hummingbirds currently visit your yard, and if so, are they using feeders or gleaning nectar from flowers? Is water naturally available? Are there established trees or shrubs where birds feed, rest, or make nests? Do you see or hear birds on your neighbors' property? Is there a nature park or greenway in the neighborhood that hosts wildlife?

Gaze out a favorite window of your home, or sit for a few moments on your patio or deck. Look around thoughtfully to answer the preceding questions, then make a list of assets present in or near your yard. You may be surprised at the elements you already have!

A LARGE patch of beebalm highlights the hummingbird–butterfly garden at the home of Connie and Pat Toops in western North Carolina.

SKETCH YOUR YARD

Now grab a blank sheet of paper and pencil with a good eraser to sketch your yard. Don't worry about your artistic skills—no one else needs to see this!

Begin by drawing the outer boundaries of your property, filling the page as much as possible with its shape. Next, add the shapes of your home, driveway, outbuildings, fences, decks, or paths, trying to keep them in proportion to the size of your map. Write *EAST* on the side of the map where the sun rises and *WEST* on the side where it sets. Then fill in *NORTH* and *SOUTH*.

Consult your list of assets and glance out the window frequently. Using squiggly circles with T in the center, mark the locations of large trees. Try to scale the amount of space they take up in your yard with the space they consume on your map. Repeat this process us-

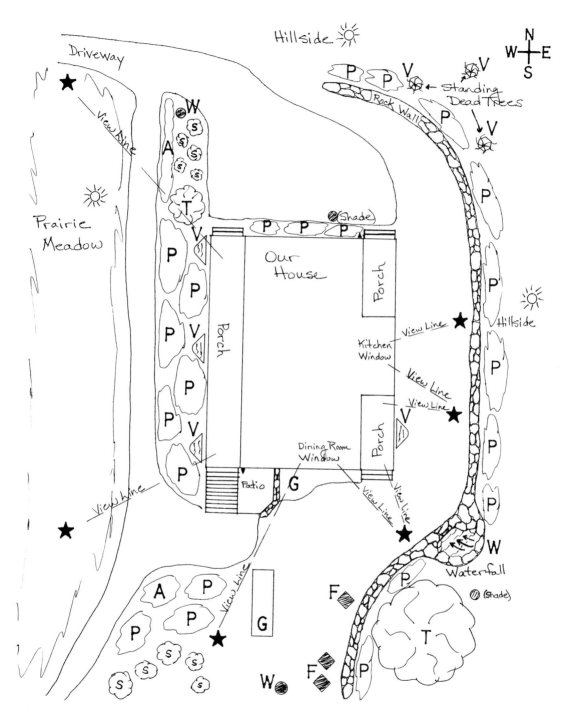

A DRAWING of author Connie Toops's yard, showing physical assets and plantings. Make a sketch of your yard, identifying areas to enhance for wildlife.

ing smaller squiggly circles with S to indicate shrubs and V for vines. Sketch the shapes of any flower beds you already have, marking P where perennials grow, A for annuals, and G for garden vegetables. If you are fortunate to have flowing water on your property, mark it with →'s showing the path of the stream. Place an F where existing bird feeders are located, and use a W to mark a birdbath or small pond. Draw a ▼ anywhere there is an outdoor faucet. If you have additional assets, such as a brush pile or dead tree, add them to the map. ★ indicates a good view.

FIVE QUESTIONS

Next, answer these basic questions:

1. DO YOU HAVE CHILDREN OR PETS? WHERE IN YOUR YARD ARE THE ACTIVE PLAY AREAS OR OTHER SPACES THEY NEED? Since loud voices, activity, and potential pet interactions are not highly compatible with traditional wildlife havens, it's best to separate these two categories of use so your wildlife oasis can be as serene as possible.

2. HOW LONG DO YOU PLAN TO LIVE AT THIS ADDRESS? WILL LANDSCAPING INCREASE THE RESALE VALUE OF THE PROPERTY? If you have a grass lawn in the midst of an urban environment, it will take several months to enhance your backyard enough to begin attracting significant wildlife. Will you live there long enough to see a payback for your efforts? Actual dollar values are hard to define, but real-estate agents and appraisers agree that tasteful landscaping increases property values. Certain buyers will pay a premium to move into a house where established trees, shrubs, and flowers attract popular wildlife species such as hummingbirds and songbirds.

3. HOW MUCH SUNLIGHT DOES YOUR YARD RECEIVE? If your yard resembles a meadow, there will be plenty of sun to grow flowers that hummingbirds use. But under trees and shrubs, and on the north side of your home, there may be too much shade. On a sunny summer day, keep track of areas that might be too shady. If they receive at least six cumulative hours of direct sunlight, sun-loving plants should survive there. Otherwise, select plants that require part or full shade.

4. WHAT ARE THE AVERAGE DATES OF THE LAST FROST IN THE SPRING AND THE FIRST FROST IN THE FALL? County extension agents or master gardener groups can provide this information, which advises when it's warm enough for tender annuals such as snapdragons and impatiens. Also consult the USDA Plant Hardiness Zone Map (http://www.usna.usda.gov/Hardzone/ushzmap.html), which assigns each region of North America a number based on minimum winter temperatures. For example, Fairbanks, Alaska, is in Zone 1, Pittsburgh is in Zone 5, Seattle is in Zone 8, and Miami is in Zone 10. Nursery stock tags and catalog descriptions usually indicate in which zones plants are best suited to grow.

5. WHAT IS YOUR SOIL TYPE AND PH? IS YOUR YARD WET OR DRY? Many county extension agents can supply low-cost soil-testing kits. Test results show soil type, fertility, and whether amendments (nitrogen, potassium, composted humus, etc.) are needed. Depending on local terrain, your yard may have additional microclimate considerations, such as whether it is on a mountainside, in a desert region, or near a swamp. These factors may require special gardening techniques, such as xeriscaping with drought-tolerant plants or terracing on steep slopes.

Not in My Backyard!

Not everyone values wildlife habitat equally. Years ago, we landscaped a suburban yard in West Virginia with so many plants and wildlife features that it was profiled on a national television series. When we later had to move and offered the property for sale, one of the first serious clients, a burly, plainspoken man, told me, "Honey, I love the house, but your yard is just too much work!" Later our home did sell to a couple who seemed anxious to live in a private wildlife refuge. —CT

Incorporate this information on your sketch by marking ☀ in sunny places and using ◉ for shady areas. Use ★ to identify good views from the deck, patio, or inside the house. Make an X if you do not wish to attract wildlife to high-energy spaces where kids and pets play. By now your sketch should reveal a developing plan. Decide where to concentrate your initial planting efforts and whether there are potentially troublesome conditions you need to address.

A garden is defined by design concepts such as paths, viewpoints, masses of color, and seasonal change. Use borders to imply order, and try to space plantings so they look informally planned rather than measured. Gentle curves, circles, and sweeps are good design elements. You can also achieve informal order by arranging similar colors to create a theme that repeats throughout the garden, or using accent colors to draw special attention. Groups of annuals or perennials planted together create high visibility. Be sure to allow enough room around the plantings so they can spread as they grow. Some landscape-design computer software forecasts future growth, showing how the garden will look in 5 or 10 years.

A FEMALE Anna's hummingbird with pollen on her bill as she gathers nectar at hummingbird sage.

A MALE Allen's hummingbird seeking nectar in a field of red delphiniums, a flower species that has a mutually beneficial relationship with hummingbirds.

Bird-friendly Plants

After the planning process is complete, visits to local garden centers or ordering from nursery catalogs become exciting opportunities, because the plants you choose will determine what critters move into your habitat. Warning: it's easy to overestimate and become overwhelmed. Start on one small area you wish to plant or rehabilitate. Do the preliminary clearing, sod removal, soil amendments, or other preparatory work. Then use labeled pieces of cardboard to mark places where you will install plants. (Moving and rearranging place markers until you achieve the spacing you desire is much easier than moving plants!) Once you define the numbers, types, and sizes of plants for this section, it's time to purchase them.

Evolution has played a huge role in determining which flowers hummingbirds use. Traits that are usually attractive include red or orange color, tubular shape, and horizontal or dangling structures that allow hummers to hover without bumping the plant as they feed. These plants also offer nectar that ranges from about 15 to 30 percent sugar content. Are the plants generous in manufacturing this sweet reward, or do they receive something in return?

Ornithologists believe ancestral hummingbirds were originally insect-eaters, and in pursuit of small insects that lived on flower blossoms, these hummingbirds occasionally sampled nectar. In the process, they may have bumped against the reproductive parts of the flower, and bits of pollen may have stuck to their bills or heads. When the hummers visited other flowers of the same species, some of these pollen grains were transferred and completed the pollination process.

Over time, these flowers displayed bright red (or orange) petals, a color hummingbirds see well and most insects do not, to advertise their sweet nectar. More hummingbirds visited these living cafeterias—drawn to color, energy-packed sugars, and insects. Increased visits helped ensure that pollen was transferred to create seeds that spread the plant to new locations. This win-win situation is embodied in North America by more than 150 native plants that now depend exclusively on hummingbirds for pollination.

In Central and South America, where more than 300 species of hummingbirds feed on nectar, numerous flowers accommodate straight, swordlike, sickle-shaped, long, and short bill designs of various hummingbirds. Hummingbirds are found only in the Western Hemisphere and have no close counterparts in Europe. Some Old

World plants now grown in North America (such as roses) have the right color to make hummers curious, but their nectar content is not adequate to entice repeat visits.

Although hummers use some nectar-producing plants from other regions of the world, it's best to include as many native plants as possible in your hummingbird garden. Plants imported from other continents have a sad history of bringing unintended diseases and insect pests that have spread beyond control and decimated large areas of natural habitat. Some imported plants have become invasive pests.

What is a *native* plant? The National Wildlife Federation defines native as any species found within 50 miles of your yard at the time of European settlement. Native plants are adjusted to the soils and climate of their homeland. Generally they are more disease resistant than plants from elsewhere. You seldom need to fertilize or treat them with chemicals that are recommended for introduced varieties. Equally important, native plants are in rhythm with the seasons, produce flowers at just the right time to be useful to visiting humming-birds, and hummers recognize them.

When you stroll through a garden center or glance at a nursery catalog, you may be intrigued by "improved" varieties, or *cultivars,* derived from wild ancestors by plant breeding. Examples include profusely flowered, giant, double, or ruffled hybrids. They certainly lend beauty to the garden, but in order to create these extraordinary specimens, characteristics such as abundant nectar production may be lost. In general, it's safest to select old-fashioned, single-flowered varieties, which usually retain their hummingbird-attracting powers. Otherwise, talk to fellow gardeners or take a few moments at the nursery to see if any hummers are using the hybrid plants.

A RUBY-THROATED hum-mingbird feeding at coral, or trumpet, honeysuckle.

BLOOMING SCHEDULE

You'll never need to worry about your hummingbird feeder going dry if you grow plants that bloom throughout the time hummers visit your backyard. Coral, or trumpet, honeysuckle is a native vine with prolific red tubular flowers that achieves this goal almost single-handedly. It begins blooming in mid-latitudes of the U.S. in late April or early May and continues until frost. You can design into your garden a progression of perennials—from early columbine to midsummer beebalm to late salvias—that will keep hummers happy while providing seasonal interest for the human eye.

At our home in western North Carolina, hummingbirds usually arrive between April 7 and April 15. They glean nectar from flowering quince, a hardy import from Japan that was planted here by previous residents and that blooms even during spring snowstorms. As the quince fades, wild columbine and coral bells burst into bloom. Then comes coral, or trumpet, honeysuckle, which flowers into autumn.

By early summer, our flower beds abound with scarlet beebalm and standing cypress. Trumpet creeper and butterfly bush kick in during July. Blood, or tropical, sage, jewelweed, and cardinal flower bloom from August until the hummers depart. —CT

Experienced gardeners know that *deadheading*—removing spent blossoms before they go to seed—stimulates plants to create a new flush of blooms. The evolutionary purpose of flowers is to induce pollination and create seeds for the next generation. If this process is interrupted, the plant forms more flowers and tries again. Thus deadheading several times during the growing season keeps annuals and perennials cloaked in color.

OUT OF THE POT, INTO THE GROUND

After planning your backyard habitat and purchasing growing stock, you'll want to give your new plants the best start possible. Transplant them on a damp, windless, overcast day to reduce stress. Or install them late in the afternoon as temperatures cool and intense sun wanes. If you must transplant on hot, windy days, provide temporary shade and windbreaks by propping cardboard boxes or overturned baskets over the transplants.

Dig slightly deeper than the plant's root ball, and widen the hole at least twice the pot's diameter. Loosen the plant from the pot by running a knife or spatula between the soil and the pot wall. Turn the plant over into your outstretched hand and tap the pot bottom with a trowel. The plant and intact root ball should slide out. If roots wrap endlessly around the outer perimeter of the soil, take a sharp knife or garden shears and slice the encircling roots, top to bottom, at one-third intervals around the perimeter. Gently straighten the outer roots so they will begin growing away from the plant's core.

Toss a little loose soil you removed, or an amended soil mix, into the hole. Center the plant in the hole, check to see that the crown (where stem meets roots) is even with the soil surface, and wiggle the root ball to seat it. Gently backfill the hole to half its depth with good soil and tamp lightly with a trowel or your hand. Apply water with a sprinkling can or fine hose spray to dampen the roots.

Fill the remainder of the hole with good soil and tamp again. Smooth the backfill dirt so it's level with the plant's soil surface. Water thoroughly, but use caution in clay or poorly drained soils so water does not collect and stand in the hole, drowning the roots. If desired, mulch around the plant's perimeter. Check soil moisture periodically by sticking your index finger into the soil. If it's dry a few inches under the surface, the plant needs a thorough watering.

GARDENING IN CONTAINERS

Backyard wildlife habitats come in all sizes, from expansive acreages to apartment rooftops to window boxes. Small-space gardening calls for creativity. It may not attract as many species as an acre with a pond, but plenty of folks have discovered the joys of luring humming-birds and butterflies to plantings on a patio or deck.

The most common way to manage plants in confined spaces is in containers, which might include a combination of hanging baskets, decorative pots, and window boxes. If your containers are large enough, try planting something tall in the back, a bushy middle-of-the-pot selection, and a trailing plant that drapes elegantly down the front or sides. Use the same technique to encourage plants to fill and spill from window boxes. If there is room on your patio, place a small trellis behind a potted vine to make use of vertical space. Consult Chapter 5 for plants suitable for containers.

Creating and tending a container garden differs from in-ground gardening in several important ways. Potted soil dries quickly, so most containerized plants require daily watering. Light-colored plastic or ceramic pots of the largest size you can handle are least prone to overheating and drying. If you can't water every day, invest in an irrigation system or choose drought-tolerant species such as aloe or cacti. Saucers placed under pots will retain root-rotting liquid if plants are overwatered. If you use saucers, add pea gravel to the bottom of the saucers so plants won't drown.

Most patio gardeners fill containers with potting mixes instead of soil. These formulations contain peat moss or cocoa fiber to retain moisture, plus porous perlite and vermiculite to encourage rooting. Many also come with bits of fertilizer distributed throughout the mix, but these energy-giving compounds are readily absorbed by plants. Feed container plants biweekly with a general-purpose, water-soluble fertilizer applied at half the recommended strength so as not to burn them.

It will be hard to keep your potted plants thriving during winter unless you have a greenhouse or lots of sunny indoor window space. For that reason, it's easiest to treat container plants as annuals and grow new ones each year. That also affords freedom to experiment with different species and combinations each season.

Completing Your Backyard Landscape

ABUNDANT FLOWERING plants and bright touches of red should bring hum-mingbirds flocking to your garden.

Customize your garden by leaving a few artistic dead branches as photoge-nic perches, placing mossy logs where ferns will grow and toads will hop, or adding accent objects such as songbird nest boxes or feeders. If humming-birds fail to find your habitat once the flowers begin blooming, make your yard more visible from a distance by purchasing a roll of bright red, pink, or orange surveyor's tape, inch-wide plastic ribbon that's available in most hard-ware stores. Drape it on branches of trees and shrubs, and tie a few stream-ers to your hummingbird feeder support. As the tape flutters in the breeze, it should catch the eye of passing hummers and beckon them to visit.

If you have the opposite problem—hummingbirds fighting over limited nectar resources—clump popular plants around several feeders, so the aggressive hummer can't defend everything at once. Nectar plants that pro-duce masses of small flowers over a long period, such as coral bells, will serve many more birds than plants offering only a few quickly fading flow-ers, such as daylily.

Backyard wildlife habitats showcase good land stewardship. They are low-maintenance landscapes that use less energy mowing and trimming, require fewer (or no) chemical sprays and fertilizers, and allow more time to observe wildlife. Once you have created a habitat that suits your needs and those of your wild guests, don't forget to spend time enjoying the serenity and the wildlife encounters. Today's children spend less time outside than children of previous generations. Encourage your kids, grandchildren, and other youngsters to share some of these special experiences. —CT

TEN PLANTS HUMMERS LOVE . . . AND YOU WILL TOO!

Hummingbirds sample nectar from thousands of plants. They have an innate curiosity to explore red—stopping at cemeteries to investigate red artificial flowers and sometimes buzzing humans wearing red clothing, lipstick, or nail polish—but they return repeatedly only to plants that offer sweet, abundant food. Here are ten plants that North American hummers find irresistible.

INVITE YOUR kids or the neighbors' kids to share the wonders of your wildlife garden.

1. CHUPAROSA. The Spanish word *chuparosa* literally means "kisses red." It's also a colloquial name for hummingbirds, describing them as "flower-kissers." In addition, chuparosa refers to several plants native to the southwestern U.S. and Mexico. All are members of the Acanthus family and are perennials recognized by their tubular red or orange flowers. These plants are ideally suited for hot climates with low rainfall, and they will thrive in large containers.

   Southwestern gardeners rate California beloperone as a prize plant in native landscapes. It grows quickly, reaching 3 to 4 feet high. In moist years it's covered with scarlet blossoms during the peak of spring hummingbird migration. Several close relatives include red justica and Mexican honeysuckle, the latter an orange-flowered shrub with velvety leaves. Both plants produce flowers almost year-round in Zones 8 and higher. Desert honeysuckle is draped in yellow-orange flowers each spring. With a name that translates to "flower-kisser," any of these chuparosas will be hummer hits in a warm, dry climate.

2. BEEBALM. The word "balm" means relief, but beebalm flowers offer comfort to more than bees. Gardeners from Georgia to southern Canada know this native wildflower as a wellspring of hummingbird nectar. Pompon heads comprise several dozen red tubes, each with a sweet reward at its base. Hummingbirds methodically hover at each floret, lingering long enough for human hosts to get good looks at them.

   Beebalm is versatile, surviving in full sun or dappled shade. Plants spread readily via shallow runners. They do best in rich, moist soil and may require water during extended dry spells. The variety 'Jacob Cline' withstands heat and powdery mildew, a fungal disease that sometimes coats the leaves. Clumps of beebalm should be divided every three to five years. Work some compost into the soil before replanting, and share the extras with someone who has not yet discovered the soothing sound of hummers feeding near the patio.

A MALE *Allen's humming-bird gathers nectar from dangling fuchsia flowers.*

3. FUCHSIA. Even though dangling fuchsias are not native to the U.S., they are highly attractive to hummingbirds. Why? Many species of fuchsia grow in the highlands of Central and South America, where migratory hummingbirds encounter them in winter. These plants are especially suited to cool, moist climates, such as the Pacific Northwest and coastal California. Usually fuchsias are sold in hanging baskets, but where protected from temperature extremes, they will survive year-round in the ground.

Although many garden-center fuchsias are hybrids lacking nectar, several species with simple blossoms do offer ambrosia. Honeysuckle fuchsia is a great choice. The popular cultivar 'Gartenmeister Bonsteadt' features orange-red flower tubes in pendant clusters. Hardy fuchsia hails from Chile and produces beautiful red-violet flowers. It thrives in moist, temperate conditions and tolerates some shade. *Fuchsia lycioides* has prolific red-purple flowers and grows to small shrub size. Any of these fuchsias make visiting hummers happy in a backyard habitat.

4. JEWELWEED. Find a stream where spotted jewelweed grows and sit quietly on a late August afternoon. The drone of hummingbird wings may amaze you. The freckled orange blossoms produce nectar that fuels the ruby-throated hummingbird's southward migration. Also called touch-me-not, these plants feature spring-loaded dispersal. Tap a fat green pod; it flings seeds far and wide. Start your own patch by collecting a few seeds and sowing immediately in rich, damp soil. Seeds need to overwinter in the ground, but once established, jewelweed renews itself annually.

Spotted jewelweed grows 3 feet tall by late summer and thrives in sun or part shade. A yellow-flowered counterpart, pale touch-me-not, tolerates full shade. Both occur naturally in damp areas throughout the East and Midwest. Jewelweed is seldom sold commercially, but the closely related impatiens is the most popular shade-tolerant bedding plant in America. Select single-flowered impatiens varieties such as 'Accent' or 'Super Elfin' for good nectar production.

5. PENSTEMON. About 250 species of penstemon have been identified, most residing in meadows, desert washes, and on rock ledges of the American West. Their tubular flowers may be blue, purple, white, or yellow—and hummingbirds will visit these colors if rewarded with ample nectar—but many western penstemons have red or hot pink flowers that especially lure hummers. Beardtongue and scarlet bugler are common names for these plants. They are drought-tolerant perennials—most requiring full sun and good drainage—and start fairly easily from seed. In the East and Midwest, beardtongues are usually white or lavender.

PINENEEDLE PENSTEMON *is one of many western species that attract hummingbirds with bright red color and sweet nectar.*

Pineneedle penstemon is a low-growing plant with numerous red blossoms. It is a great choice for rock gardens. Native to southern New Mexico, Arizona, and Mexico, it adapts well in dry soils north into Zone 4. Beardlip penstemon and cardinal penstemon—both of which produce snapdragon-shaped red flowers—thrive in the mountainous Southwest.

Desert species seen at hummingbird hotspots in southeastern Arizona include Parry's penstemon, which is covered in spring with small rose-magenta flowers, and firecracker penstemon, well named for its yard-long plumes of scarlet flowers. It requires dry conditions and grows north into Zone 4.

Natives suited to southern California and Baja California include desert beardtongue with rose-purple blossoms on 3-foot plants, and scarlet bugler, which flourishes on dry sites in Zone 8 and warmer. It bears brilliant inch-long red flowers. In the moist habitat of the California coast, honeysuckle penstemon, or heartleaf keckiella, climbs to 10 feet and has small red flowers with yellow beards. Redwood keckiella, a shrub with brick red blossoms, also entices California hummers.

6. SALVIA. Like penstemons, plants in the genus *Salvia* are widespread, and many have evolutionary relationships with hummingbirds. Blood, or tropical, sage is native from Texas to Central America and the West Indies. It has naturalized from Florida to South Carolina and can be grown as a summer

AN IMMATURE *Anna's hummingbird seeking nectar at Cleveland sage.*

annual throughout most of the U.S. This scarlet-blossomed beauty is perfect for hummingbird gardens because it flowers prolifically over a long season and is easy to grow. Though a sun lover, it can tolerate some shade and excels in moist to dry climates.

Autumn sage is another attractive, adaptable choice. In Texas and Mexico, the shrubby plant prospers in dry, sunny locations. It is perennial into Zone 7, with showy red-purple blossoms timed to fuel hummingbirds on their southward migrations. Mexican bush sage offers silvery green foliage and woolly purple and white flowers on tall spikes. Native to Mexico, it adapts well in the southern U.S., providing more nectar for autumn migration.

Blue-flowered Cleveland sage is an evergreen shrub of dry regions in southern California and Baja California. In addition to pleasing hummers, its fragrant leaves are dried for tea and potpourri. *Salvia* species belong to the mint family, typically recognized by square stems, distinct fragrance, and diverse culinary uses. Pineapple sage has the odor of ripe pineapple and is used in refreshing drinks. Native to Mexico and Guatemala, its elegant scarlet tubes are instantly recognized and eagerly sampled by hummingbirds that know the plant from their winter range. Anise-scented sage is a South American species with rich blue-purple flowers. It is well suited to container gardens. Both pineapple and anise-scented sage are widely grown as summer annuals in North America.

7. TRUMPET CREEPER. Flowers that attract hummingbirds typically fit the size and shape of their pollinators' bills, which for North American species means a floral tube ¾ to 1½ inches long. The exception is trumpet creeper, with 3-inch blossoms. Usually hummingbirds avoid immersing their head all the way into a flower, because they cannot see predators approaching while they gather nectar. But trumpet creeper offers so much food that hungry hummers can't resist.

This sprawling vine, which can grow 30 feet long, is not for small spaces or shy gardeners. Eliminate any shoots that pop up uninvited in flower beds! Trained on a sturdy trellis or allowed to cling to the trunk of a stout dead tree, the vine will become established in three or four years and then drip with orange-red flowers each summer. The hybrid cultivar 'Madame Galen' has less exuberant growth yet offers sweet rewards. Trumpet creeper is native from Florida to Pennsylvania, Iowa, and Texas. In the West, it grows in Zones 5 through 9.

8. CORAL, OR TRUMPET, HONEYSUCKLE. The difference between trumpet creeper and coral (also called trumpet) honeysuckle is like comparing a sprinter with a marathon runner. The trumpet creeper grows rapidly and pumps out showy flowers during late summer. Trumpet honeysuckle grows more slowly and produces long-lasting clusters of red flowers that envelop the vine from early May until frost. It retains glossy leaves, and sometimes a few blossoms, through southern winters and behaves beautifully on a trellis. If I were limited to only one plant that could attract hummingbirds to my North Carolina home, I would choose coral honeysuckle. The vine is native to the eastern and midwestern United States and hardy north into Zone 4. If nurseries near you don't stock the wild, red-blossomed vine, the cultivars 'Goldflame' or 'Dropmore Scarlet' will satisfy hummers' nectar cravings. Although hummingbirds abandon feeders during peak bloom of Japanese honeysuckle, *don't be tempted* to plant this highly invasive Asian species, which chokes fields and woodlands in the eastern U.S.

Coral honeysuckle has several yellow-flowered, summer-blooming counterparts. Yellow honeysuckle grows in sun or part shade in mid-latitudes from North Carolina west to Oklahoma. Orange honeysuckle is a similar vine with orange-red blossoms. It is native to Zone 6 and warmer climates from British Columbia, Washington, and Montana south through Utah and California. Chaparral honeysuckle tolerates the hot, dry conditions in southern California and Arizona.

All of the native honeysuckle vines grow well with little care. It's best to shape and prune them in winter. Sometimes aphids infest the tender shoots. They can be controlled with applications

IN THE Pacific Northwest, hummingbirds such as this male rufous swarm around red-flowering currant bushes in spring.

A MALE broad-billed hummingbird samples nectar from ocotillo.

of ladybugs or insecticidal soap. Don't use stronger chemicals, because hummingbirds often glean small spiders, gnats, and aphids from honeysuckle foliage and blossoms.

9. RED-FLOWERING CURRANT. It is no accident that rufous hummingbirds arrive in the Pacific Northwest as red-flowering currant bursts into bloom each spring. Scientists believe the red, or deep pink, blossoms have evolved to be pollinated by hummers, and sometimes swarms of them feed at the drooping flowers. These attractive shrubs reach 8 to 10 feet tall and bear small blue-black fruits that songbirds eat. Red-flowering currant is native to the coastal mountains of British Columbia, south into California, but it grows well elsewhere in dry areas to Zone 5. Widely available at nurseries and garden centers, this shrub is a tremendous hummingbird magnet.

Another stunning shrub, native from coastal central California to Baja California, is fuchsia-flowering gooseberry. In late winter it produces dangling crimson flowers, tempting resident and migrant hummers to drink nectar and brush against protruding, pollen-covered stamens. Several other related currants (thornless) and gooseberries (with thorns) are common in the West and are eagerly visited by hummers. They include the delightfully named gummy gooseberry and mountain gooseberry, both producing red-purple flowers, and the golden currant, with spicy-smelling yellow blossoms.

10. OCOTILLO. If you live in the desert Southwest where intense sun and baking heat govern what succeeds in your garden, and you don't waste precious water irrigating, try ocotillo. This tough shrub, native to parched landscapes from Texas west to California and south to Mexico, thrives where most other plants wither. Ocotillos shed their leaves during drought, but after winter rains, they green up and form foot-long clusters of red florets at the tips of their spiny branches. Ocotillo's bright advertisement entices Anna's, Costa's, black-chinned, broad-billed, and broad-tailed hummingbirds, which jockey for nectar as well as favorite perches atop the tall shrubs. Using a lanky ocotillo as a focal point in a native desert landscape will not disappoint!

Chapter 5: A Hummer Garden Plan

ON THE FOLLOWING PAGES you will find three plans for backyard hummingbird habitats. The first shows a design for a typical quarter- to half-acre residential backyard. This layout can be customized for smaller, larger, or irregularly shaped spaces of your yard by deleting or adding plants. If your yard has a different directional orientation, determine which places are sunny or shady, then select plants accordingly.

The second plan typifies views from a patio or favorite window. In addition to an overhead perspective of the planting layout, it visualizes the vertical space that trees, shrubs, vines, and other features will occupy. The third plan takes a similar approach for a container garden, appropriate for a deck or small patio.

To adapt any plan to your specific needs, imagine your yard as a bird cafeteria. Each space is an opportunity to plant something yummy that will attract hummingbirds. Use the symbols on generic plans to identify the category (tree, shrub, etc.), then go to the appropriate regional plant list to choose plants that should do well in your yard.

Key for All Plans

T—Tree	**A**—Annual	☀—Sun
S—Shrub	**G**—Garden plants	◉—Shade
V—Vine	**W**—Water	
P—Perennial	**F**—Feeder	

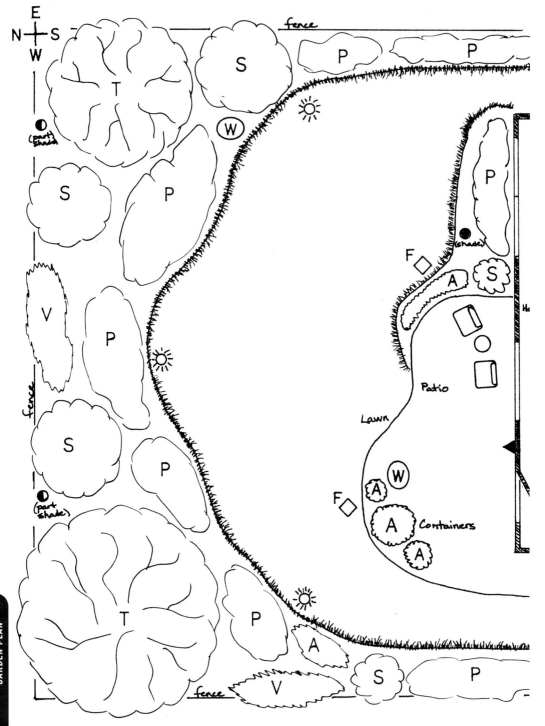

USE THIS generic plan as a guide to customize a backyard hummingbird habitat at your home.

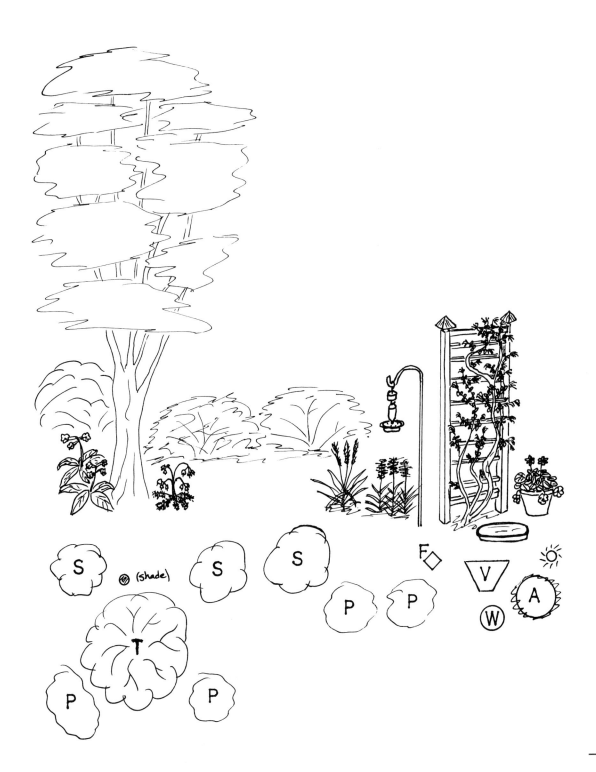

THIS GENERIC hummingbird habitat plan will help you visualize how to use vertical space.

TAKE IDEAS *from this generic plan for a container-based hummingbird habitat if you only have a deck or tiny yard to support plants.*

Regional Plant Lists

The following lists are based on average climatic conditions in the eight regions shown below. Listed plants have proven their ability to attract hummingbirds, but many other species also work well. Substitute freely if other plants better fit your situation. Red is key to attracting a hummer's attention, but pink, orange, purple, blue, yellow, and white flowers also lure them if blossoms are appropriately shaped and offer abundant nectar. Some native species may be available only from native plant nurseries. Make certain plants are responsibly grown rather than dug from the wild. Unless noted, all listed plants require at least six hours of daily sun.

Numerous common names can describe the same plant, and these names may vary from region to region. Plant names in this book follow the U.S. Department of Agriculture Plant Database. By selecting the Latin name of a plant that interests you, you can define it precisely at your local nursery or garden center.

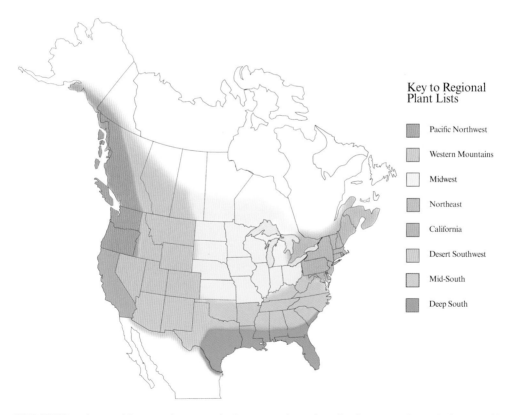

Key to Regional
Plant Lists

Pacific Northwest

Western Mountains

Midwest

Northeast

California

Desert Southwest

Mid-South

Deep South

FIND YOUR region on this map, then consult the appropriate plant list for suggestions of what to add to your yard to entice hummingbirds.

Key to Plant List Symbols

N—Native to region

* —Attracts hummers and butterflies

◉ —Tolerates shade

!—Use caution

A MALE *black-chinned hummingbird feeding at a snapdragon.*

PACIFIC NORTHWEST

ANNUALS

Snapdragon (*Antirrhinum majus*) *****

Farewell-to-spring (*Clarkia amoena*) **N**

Grand collomia (*Collomia grandiflora*) **N**

Impatiens (*Impatiens walleriana*) ***** ◉

Shrimpplant (*Justicia brandegeeana*)

Painted tongue (*Salpiglossis sinuata*)

Blood, or tropical, sage (*Salvia coccinea*)

Pineapple sage (*Salvia elegans*)

Nasturtium (*Tropaeolum majus*) *****

PERENNIALS

Western red columbine (*Aquilegia formosa*) **N ***

Indian paintbrush (*Castilleja miniata*) **N**

Fireweed (*Chamerion angustifolium*) **N ***

Scarlet larkspur (*Delphinium nudicaule*) **N**

Western bleeding heart (*Dicentra formosa*) **N *** ◉

Common foxglove (*Digitalis purpurea*) ◉ **!** (poisonous if eaten) (biennial)

Hummingbird trumpet, or California fuchsia (*Epilobium canum*) **N ***

Coral bells (*Heuchera sanguinea*)

Red-hot poker (*Kniphofia uvaria*)

Columbia lily (*Lilium columbianum*) **N ***

Cardinal flower (*Lobelia cardinalis*) **N** * ! (poisonous if eaten)
Scarlet monkeyflower (*Mimulus cardinalis*) **N**
Lewis' monkeyflower (*Mimulus lewisii*) **N**
Beebalm (*Monarda didyma*) *
Bird's beak lousewort (*Pedicularis ornithorhyncha*) **N**
Mountain pride (*Penstemon newberryi*) **N**
Richardson's penstemon (*Penstemon richardsonii*) **N**
Spreading phlox (*Phlox diffusa*) **N** *
Cape fuchsia (*Phygelius capensis*)

VINES

Trumpet creeper (*Campsis radicans*)
Chilean bellflower (*Laphgeria rosea*) ◉
Orange honeysuckle (*Lonicera ciliosa*) **N** *
Scarlet runner bean (*Phaseolus coccineus*) *

SHRUBS

Hairy manzanita (*Arctostaphylos columbiana*) **N**
Winter-blooming camellia (*Camellia sasanqua*) ◉
Hardy fuchsia (*Fuchsia magellanica*) ◉
Winter jasmine (*Jasminum nudiflorum*)
Twinberry (*Lonicera involucrata*) **N** *
Western rhododendron (*Rhododendron macrophyllum*) **N**
Red-flowering currant (*Ribes sanguineum*) **N** *
Salmonberry (*Rubus spectabilis*) **N** *
Red elderberry (*Sambucus racemosa*) **N**
Red huckleberry (*Vaccinium parvifolium*) **N** *

TREES

Red horsechestnut (*Aesculus* × *carnea*)
Red buckeye (*Aesculus pavia*) *
Pacific madrone (*Arbutus menziesii*) **N** *
Strawberry tree (*Arbutus unedo*)
Chilean flame tree (*Embothrium coccineum*)
Black locust (*Robinia pseudoacacia*) *
Australian flame tree (*Telopea oreades*)

A FEMALE Anna's hummingbird sipping nectar at autumn sage.

CALIFORNIA

ANNUALS
Spider flower (*Cleome hasslerana*) *
Impatiens (*Impatiens walleriana*) * ◉
Blood, or tropical, sage (*Salvia coccinea*)

PERENNIALS
Medicinal aloe (*Aloe vera*)
Western red columbine (*Aquilegia formosa*) **N** *
Coast paintbrush (*Castilleja affinis*) **N**
California paintbrush (*Castilleja californica*) **N**
Scarlet delphinium (*Delphinium cardinale*) **N**
Hummingbird trumpet, or California fuchsia (*Epilobium canum*) **N** *
Shrimpplant (*Justicia brandegeeana*)
Red-hot poker (*Kniphofia uvaria*)
Tree mallow (*Lavatera assurgentiflora*) **N** *
Scarlet monkeyflower (*Mimulus cardinalis*) **N**
Scarlet bugler (*Penstemon centranthifolius*) **N**
Royal penstemon (*Penstemon spectabilis*) **N**
Pineapple sage (*Salvia elegans*)

Anise sage (*Saliva guaranitica*)
Mexican bush sage (*Salvia leucantha*)
Hummingbird sage (*Salvia spathacea*) **N**
Woolly blue-curls (*Trichostema lanatum*) **N** *

VINES

Trailing abutilon (*Abutilon megapotamicum*)
Trumpet creeper (*Campsis radicans*)
Blood-red trumpet vine (*Disticus buccinatoria*)
Chilean glory vine (*Eccremocarpus scaber*)
Coral, or trumpet, honeysuckle (*Lonicera sempervirens*) * ◉

SHRUBS

Common manzanita (*Arctostaphylos manzanita*) **N**
Yellow bird-of-paradise (*Caesalpinia gilliesii*)
Baja fairy duster (*Calliandra californica*) **N** *
Pink powder puff (*Calliandra haematocephala*)
Wild lilac, or felt leaf ceanothus (*Ceanothus arboreus*) **N** *
Pride of Madeira (*Echium candicans*) *
Escallonia (*Escallonia* × *exoniensis* 'Frades') *
Hardy fuchsia (*Fuchsia magellanica*) ◉
Grevillea 'Robyn Gordon'
Chuparosa, or hummingbird bush, or California beloperone (*Justicia
    californica*) **N** *
Honeysuckle penstemon, or heartleaf keckiella (*Keckiella cordifolia*)
    N *
Redwood keckiella (*Keckiella corymbosa*) **N**
Lantana (*Lantana camara*) *
Lion's tail (*Leonotis leonurus*)
Chaparral honeysuckle (*Lonicera interrupta*) **N** *
Indian hawthorn (*Rhaphiolepis indica*) *
Red-flowering currant (*Ribes sanguineum*) **N** *
Fuchsia-flowered gooseberry (*Ribes speciosum*) **N**
Cleveland sage (*Salvia clevelandii*) **N** *
Cape honeysuckle (*Tecoma capensis*)

TREES

Mimosa (*Albizia julibrissin*) *
Pacific madrone (*Arbutus menziessi*) **N** *
Strawberry tree (*Arbutus unedo*)

Key to Plant List
Symbols

N—Native to region
*—Attracts hummers and
    butterflies
◉—Tolerates shade
!—Use caution

Lemon bottlebrush (*Callistemon citrinus*)
Chilean flame tree (*Embothrium coccineum*)
Red-flowering gum (*Eucalyptus ficifolia*)
Blue gum (*Eucalyptus globulus*)
White ironbark (*Eucalyptus leucoxylon megalocarpa*)
Red ironbark (*Eucalyptus sideroxylon*)
Silk oak (*Grevillea robusta*)

California Hummingbird Paradise

HUGH AND Sue Smith's backyard in Solvang, California, with wild lilac (left) and breath of heaven (right) in bloom.

After Hugh P. Smith Jr. retired as a medical doctor and radiologist, he began photographing birds, especially hummingbirds. His wife, Sue, loves to garden, so together they planned and planted a three-acre suburban yard to attract wildlife around their home in Solvang, California. Later they downsized to a smaller home in Solvang but continued to garden for hummingbirds. Now, at their retirement villa, they spend lots of time watching hummingbirds and songbirds that visit plants and feeders on their patio. Sue shares recommendations from more than two decades of gardening in this balmy Mediterranean climate.

Our favorite tree is mimosa. It is messy, but the hummers fight over it and we don't mind the mess. Another tree we discovered is chitalpa. This hybrid comes from southern catalpa, which offers large flowers, and drought-tolerant desert willow. It grows quickly to a nice rounded shape, about 20 to 30 feet tall.

Ours had tubular pink blossoms, but I've also seen lavender and white. Dropped blossoms can be messy, and trees sometimes get powdery mildew or anthracnose, but the one we had in Solvang was problem-free and bloomed all summer. It was great.

Trumpet creeper is tops for attracting hummers. It is a big heavy vine and needs a sturdy fence. Cape honeysuckle has a red flower and can be trained as a shrub or vine. Both require a bit more water than the native plants.

When we first came to California we couldn't get enough of the flowers, so we chose ivy geraniums, but it was too cold for them in Solvang. A number of plants will grow here on the coast that won't grow in Solvang. Periwinkle (Vinca major or Vinca minor) works well as a ground cover but requires a lot of water and does better with some shade. If you have full sun you could go with rock rose. There are many choices. We like Cistus X purpureus for size and color. This isn't a true ground cover, but you can get very low-growing varieties. The foliage is interesting, and the color is glorious when it blooms. It makes a good bank cover.

A great shrub is Escallonia rubra or Escallonia X langleyensis. It has pink flowers throughout most of the summer, and hummers like it. Bottlebrush is a real hummer favorite that requires moderate water. Rhaphiolepis has pink flowers and will tolerate all types of soil. It seems to do well with moderate or skimpy water but needs some sun. There are many varieties and sizes, but our first choice is Rhaphiolepis 'Ballerina' (2 to 3 feet).

Penstemon is a fabulous native perennial that survives on moderate water. Lots of colors, long bloom, and hummers love it. They also swarm to fuchsias, a wonderful choice, though they need some moisture. If you put hardy fuchsia (Fuchsia magellanica) on the north side of the house with almost no sun, it will do very well. Lavender gets by on very little water and attracts both hummers and butterflies. We have English lavender and Lavandula 'Goodwin Creek Grey'. Another dry lover is Mexican sage. Great for hummers. We've grown lots of varieties of sage, all of which survive with almost no water but thrive with moderate moisture. We are very partial to red-hot poker because the hooded orioles also love it. We leave one feeding hole open in the hummer feeder to attract the orioles as well.

We discovered an annual the hummers love—cleome. It's like a spider lily—super plant! Cosmos is another great all-around choice. It blooms almost all summer and into fall. It attracts butterflies, as well as goldfinches that visit when it goes to seed. —Sue Smith, Santa Barbara, California

A MALE black-chinned hummingbird nectaring at aloe.

DESERT SOUTHWEST

ANNUALS

Hummingbird mint (*Agastache cana*) **N** *

Mexican hyssop (*Agastache mexicana*) *

Threadleaf giant hyssop, or sunset hyssop, or licorice mint
   (*Agastache rupestris*) *

Annual phlox (*Phlox drummondii*) *

PERENNIALS

Aloe (*Aloe karasburgensis, A. vera*)

Bouvardia (*Bouvardia glaberrima*) **N**

Hummingbird trumpet, or California fuchsia
   (*Epilobium canum*) **N** *

Coral bells (*Heuchera sanguinea*) **N**

Cardinal flower (*Lobelia cardinalis, L. laxiflora*) **N** * !
   (poisonous if eaten)

Scarlet monkeyflower (*Mimulus cardinalis*) **N**

Beardlip penstemon (*Penstemon barbatus*) **N**

Firecracker penstemon (*Penstemon eatonii*) **N**

Parry's penstemon (*Penstemon parryi*) **N**
Desert beardtongue (*Penstemon pseudospectabilis*) **N**
Royal penstemon (*Penstemon spectabilis*) **N**
Autumn sage (*Salvia greggii*) **N**
Lemmon's sage (*Salvia lemmonii*) **N**
Baby sage (*Salvia microphylla*) **N**
Mountain sage (*Salvia regla*) **N**
Mexican pink (*Silene laciniata*) **N**
Scarlet hedge nettle (*Stachys coccinea*) **N**

VINES
Trumpet creeper (*Campsis radicans*)
Scarlet creeper (*Ipomoea hederifolia*) **N**
Snapdragon vine (*Maurandella antirrhiniflora*) **N**

SHRUBS
Desert honeysuckle (*Anisacanthus quadrifidus brevilobus, A. quadrifidus wrightii*) **N ***
Chuparosa, or desert honeysuckle (*Anisacanthus thurberi*) **N**
Red bird-of-paradise (*Caesalpinia pulcherrima*)
Fairy duster (*Calliandra californica, C. eriophylla*) **N ***
Coral bean (*Erythrina flabelliformis*) **N**
Ocotillo (*Fouquieria splendens*) **N**
Hesperaloe (*Hesperaloe parviflora*) **N**
Chuparosa, or hummingbird bush, or California beloperone (*Justicia californica*) **N ***
Arizona water-willow, or chuparosa (*Justicia candicans*) **N**
Water-willow, or chuparosa, or Mexican honeysuckle (*Justicia sonorae, J. spicigera*)
Cape honeysuckle (*Tecoma capensis*)
Yellow bells (*Tecoma stans angusta, T. s. stans*) **N**

TREES
Desert willow (*Chilopsis linearis*) **N**
Mexican elderberry (*Sambucus nigra canadensis*) **N** (flowers not as attractive as potential for nesting cover)

Key to Plant List Symbols

N—Native to region
*—Attracts hummers and butterflies
◉—Tolerates shade
!—Use caution

A MALE broad-tailed hummingbird feeding at orange honeysuckle.

WESTERN MOUNTAINS

ANNUALS
Snapdragon (*Antirrhinum majus*) *
Blood, or tropical, sage (*Salvia coccinea*)
Nasturtium (*Tropaeolum majus*) *

PERENNIALS
Threadleaf giant hyssop, or sunset hyssop, or licorice mint (*Agastache rupestris*) *
Western red columbine (*Aquilegia formosa*) **N** *
Wyoming paintbrush (*Castilleja linariifolia*) **N**
Giant red paintbrush (*Castilleja miniata*) **N**
Fireweed (*Chamerion angustifolium*) **N** *
Hummingbird trumpet, or California fuchsia (*Epilobium canum*) **N** *
Coral bells (*Heuchera sanguinea*)
Scarlet gilia (*Ipomopsis aggregata*) **N** * (biennial)
Scarlet monkeyflower (*Mimulus cardinalis*) **N**
Lewis' monkeyflower (*Mimulus lewisii*) **N**
Horsemint (*Monarda menthaefolia*) **N** *

Beardlip penstemon (*Penstemon barbatus*) **N**
Cardinal penstemon (*Penstemon cardinalis*) **N**
Pineneedle penstemon (*Penstemon pinifolius*) **N**
Longleaf phlox (*Phlox longifolia*) **N** *****

VINES
Trumpet creeper (*Campsis radicans*)
Red morning glory (*Ipomoea coccinea*)
Orange honeysuckle (*Lonicera ciliosa*) **N** *****
Coral, or trumpet, honeysuckle (*Lonicera sempervirens*) ***** ◉

SHRUBS
Green-leaf manzanita (*Arctostaphylos patula*) **N**
Buckbrush (*Ceanothus fendleri*) **N** *****
Flowering quince (*Chaenomeles japonica*)
Twinberry (*Lonicera involucrata*) **N** *****
Golden currant (*Ribes aureum*) **N** *****
Salmonberry (*Rubus spectabilis*) **N** *****
Huckleberry, blueberry (*Vaccinium membranaceum, V. ovalifolium*) **N** *****

TREES
Catalpa (*Catalpa speciosa*)
Chokecherry (*Prunus virginiana*) **N** *****
New Mexico locust (*Robinia neomexicana*) **N**
Black locust (*Robinia pseudoacacia*) *****

Key to Plant List Symbols

N—Native to region
*****—Attracts hummers and butterflies
◉—Tolerates shade
!—Use caution

A YOUNG ruby-throated hummingbird nectaring at trumpet creeper.

MIDWEST

ANNUALS
Spider flower (*Cleome hasslerana*) *
Blood, or tropical, sage (*Salvia coccinea*) *
Zinnia (*Zinnia elegans*) *

PERENNIALS
Hollyhock (*Alcea rosea*) * (biennial)
Columbine (*Aquilegia canadensis*) **N** *
Butterfly milkweed (*Asclepias tuberosa*) **N** *
Wild bleeding heart (*Dicentra eximia*) ◉
Foxglove (*Digitalis purpurea*) ◉ **!**
   (poisonous if eaten) (biennial)
Coral bells (*Heuchera sanguinea*)
Spotted jewelweed (*Impatiens capensis*) **N** *
Cardinal flower (*Lobelia cardinalis*) **N** * **!**
   (poisonous if eaten)
Beebalm (*Monarda didyma*) *
Wild bergamot (*Monarda fistulosa*) **N** *

Dotted mint, or spotted beebalm (*Monarda punctata*) **N** *
    (biennial)
Fire pink (*Silene virginica*) **N**

VINES

Trumpet creeper (*Campsis radicans*) **N**
Chilean glory vine (*Eccremocarpus scaber*)
Red morning glory (*Ipomoea coccinea*)
Coral, or trumpet, honeysuckle (*Lonicera sempervirens*) **N** * ◉

SHRUBS

Butterfly bush (*Buddleja davidii*) * ◉
Buttonbush (*Cephalanthus occidentalis*) **N** * ◉
Flowering quince (*Chaenomeles japonica*)
Rose of Sharon (*Hibiscus syriacus*)
Coralberry (*Symphoricarpos albus*) **N** *
Lilac (*Syringa vulgaris*) *

TREES

Ohio buckeye (*Aesculus glabra*) **N**
Horsechestnut (*Aesculus hippocastanum*)
Catalpa (*Catalpa speciosa*)
Tuliptree (*Liriodendron tulipifera*) **N** *
Crab apple (*Malus floribunda*) *
Black locust (*Robinia pseudoacacia*) *

Key to Plant List Symbols

N—Native to region

*—Attracts hummers and butterflies

◉—Tolerates shade

!—Use caution

AN IMMATURE *ruby-throated hummingbird feeding at blood, or tropical, sage.*

MID-SOUTH

ANNUALS
Spider flower (*Cleome hasslerana*) *
Blood, or tropical, sage (*Salvia coccinea*) *
Pineapple sage (*Salvia elegans*)
Mexican sunflower (*Tithonia rotundifolia*) *

PERENNIALS
Hummingbird mint (*Agastache cana*) *
Bleeding heart (*Dicentra spectabilis*) ○
Foxglove (*Digitalis purpurea*) ○ ! (poisonous if eaten) (biennial)
Spotted jewelweed (*Impatiens capensis*) **N** *
Standing cypress (*Ipomopsis rubra*) **N**
Red-hot poker (*Kniphofia uvaria*)
Cardinal flower (*Lobelia cardinalis*) **N** * ! (poisonous if eaten)
Beebalm (*Monarda didyma*) **N** *
Wild bergamot (*Monarda fistulosa*) **N** *

Dotted mint, or spotted beebalm (*Monarda punctata*) **N** * (biennial)
Fire pink (*Silene virginica*) **N**
Indian pink (*Spigelia marilandica*) **N**

VINES
Cross vine (*Bignonia capreolata*) **N**
Trumpet creeper (*Campsis radicans*) **N**
Cardinal climber (*Ipomoea × multifida*)
Cypress vine (*Ipomoea quamoclit*)
Coral, or trumpet, honeysuckle (*Lonicera sempervirens*) **N** * ◉

SHRUBS
Butterfly bush (*Buddleja davidii*) * ◉
Buttonbush (*Cephalanthus occidentalis*) **N** * ◉
Flowering quince (*Chaenomeles japonica*)
Rose of Sharon (*Hibiscus syriacus*)
Azalea (*Rhododendron* spp.) **N** *
Coralberry (*Symphoricarpos orbiculatus*) **N**

TREES
Red buckeye (*Aesculus pavia*) **N** *
Catalpa (*Catalpa bignonioides*) **N**
Tuliptree (*Liriodendron tulipifera*) **N**
Crab apple (*Malus floribunda*)
Black locust (*Robinia pseudoacacia*) **N** *

Key to Plant List Symbols

N—Native to region
*—Attracts hummers and butterflies
◉—Tolerates shade
!—Use caution

A YOUNG *male ruby-throated hummingbird seeking nectar at scarlet bush.*

DEEP SOUTH

ANNUALS
Impatiens (*Impatiens walleriana*) *
Star cluster (*Pentas lanceolata*) * (choose old-fashioned varieties with dark throats)
Annual phlox (*Phlox drummondii*) **N** *
Blood, or tropical, sage (*Salvia coccinea*) **N** *

PERENNIALS
Butterfly milkweed (*Asclepias tuberosa*) **N** *
Canna (*Canna indica*) *
Mexican cigar (*Cuphea micropetala*)
Scarlet hibiscus (*Hibiscus coccineus*) **N** *
Standing cypress (*Ipomopsis rubra*) **N**
Shrimpplant (*Justicia brandegeeana*)
Cardinal flower (*Lobelia cardinalis*) **N** * ! (poisonous if eaten)
Fountain, or firecracker, plant (*Russelia equisetiformis*)

Pineapple sage (*Salvia elegans*)
Mexican bush sage (*Salvia leucantha*) *****
Indian pink (*Spigelia marilandica*) **N**
Porterweed (*Stachytarphaeta urticifolia*) *****

VINES

Cross vine (*Bignonia capreolata*) **N**
Trumpet creeper (*Campsis radicans*) **N**
Cypress vine (*Ipomoea quamoclit*)
Coral, or trumpet, honeysuckle (*Lonicera sempervirens*) **N *** ◉

SHRUBS

Flame flower (*Anisacanthus wrightii*) **N**
Pride-of-Barbados (*Caesalpinia pulcherrima*) *****
Purple cestrum (*Cestrum elegans*)
Coral bean (*Erythrina herbacea*) **N**
Scarlet bush (*Hamelia patens*) **N ***
Mexican honeysuckle (*Justicia spicigera*) *****
Lantana, or West Indian shrub-verbena (*Lantana urticoides*) **N ***
Turk's cap (*Malvaviscus arboreus drummondii*) **N ***
Giant Turk's cap (*Malvaviscus penduliflorus*) *****

TREES

Weeping bottlebrush (*Callistemon viminalis*)
Desert willow (*Chilopsis linearis*)
Orange, lemon, grapefruit (*Citrus* spp.) *****
Texas olive (*Cordia boissieri*)
Royal poinciana (*Delonix regia*)
Loquat (*Eriobotrya japonica*)

Key to Plant List Symbols

N—Native to region
*—Attracts hummers and butterflies
◉ —Tolerates shade
!—Use caution

South Texas Hummingbird Hotspot

A PATIO garden with hummingbird feeders in the backyard of Curt and Anna Reemsnyder in Fulton, Texas.

A HUMMER GARDEN PLAN

Does one small bird have the power to change two lives? For Curtis and Anna Reemsnyder, the answer is a resounding *yes*. Three decades ago, Curt bought a hummingbird feeder for their weekend cottage, located north of Corpus Christi, Texas. The novice birders noticed a hummer, but not the ruby-throated variety their bird book predicted. Jesse Grantham, from the National Audubon Society, identified the mystery guest as a buff-bellied hummingbird.

"At that time, it was an unusual sighting," Anna recalled. "Jesse also told us about the huge numbers of rubythroats that funnel south along the Texas Gulf Coast each September. He suggested we add certain nectar plants to the yard."

When Curt retired, the Reemsnyders sold the cottage and purchased a lovely home on 55 acres that had been used for oil and gas exploration. For nearly 20 years, they labored to restore the shady canopy of live and laurel oaks. Smaller native trees and shrubs create a dense understory. Patches of manicured St. Augustine grass accent magnificent oaks in the front and side yards and provide clear vistas of bird-feeding areas from windows and patios. Sun-drenched woodland edges are perfect for hummer and butterfly plants, creating colorful transitions between lawn and tree islands. The property is a registered Texas Wildscape and a showplace for backyard wildlife.

Early on, the Reemsnyders learned that hummingbirds love the tubular red blossoms of scarlet bush and fountain plant. Throughout the spring, summer, and fall, hummers sip at native coral honeysuckle vines, fragrant passionflowers, feathery pride-of-Barbados, and Cape honeysuckle, a shrub from South Africa. Autumn migrants flock to bright red Turk's cap and to long-blooming blood, or tropical, sage, which is a perennial in subtropical climates.

In beds near the driveway, carrot-colored blossoms of butterfly milkweed provide eye-catching contrast with purple wild petunias (*Ruellia nudiflora* and *R. dyschoriste linearis*). Above them, the delicate lilac blossoms of sky-flower arch gracefully near the orange trumpet creeper hybrid 'Madame Galen', which Curt and Anna prefer over the more exuberant native. All of these plants perform dual duty as hummingbird and butterfly attractors.

Hummer watching here is world class. Each September, hundreds of ruby-throated hummingbirds zip around the feeders like bees drawn to honey. Black-chinned and rufous hummers have visited in winter. Buff-bellied hummingbirds, perhaps descendents of the individual that captured Curt and Anna's hearts decades ago, reside in the yard and flutter to a feeder inches from the deck. Emerald throat, bronze back, chestnut tail, jaunty red beak—Curt and Anna still take special notice whenever one arrives. Perhaps because they discovered birding through an interest in plants, the Reemsnyders regard their yard as a functioning ecosystem. What started with one bird has made a huge impact on their lives and on the habitat that surrounds them. —*CT*

SPOTTED JEWELWEED *is a favorite late-summer nectar source for ruby-throated hummingbirds.*

NORTHEAST

ANNUALS

Snapdragon (*Antirrhinum majus*) *

Spider flower (*Cleome hasslerana*) *

Egyptian star cluster (*Pentas lanceolata*) * (choose old-fashioned varieties with dark throats)

Nasturtium (*Tropaeolum majus*) *

Zinnia (*Zinnia elegans*) *

PERENNIALS

Columbine (*Aquilegia canadensis*) **N** *

Butterfly milkweed (*Asclepias tuberosa*) **N** *

Bleeding heart (*Dicentra eximia*) **N** ◎
Foxglove (*Digitalis purpurea*) ◎ **!** (poisonous if eaten) (biennial)
Coral bells (*Heuchera sanguinea*)
Plantain lily (*Hosta plantaginea*) ◎
Spotted jewelweed (*Impatiens capensis*) **N ***
Red-hot poker (*Kniphofia uvaria*)
Blazing star (*Liatris spicata*) **N ***
Cardinal flower (*Lobelia cardinalis*) **N * !** (poisonous if eaten)
Beebalm (*Monarda didyma*) **N ***
Wild bergamot (*Monarda fistulosa*) **N ***

VINES
Red morning glory (*Ipomoea coccinea*)
Coral, or trumpet, honeysuckle (*Lonicera sempervirens*) **N *** ◎
Scarlet runner bean (*Phaseolus coccineus*)

SHRUBS
Butterfly bush (*Buddleja davidii*) ***** ◎
Buttonbush (*Cephalanthus occidentalis*) **N *** ◎
Flowering quince (*Chaenomeles japonica*)
Coralberry (*Symphoricarpos albus*) **N ***
Lilac (*Syringa vulgaris*) *****
Cardinal shrub (*Weigela florida*) *****

TREES
Redbud (*Cercis canadensis*) **N ***
Downy hawthorn (*Crategus mollis*) **N**
Tuliptree (*Liriodendron tulipifera*) **N ***
Black locust (*Robinia pseudoacacia*) **N ***

Key to Plant List Symbols

N—Native to region
*—Attracts hummers and butterflies
◎—Tolerates shade
!—Use caution

Plants for Container Gardens

The following plants adapt well to growing in containers in most areas. If you live in a mild climate, some will successfully overwinter outdoors. In cooler regions, these plants die without winter protection and will need to be restarted from seeds or bedding plants the following spring.

A RUBY-THROATED hummingbird feeding at the popular bedding plant scarlet sage, which is ideal for container gardens.

ANNUALS

Snapdragon (*Antirrhinum majus*) *

Spider flower (*Cleome spinosa*) *

Honeysuckle fuchsia (*Fuchsia triphylla* 'Gartenmeister Bonstedt')

Impatiens (*Impatiens walleriana*) * ○

Shrimpplant (*Justicia brandegeeana*) (part ○ in hot regions)

Egyptian star cluster (*Pentas lanceolata*) * (choose old-fashioned varieties with dark throats)

Petunia (*Petunia* × *hybrida*) (choose old-fashioned single-flowered varieties)

Fountain, or firecracker, plant (*Russelia equisetiformis*)

Blood, or tropical, sage (*Salvia coccinea*) *

Nasturtium (*Tropaeolum majus*) *

Zinnia (*Zinnia elegans*) *

VINES

Red morning glory (*Ipomoea coccinea*)

Cardinal climber (*Ipomoea × multifida*)
Cypress vine (*Ipomoea quamoclit*)
Scarlet runner bean (*Phaseolus coccineus*) *

Seasonal Progression of Blossoms

In addition to incorporating a variety of plant sizes (trees, shrubs, perennials) into your landscape, create a progression of blooming times, so that something is always flowering from spring through early fall. The following table suggests plant choices (appropriate for the eastern U.S.) to create a continuous nectar buffet.

SPRING	EARLY SUMMER	LATE SUMMER
Columbine (*Aquilegia canadensis*)	Beebalm (*Monarda didyma*)	Autumn sage (*Salvia greggii*)
Coral bells (*Heuchera sanguinea*)	Spider flower (*Cleome hasslerana*)	Blood, or tropical, sage (*Salvia coccinea*)
Creeping phlox (*Phlox subulata*)	Foxglove (*Digitalis purpurea*)	Cardinal flower (*Lobelia cardinalis*)
Bleeding heart (*Dicentra eximia*)	Blazing star (*Liatris spicata*)	Mexican sunflower (*Tithonia rotundifolia*)
Flowering quince (*Chaenomeles japonica*)	Standing cypress (*Ipomopsis rubra*)	Lantana (*Lantana camara*)
Lilac (*Syringa vulgaris*)	Trumpet creeper (*Campsis radicans*)	Cypress vine (*Ipomoea quamoclit*)
Weigela (*Weigela florida*)	Coral, or trumpet, honeysuckle (*Lonicera sempervirens*)	Butterfly bush (*Buddleja davidii*)

Chapter 6: Troubleshooting

BY THEIR VERY HIGH-ENERGY NATURE, their small size, and their high-speed lifestyle, hummingbirds have the potential to get into a lot of trouble. Over my three-plus decades of attracting and feeding hummingbirds, I've seen and experienced most of this trouble and tried to forge solutions. It's impossible to address all the hummingbird troubles you might encounter, but I'm going to try to hit the most common ones here in this chapter.

THE BEST way to foil a bully hummingbird is to group several feeders together. This effectively swamps the bully with competition and eventually he (though female hummers can be bullies too) will give up.

FOILING BULLIES

"Why do the hummers fight over the feeder, Daddy?" my son Liam asked me. "Well, because they are all hungry, and they want to eat first in case the food runs out." "Sounds like my lunch line at school!" Liam was right about that! Hummingbirds are notoriously feisty defenders of a reliable food source such as a feeder or a patch of nectar-rich flowers. They will chase, poke, smack into, and chatter at any other birds that try to come in for a drink.

Conventional wisdom used to dictate that putting out other food sources in distant parts of your yard or garden was the answer. But for those of us catering to large numbers of hummers, that only resulted in several more little fiefdoms being established. Late summer is when it gets the craziest. Adult males are still around looking for a fight. Adult females are frantically trying to get enough food to feed nestlings or fledglings. And the first round of newly fledged hummers may also be there, naively hovering near the feeders without a clue that they are about to get the smack-down from the resident bully adult male (or sometimes an aggressive adult female).

This is the time of year when we struggle to keep the feeders full and add a few more feeders to our front-porch station. Ganging the feeders makes it harder for the bully to keep everyone away, and sometimes he tires enough to let the others feed in peace, at least for a while. If bullies are a problem, add more feeders in a group and see if this makes it easier for the less-aggressive nectar-seekers.

NO HUMMINGBIRDS AT MY FEEDER

Every year I get the call. Often it comes early in the summer, from someone who is worried that there are no hummers coming to the feeders. There are a few possible explanations: (1) The natural sources of nectar (flowering plants) may be at peak production and availability. This will lure hummingbirds away from even the most well-stocked feeding station. (2) A predator, such as a cat or a hawk, may have temporarily scared the birds away. Even very aggressive bees and wasps can force hummingbirds to forsake a feeder. Watch for signs of such interference. There's little you can do other than wait for the predator to move on, unless it's a free-roaming cat, in which case I normally resort to the super-soaker squirt gun filled with vinegar. If it's bees and wasps, read on.

BEES, WASPS, ETC.

If the insects are swarming your feeders, check to see if your feeder's manufacturer offers bee guards to prevent access to the feeding port. If not, consider switching to a feeder model that offers bee guards or one of the newer feeder models that are designed to be insect-resistant. You can also try to lure the insects away from the feeder by offering a small amount of nectar in a jar lid. Start this lid feeder near the regular feeder, then slowly move it farther and farther away. The insects usually follow, because this source of nectar is easier to access than the feeders.

AN ANT moat filled with water acts as a barrier, preventing ants from gaining access to feeder ports.

ANTS AT THE FEEDER

In cartoons, ants always find the picnic food, and it's no different with the sugary goodness of nectar in our feeders. Most feeders give themselves away to ants by dripping or sloshing out a bit of nectar, and this is when the ants begin trying to find the source. And believe me, they are ingenious. I've watched ants find nectar drips on our concrete patio and then, over the course of a day, find their way up the back stairs to the feeder hanging from the deck railing a full story above the drip zone.

Ants are nothing more than a nuisance at a hummer feeder. The worst result may be that your feeders get clogged with ants, some of which will have entered the feeder. This gives you a good clue that it's time to clean and refill the feeder and get an ant baffle in place.

So, how do you stop them?

The best way is to use an ant moat between the feeder support and the feeder. Most ant baffles look like an upturned cap from a can of spray paint. Inside the upturned cap is water, and in the center is a hook for suspending the moat above the feeder. The water prevents the ants from getting past the moat to the feeder. Of course, if you use one of the better feeders—one that promises it does not leak—you may not have this problem at all. But more likely, the feeder will drip and the ants will find it.

Here are some things not to do. Don't ever use any kind of pesticide or insecticide on or near your feeders. This is only a temporary solution and may be harmful to your hummingbirds. Also, avoid the temptation to put grease or petroleum jelly on the feeder or its hanging support. A hummingbird coming in contact with this gunk will not be able to preen it out of its feathers, which may compromise its chances for survival.

AVIAN COMPETITORS

There are other birds that may become regulars at your nectar feeders, including orioles, tanagers, woodpeckers, house finches, and others. I'd welcome them at the feeder, unless one of the woodpeckers is enlarging the holes on the feeding ports (we had a red-bellied woodpecker that used to do that) and ruining the feeders. The best solution is to lure the birds away to another feeder or food source. Halved oranges, suet dough, or a small dish of jelly can be highly attractive to orioles and woodpeckers. There are more durable plastic and glass nectar feeders designed for use by orioles and, by default, woodpeckers.

PREDATORS

There aren't a lot of creatures on this planet that can chase and catch a hummingbird. Those that do catch hummingbirds use the element of surprise—hiding near a feeder and leaping or flying out to grab these tiny buzz bombs. If you have a house cat nabbing hummers at your feeder, raise the feeder higher than 6 feet from the ground and move it away from any potential hiding spots for kitty. It's harder to stop birds from killing hummingbirds. American kestrels and merlins are two speedy falcon species that have been known to catch and eat hummingbirds. There's really no way to prevent this, and it's illegal to harm birds of prey.

DOZENS OF other bird species will drink nectar from hummingbird feeders, once they identify this as a food source. These are acorn woodpeckers.

In the Southwest, greater roadrunners are sometimes observed leaping up to nab hummingbirds at busy feeding stations. Again, the only solution is to raise the feeders up out of the roadrunner's leaping range. As much as I adore hummingbirds, I'd love to see this happen just once because it shows the incredible resourcefulness of the roadrunner's foraging strategy.

SPOILAGE

Sooner or later, your clear nectar is going to spoil and get gunky and dark. During warm weather and in direct sunlight, this can happen in as little as a day or two. Feeders in the shade may last a week or more before the nectar begins to get cloudy. Before it does, it's time to dump out the old solution, clean the feeder thoroughly, and refill it with fresh nectar. If your nectar regularly spoils more quickly, there are two possible problems for you to correct: (1) You may not be boiling your solution long enough. Letting the water come to a full boil before mixing in the sugar helps remove impurities and makes the nectar more stable. (2) Your feeder may need a more thorough cleaning. Perhaps there are some tiny corners or crevices harboring mold, fungus, or other nasty things. A good soaking in hot bleachy water (10 parts water, 1 part chlorine bleach) followed by a thorough rinsing should solve this problem.

LEAKY FEEDERS

Some hummingbird-feeding veterans will tell you there's no such thing as a hummer feeder that doesn't leak. The feeder manufacturers would beg to differ. But the reality is that nectar is a liquid, and there are many ways for it to escape the confines of a feeder. Sunlight and warm air temperatures warm a feeder, expanding its materials and contents and making it easier for a leak to start. Wind can cause a feeder to sway and slosh. Lots of active feeding from hummers can result in the occasional drip falling to the ground.

And other creatures, such as larger birds, mammals, and insects, may chew or otherwise damage a feeder, making it leak. In the Southwest, some feeder operators have to deal with bats visiting their feeders. Flying squirrels and raccoons have visited our feeders. The raccoons will steal feeders if we don't fasten them tightly to our feeder pole. I'm sure the flying squirrels would too, if they could still manage to glide into the woods with a feeder in their clutches.

PERCHES ON FEEDERS

"Is it true that perches on hummingbird feeders are bad?" In the late 1990s, there was a swirling controversy over whether perches on feeders were bad for hummingbirds. Most of the evidence supporting the theory that perches were harmful came from a feeder operator in the mountain region of the West. The hypothesis was this: A hummingbird wakes up after a long, cool or cold night and visits a feeder, where it perches and takes a big drink of chilled nectar. The cold nectar causes the bird's body temperature to drop, slowing its metabolism and sending the hummer into a trancelike torpor. Pictures of hummingbirds hanging upside down at feeders on cold Rocky Mountain mornings were circulated. And the conclusion was drawn that the birds were going torpid because they were perching, not hovering, while drinking the cold nectar. A "ban the perches" grassroots movement was started, because torpid hummingbirds are vulnerable to predators and competitors.

I can understand the apparent logic of this, but it's actually the large cold jolt of nectar that is causing the birds' reaction. So if we want to ban something, shouldn't we ban the feeders? In nature, if a hummer can perch and still reach a flower for nectar, it will, so I still like to offer perches on some of my hummer feeders. Feeders with perches often have a bird at every port, feeding peacefully. Feeders

PERCHES ON *feeders permit hummers to rest while feeding, rather than having to hover constantly.*

without perches seem to cause more jostling and fighting for position at the feeding port.

If you live in a region where nighttime temperatures chill your nectar, consider bringing your feeders inside on cold nights and putting them back outside in the morning. This is what we do in early spring and late fall here in southeastern Ohio, primarily to avoid having the nectar freeze cracking the plastic feeder.

AVOID RED DYE IN NECTAR

Avoid adding red food coloring to your hummingbird solution. Do not buy the nectar mixes that include red dye. The dye used in food coloring is unnecessary to attract hummers (most feeders have red or orange parts), and it may very well be unhealthy for the birds.

Red Food Coloring and Hummingbirds

THESE HUMMER *droppings show traces of red dye more than 24 hours after the bird was no longer being fed dyed nectar. It's unnecessary to use dye in nectar, and it may cause health problems in hummingbirds.*

Is the red food coloring in hummingbird nectar really harmful? I decided to research this question when an injured hummingbird came into my care in the summer of 2009. She had had just two feedings of a commercial nectar preparation containing artificial dye. She was still excreting brilliant red droppings 24 hours later. Many commercial hummingbird food preparations contain red dye #40, which is an artificial colorant derived from petrochemicals, more specifically coal tar. Rumors have been rampant for years about the effects of artificial food coloring on hummingbirds. There have been claims that it impairs hatching in hummingbird eggs, and hummingbird rehabilitators report seeing an increased incidence in skin and bill tumors in hummingbirds. Here are the facts.

Red dye #40 has proven carcinogenic and mutagenic (meaning it induces tumors) in rats and mice. Furthermore, it decreases reproduction rates and increases the incidence of both internal and skin tumors in these animals. It is banned in Denmark, Belgium, France, Germany, Austria, Sweden, and Norway but is still in use in the U.S.

Because it has not been tested directly on hummingbirds, manufacturers of artificial nectars containing red dye are on solid ground when they claim that no proof exists that it is harmful to hummingbirds. That's true. But neither is there any research that indicates that red dye is not harmful to hummingbirds. They also state that the dyes used are FDA-approved for human consumption. That's true, but the FDA has also set limits for consumption and recommends that people not ingest large quantities of a single dye product. However, when we set up a hummingbird feeder with dyed nectar, this is just what we're encouraging hummingbirds to do. And that's the core of the problem.

How much red dye does a hummingbird consume when it visits a feeder containing artificially colored nectar? A banded and color-marked rufous hummingbird observed by Louisiana master hummingbird bander W. D. (Dave) Patton took an average of 10 grams of nectar from the same feeder each day. This corresponds with my observations of convalescing hummingbirds, for which I mix 15 grams (three teaspoons) of nectar each day, allowing for waste in dripping. A popular dry nectar mix contains .21 mg of dye per gram of dry mix. Combined with water as directed, a gram of the solution contains .04 mg of red dye #40. A hummingbird taking 10 grams of the mix ingests about .42 mg of red dye per day. This works out to .12 mg of dye per gram of body weight. It doesn't sound like much, until you note that the World Health Organization recommends a daily limit of only .007 mg per gram of body weight in humans. And DNA damage in mice showed up at concentrations as low as .01 mg per gram of body weight.

The truth is that a hummingbird taking artificially dyed nectar may be ingesting the dye in concentrations that are 17 times the accepted daily intake recommended for humans, and 12 times higher than the concentration found to induce DNA damage in mice. And they may be ingesting it every single day, all summer long.

It's true that no solid research yet exists to prove that red dye is harmful to hummingbirds. Hummingbirds are not humans; they are not mice. But all hummingbird feeders have red parts that serve to attract the birds, so the dye is unnecessary at best, and potentially harmful at worst. Artificial nectars have little if any added nutritional value over sugar water. To avoid causing any possible harm, I stick to the homemade formula of one part white table sugar to four parts boiled water and let the red feeder parts do the work of attracting hummingbirds to my door. —*Julie Zickefoose, writer and bird rehabilitator*

When we find a sick or injured hummingbird, we pick it up gently and poke its bill into a teaspoon full of fresh nectar. Sometimes this shot of nectar is all the bird needs to revive. But all hummers need to eat often, so until you can get an ill bird to a rehabber, it's a good idea to offer it a sip of nectar every 15 minutes or so. Once they taste the nectar, most hummers will drink eagerly.

SICK AND INJURED HUMMINGBIRDS

If you find a sick or injured hummingbird, the first thing to do is to make sure it's safe. If you don't want to touch it, then place a cardboard box over it to protect it from danger until you take the next step. For an injured bird—say, one that has been stunned by hitting a window or in a fight with another hummingbird—the time inside the box may be all it needs to recover. If so, you may hear it buzzing in flight inside the box. Release it and watch to see that it flies well and makes it to safety in a nearby tree or bush. For a sick or badly injured hummingbird, the best thing is to get it to a rehabilitator. You can find a rehabber by searching online (search your town or the nearest city plus "wildlife rehabilitator"). You can also consult the website of the National Wildlife Rehabilitators Association (www.nwrawildlife .org) for a local contact. Only a licensed rehabilitator is qualified to diagnose and treat a sick or injured bird. It's illegal for anyone without a license to possess a wild bird.

HUMMINGBIRDS TRAPPED INSIDE

Occasionally, a hummingbird may zip in an open door or window of your house or garage. The red knobs on electric garage-door release ropes seem to be insidiously attractive to hummingbirds, luring them into garages, where they often starve unless you notice them and help them escape.

Once it realizes it is trapped, a hummingbird will fly upward to the highest point in the room. Your challenge is to get it down and back outside as soon as possible. First I will tell you what we do with garage-trapped hummers.

Our garage is huge, and the ceiling has roofing nails poking down through it—not a safe place for a frantic hummingbird. When we find a hummer inside, we immediately open all the doors to create numerous escape routes. Then we get a small hummer feeder (preferably one with bright red parts) and fill it with nectar, attach it to a hook on the end of a long pole, and raise it up near the hummer. As the bird sees it and begins feeding from it, we slowly lower the feeder until the bird is back near the ground. Once we get the bird down to this level, it almost always stops feeding from the feeder and zips toward the light and freedom. Occasionally, this takes several attempts. Once in a great while we have to wait until the hummer is tired of hovering and drops to a perch to rest. Then we get a ladder and try to catch the hummer gently in our hands. We never use a net, for fear of striking and hurting the bird.

We painted the red knobs on our garage-door release ropes black, which has nearly eliminated the problem.

For birds in our house, which has a 20-foot-high ceiling in the foyer and living room, we have to get the extension ladder from the garage. Then we put the ladder up near where the hummer is hovering and wait for it to tire. This seldom takes more than 20 minutes.

When catching a hummingbird in your hands, be very gentle. Try to close your hand around its body to restrict wing movement without squeezing too tightly. When first caught, a hummingbird will often utter a high-pitched squealing cry. This is not necessarily because you are hurting it. It's just the bird's way of trying to startle you into opening your hand. Trust me, you'll want to wait to open your hand until you get the bird outside. And you may want to offer the tired, scared hummer a sip or two from a teaspoon of fresh nectar before you release it.

WINTER FEEDING AND VAGRANTS

If you have a hummingbird show up at your feeders long after the birds should be gone, what do you do? First of all, try to identify the species. It could be that you have a rare vagrant from far away. If you cannot determine the bird's identity, contact a local birding expert to help you. Try to take a few digital photographs or some video to help document and identify the bird.

Next it's time to make sure the bird has regular access to food. If you live in an area where the winters are cold and snowy, keeping the nectar from freezing will be a tricky task. I know of many folks who have installed heating pads, heat lamps, or other warming devices on or near the feeder to keep it from freezing. Others simply rotate feeders from inside to keep a constant source of food available. Hummingbird expert Sheri Williamson recommends offering a 3:1 nectar ratio to vagrant hummers to help these birds get enough energy.

We learn a lot about these so-called vagrant or lost hummingbirds as more and more of them show up where they don't belong. Some even return year after year, which seems to be one way a bird population works to expand its distribution. Surviving vagrants may pass on this behavior to future generations.

I cannot wait until a marvelous spatuletail from Peru shows up at my feeders. I'll be sure to let you know if and when this does happen. But more than likely I'll have to be content with the good old ruby-throated hummingbirds that seem to love our farm here in Ohio. And that's plenty good enough for me!

Chapter 7: Hummingbird Species Profiles

HUMMINGBIRDS ARE OUR SMALLEST birds by size, but their flying ability, high-energy lifestyles, and pugnacious behavior belie their physical stature. Our hummingbird species are not evenly distributed across North America. The greatest numbers of hummingbirds are found where the habitat is best suited to their needs. The West, with its greater habitat diversity, is home to most of our 15 species of hummingbirds that regularly breed in North America north of Mexico.

Identifying Hummingbirds

Identifying a hummingbird is very similar to identifying other bird species—if the hummer is sitting or hovering in one place long enough for you to get a reasonably good look at it. If the hummingbird is behaving like most hummers do, getting a good look may take some time and a bit of patience on your part.

I always recommend that bird watchers looking at an unfamiliar bird start at the top of the bird's head (or tip of the bill) and visually work their way down the body and back toward the tail, noting any obvious field marks. For most North American bird species, the key field marks (unique physical features used for identification) are located on the top or front half of a bird—above the midway point.

Here are a few easy steps to help you identify a hummingbird.

RANGE

Where, geographically, you are seeing the bird is important. Only one species, the ruby-throated hummingbird, summers in the eastern half of the United States. If you are trying to identify a hummingbird in Tennessee in July, it's almost certainly a rubythroat. In the West, and particularly in the Southwest, there are many more hummingbirds to identify. Check the range maps in this book (or in your field guide) to see what species are found in your region in any particular season. In the maps that accompany the 15 hummingbird species profiles, the map colors are as follows: red = summer range; blue = winter range; purple = year-round range.

In fall and winter, a stray hummingbird can show up almost any-where, so it's good to bear this in mind when looking at late-season birds. Dashed or dotted lines on the maps in this book indicate areas outside the species' normal range where the species occasionally occurs.

Key to Range Maps

▭ **Red:** summer range

▭ **Blue:** winter range

▭ **Purple:** year-round range

······ **Red dash line:** approximate limits of irregular summer range and/or post-breeding dispersal

······ **Blue dash line:** approximate limits of irregular winter range

······ **Purple dash line:** approximate limits or irregular year-round range

SEX

All of our widespread hummingbird species are sexually dimorphic, meaning that adult males and females look different from one another. In most cases, the males sport brighter colors, especially on the gorget. Determining the sex of a hummingbird you are trying to identify can help you narrow down the possibilities. If a bird has an obvious gorget, it's likely to be a male. Knowing which hummingbird species are commonly found in your region then can narrow the possibilities further.

A word about gorgets: on male hummingbirds, the iridescent feathers on the throat (called the gorget) are probably the most noticeable field mark. However, as we've discussed earlier in this book, these gorget feathers get their color from the way they reflect sunlight. So most of the time they will appear dark to your eyes. Watch a male hummingbird for a few minutes, and you are almost certainly going to get a flash of the gorget feathers as they reflect sunlight. Note the color and placement of the color on the hummer's throat or head.

Juvenile hummingbirds (those born in the same nesting season in which you are seeing them) are often the most difficult birds to identify. They lack many of the field marks of the adults—even young males will have almost no noticeable gorget feathers.

GENERAL IMPRESSION

Take a moment to look at your mystery hummingbird and gather a general impression of its overall size and shape. Is it larger or smaller than other birds and hummingbirds present? What are the proportions of its bill and tail to its body? Is it exhibiting any unusual behavior, such as tail flicking, or any notable vocalizations? Is it highly aggressive toward other birds? The answers to these questions, combined with any physical field marks you note, may be valuable clues to a positive identification.

BILL COLOR, SHAPE, AND LENGTH

Most of our North American hummingbirds have a relatively straight black bill. A few have a longer, curved bill, and some hummer bills are two-toned in color—usually red or orange with a black tip. While bill color isn't the first field mark to look for, if the bill has color it should be an obvious clue.

TAIL SHAPE AND COLOR

As you work your way to the bottom of a mystery hummingbird, looking for field marks, don't overlook the tail. The shape and size of the tail can be good clues, as can the amount of white present on the feather tips. Rufous, Allen's, and buff-bellied hummingbirds have mostly rufous tails. Lucifer, violet-crowned, and broad-billed hummingbirds all have notched tails. Black-chinned hummingbirds usually pump their tails while hovering, whereas the similar ruby-throated hummingbird usually holds its tail still. There are many other subtle field marks in the tails of hummingbirds, so don't give up your search for clues until you reach the "tail end"!

SOUNDS

Hummingbirds can be quite vocal. Most give some basic chip notes or call notes, but some, like the male Anna's hummingbird, sing actual songs from a territorial perch. Hummingbirds also produce sound with their wings. This is usually described as a high trill or ringing buzz. Males of other species, including broad-tailed, Allen's, and rufous, produce a high, buzzy trill with their wings whenever they fly.

CONFUSINGLY SIMILAR

As with the aforementioned black-chinned versus ruby-throat ID challenge, or the even tougher Allen's versus rufous hummingbird (and that's just the males; females are tougher still), some hummingbirds are nearly impossible to identify based on field marks viewed from a distance. In fact, when a vagrant rufous or Allen's shows up at a feeder in the East or Southeast, hummingbird banders are sometimes called in to capture the bird to view it in the hand, which is one of the only ways to get a positive ID. There are minute differences in the notching on the central tail feathers that are most easily seen in the hand.

So don't be discouraged if you find yourself unable to identify a hummingbird that offers few clear field marks. It happens, even to the experts.

JUST PLAIN WEIRD

Every individual hummingbird is unique, and sometimes this uniqueness shows in plumage and behavior. For years we had a male rubythroat in our yard that had one drooping wing—probably the result of an accident. We could always identify "Droopy" as an individual. Plumage anomalies are not very common, but discoloration from pollen or other things encountered in the environment is normal. Part of the natural relationship between hummers and flowering plants is that the birds help distribute the flowers' pollen from plant to plant. It is quite common to see an otherwise normal hummingbird with a bright orange or yellow crown—something you won't find in most field guides. This is most likely pollen from a plant the bird has recently visited.

If you see a hummingbird that looks just plain weird, try to look beyond the weirdness to its essential hummingbird-ness—the subtle clues that will help you solve the mystery of its identity. It's probably not a species new to science, but if it is, good for you. And since you cannot name a species you've discovered after yourself, I'll let you name it after me. Thompson's hummingbird has a nice ring to it, don't you think?

Happy hummingbird watching!

Note: The size measurements given in these species accounts indicate the bird's length measured from bill tip to tail tip.

Species Profiles

In this chapter you'll find profiles for the 15 most commonly encountered hummingbird species found in North America north of the Mexican border. Each profile includes the species name and Latin name, the species' size, measured from bill tip to tail tip, a range map, and one or more photographs showing key field marks for identification. The text includes sections on the species' description, the important field marks, sounds, behavior, and preferred habitat.

All of these species visit both flowering plants and feeders, but some are more widely distributed and common than others. The range maps give seasonal distribution and range for each species, which can be an important clue to a hummingbird's identification. While hummingbirds can be found far from their expected ranges, especially in fall and winter, such vagrant birds are very rare.

Hummingbird Species Profiles

Ruby-throated Hummingbird

Archilochus colubris   SIZE: 3¾"

DESCRIPTION
The rubythroat is the only common hummingbird of the East in spring and summer. Most rubythroats leave for the Neotropics in winter, though a few overwinter in the Gulf states. In fall and winter, any hummingbird visiting a feeder should be carefully checked—it may be a vagrant species from the West.

FIELD MARKS
Adult males have a ruby gorget, which can appear black in bright sunlight, and a black chin strap above the gorget. The chest is pale, the belly greenish, and the crown, back, and tail iridescent green. Females and young birds are green above, white below.

SOUNDS
Calls are high squeaky or sputtering notes. The male's wings hum or whine in display flights.

BEHAVIOR
May flick its tail occasionally when hovering at flower or feeder. Other food sources include flying insects and sap at sapsucker wells. Male uses swooping, U-shaped pendulum display flights both for courting females and in territorial disputes with other males. Short zigzag display flights are performed in front of perched female. Bathes in rain, mist from birdbaths, or on water-soaked leaves.

HABITAT
Usually seen at or near flowering plants, vines, and trees in gardens, woodland edges, and backyards.

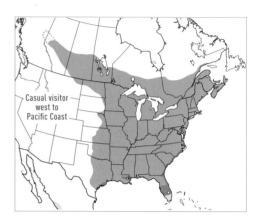

Casual visitor west to Pacific Coast

Adult female

Adult male

Adult male

Adult female

Black-chinned Hummingbird

Archilochus alexandri   SIZE: 3¾"

DESCRIPTION
This is the most widespread hummingbird in the West. The male's gorget flashes deep purple at the bottom in the right light; in poor light it can appear black.

FIELD MARKS
Both sexes are bright green on the head, back, and tail. Males show a clean white bib below the dark purple gorget. Females look similar to female ruby-throated hummingbirds.

SOUNDS
The wings of adult males make a dry buzz in flight. Chasing birds give a series of twitters and buzzes. Call is a soft *chew!*

BEHAVIOR
This species pumps its tail consistently while hovering. Courting males perform both a U-shaped dive display and a back-and-forth shuttle display (a series of short zipping flights back and forth) for perched females. Both displays are accompanied by vocal or wing sounds.

HABITAT
Common in wooded foothills and canyons and along the Pacific Coast.

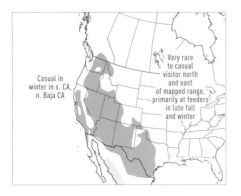

Casual in winter in s. CA, n. Baja CA

Very rare to casual visitor north and east of mapped range, primarily at feeders in late fall and winter

Costa's Hummingbird

Calypte costae   SIZE: 3½"

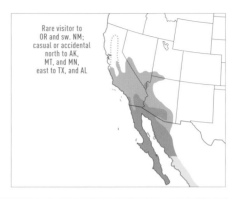

Rare visitor to OR and sw. NM; casual or accidental north to AK, MT, and MN, east to TX, and AL

DESCRIPTION

Male Costa's hummingbirds have a striking, deep purple crown and a gorget that extends downward like a Fu Manchu mustache. This small hummingbird has a diagnostic call—see below.

FIELD MARKS

The male's gorget shape and color are unique among our hummingbirds. The female is green above and white below. This species is similar to the black-chinned hummingbird, which is slightly larger. The male black-chinned lacks the extended gorget and purple crown of the male Costa's.

SOUNDS

Call is a high-pitched, tinny *tink-tink-tink-tink.* Male's song and dive display sound is a rising, then falling *ziiiing!*

BEHAVIOR

Males sing from a prominent perch within their breeding territories and as they perform elaborate looping courtship flights for perched females. These flights may include more than 35 vertical loops above a watching female.

HABITAT

Desert scrub, chaparral, dry washes with flowering plants, backyards, and gardens.

Adult male

Adult female

Anna's Hummingbird

Calypte anna **SIZE: 4"**

DESCRIPTION
The male Anna's is our only hummingbird with a bright magenta to cherry red crown, which combined with his magenta to cherry red gorget and emerald green back, makes for an impressive bird. This species is common along the Pacific Coast all year long. In winter and spring, the male performs a remarkable courtship flight: soaring in a pendulum-shaped loop in view of a perched female, he makes a loud popping sound at the bottom of each loop.

FIELD MARKS
The male's crown and gorget are brilliant ruby in good light but can appear black in poor light. A greenish back and smudgy green belly make the Anna's appear "messier" than other hummers. Females usually have some red spots on the otherwise white throat. At 4 inches in length, the Anna's is larger than most other widespread western hummingbirds.

SOUNDS
A series of raspy notes and chattery buzzes is what passes for the Anna's song, which the male usually delivers while perched.

BEHAVIOR
Males can erect gorget and head feathers and move back and forth to flash bright colors at intruders, rivals, and potential mates. Display flights are spectacular: the male hovers over its rival, potential mate, or an intruder, then rises into the sky—sometimes more than 120 feet—before swooping speedily back down, with wings and tail whining through the air. While hovering, the Anna's does not pump its tail, unlike many other common hummingbird species.

HABITAT
Common in brushy habitat in the westernmost states from Canada to Mexico and in the desert Southwest north to Nevada and east to Texas. Any habitat with nectar-producing flowers, including parks, gardens, and backyards, can host this species.

Adult male

Adult female

A few wander casually north to AK and east to Great Plains, primarily in fall and winter; accidental farther east

Broad-tailed Hummingbird

Selasphorus platycerus   SIZE: 4"

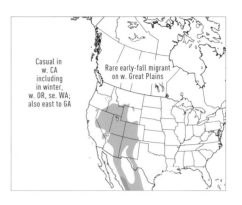

Casual in w. CA including in winter, w. OR, se. WA; also east to GA

Rare early-fall migrant on w. Great Plains

DESCRIPTION
This hummingbird is often heard before it is seen, because the wings of the adult male produce a loud, whistled trill as he flies. The species is common throughout the inland mountain West and is the most commonly encountered hummer in the Rocky Mountains.

FIELD MARKS
Males and females are metallic green above with a white breast and belly. Males have a magenta gorget with no black chin strap. Females have a speckled throat and buffy sides. Both sexes are longer and slimmer than the ruby-throated hummingbird of the East.

SOUNDS
In addition to the wing trill of the male in flight, broad-taileds produce high-pitched chattering calls, usually from a perch. Call is a loud *chit!*

BEHAVIOR
This relatively unaggressive hummingbird frequently gets dominated by other species at feeders. Returns early to breeding habitat and survives on sap at tree holes and on insects until flower nectar is available. The male performs a swooping dive display with trilling wings for females and at rival males. He also performs a bouncing shuttle display in front of the perched female.

HABITAT
Mountain forests, meadows, and wooded canyons.

Adult male

Adult female

Rufous Hummingbird

Selasphorus rufus   SIZE: 3¾"

DESCRIPTION
Rusty, red, and white overall, this is our only North American hummingbird with an all-rufous back. Only males can be separated visually from the very similar Allen's hummingbird. Female rufous and Allen's hummingbirds are indistinguishable.

FIELD MARKS
The male usually has an entirely rufous back and tail, bright red gorget, and white chest. Some males have extensive green, similar to Allen's hummingbird male.

SOUNDS
Makes a variety of vocal chips and twitters. The male's wings whine in flight, especially during courtship display.

BEHAVIOR
The rufous hummingbird aggressively defends food sources, even against larger birds. This species is increasingly regular as a fall and winter vagrant to feeders and gardens in the East and Southeast. Males perform an oval-shaped dive display accompanied by loud, descending sputtering calls and snapping sounds from flared feathers.

HABITAT
Forests, woodland edges, mountain meadows, gardens, backyards, parks.

Casual in winter along coast north to WA

Regular fall migrant through w. Great Plains, very rare farther east

Recent increases in small wintering population at southeastern feeders

Adult male

Adult female

Allen's Hummingbird

Selasphorus sasin

SIZE: 3¾"

Accidental north to WA, east to Atlantic Seaboard

Regular late-summer migrant through AZ; casual to NV, NM, TX

DESCRIPTION
This rufous, green, and white hummingbird is found along the Pacific Coast. It is very similar to the more widespread rufous hummingbird. Females of the two species are indistinguishable (except to the birds themselves).

FIELD MARKS
Males have a bright orange gorget, white belly, green crown and back, and rufous tail. (Male rufous hummingbirds have a mostly rufous back and tail.)

SOUNDS
In flight, the male's wings make a loud whine. Call is a loud, piercing *kvikk!* The male often gives it during swooping, pendulum courtship display flights.

BEHAVIOR
The Allen's is less aggressive than the similar-looking rufous hummingbird but is still territorial around food sources. The male's J-shaped dive display is used both for courtship and in aggressive encounters with rival males. The back-and-forth shuttle display is performed by the male toward the female.

HABITAT
Woodlands, wooded parks, brushy gardens, backyards.

Adult male

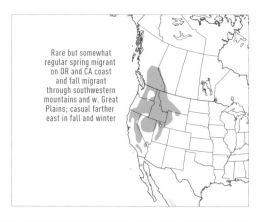

Rare but somewhat regular spring migrant on OR and CA coast and fall migrant through southwestern mountains and w. Great Plains; casual farther east in fall and winter

Calliope Hummingbird

Stellula calliope   SIZE: 3¼"

DESCRIPTION
This is the smallest bird in North America north of Mexico. A common visitor to feeders and gardens within its range, the Calliope sometimes holds its tail cocked upward while hovering to feed.

Adult male

FIELD MARKS
The male's gorget of magenta feathers may be flared open or held together, forming an inverted V on the throat. The male is green above, white below. The female is green above and white-bellied with buffy flanks. Calliopes look very short-tailed and small compared with other hummingbirds.

SOUNDS
Despite its name, this species is not very vocal. It makes various chips and twitters in flight. The male gives a high-pitched *tsee-see* in courtship flight.

BEHAVIOR
Often visits flowers very low to the ground. The male performs a U-shaped dive display in courtship, which finishes with a loud *zit-ziing* and a flaring of the brilliant gorget feathers. Shorter shuttle displays may involve both male and female.

HABITAT
Mountain meadows and open canyons. Often found near water. Present in summer only, though a few winter in the Gulf Coast states.

Adult female

Broad-billed Hummingbird

Cynanthus latirostris   SIZE: 4"

DESCRIPTION
This small and mild-mannered hummer has a very limited range in the Southwest. The male is richly colorful with a deep blue gorget and green body and has an orange bill tipped in black. In poor light, however, he may appear all dark.

FIELD MARKS
The blue and green male has an obvious two-toned bill and a long notched tail. The female is green above and grayish white below with an obvious white eye stripe that broadens behind the eye. Her bill is mostly dark.

SOUNDS
Vocal sounds include actual singing by males from a prominent perch, described as *jeejeejeejeejee* broken up by scattered chips. Calls are harsh *chit* notes, sometimes given in a series. During the male's pendulum display flights, his wings make a high whine.

BEHAVIOR
Notably less aggressive than many other species. It twitches its tail while flying or foraging.

HABITAT
Wooded canyons and shrubby foothills of southeastern Arizona and southwestern New Mexico.

Fall and winter vagrant to many states north and east as far as Maritimes

Adult male

Adult female

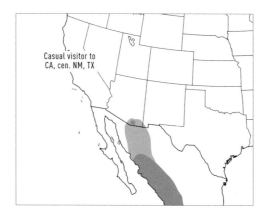

Casual visitor to
CA, cen. NM, TX

Violet-crowned Hummingbird

Amazilia violiceps

SIZE: 4½"

DESCRIPTION
Bright white below with a dark green-brown back and a bright orange bill, this medium-sized hummingbird is very aggressive at feeders and food plants. It is distributed very locally in southeasternmost Arizona and southwestern New Mexico.

FIELD MARKS
Sexes look identical. The bright white throat, chest, and belly contrast with the orange bill tipped in black. The crown is dark blue, and upperparts are green fading to brown near the tail.

SOUNDS
Song is more musical than that of other hummingbirds, consisting of four to six *chew* notes descending in pitch. Calls are hard, sputtering *chip* notes, often given in aggressive encounters.

BEHAVIOR
Aggressively chases other hummingbirds. Males sing from a prominent perch, often early in the day.

HABITAT
Breeds in streamside woods. Forages in areas with thick vegetation.

Violet-crowned hummingbird, male (the female's crown is less violet).

Buff-bellied Hummingbird

Amazilia yucatanensis   SIZE: 4¼"

DESCRIPTION
This large hummingbird is well named for its obvious buff belly patch. It is a primarily Neotropical species that is expanding its range northward along the Texas Gulf Coast.

FIELD MARKS
Iridescent green on the head and throat contrasts with a tan belly and rufous tail and wings. The bill is coral red tipped in black. Sexes are similar, but the male is slightly more colorful overall.

SOUNDS
A very vocal species. It gives a variety of calls, including harsh *chik* notes and a nasal *mew*. Aggressive calls include a long staticlike rattle. Males sing a complex burbling song, often from cover.

BEHAVIOR
Males are highly aggressive, especially toward rival males. Flicks tail irregularly in flight. The male's dive display may be accompanied by whirring or whistling wings.

HABITAT
Coastal scrub and woodlands from the lower Rio Grande Valley northward. Increasingly common at feeding stations in residential areas. Some birds move north and east along the Gulf Coast in winter, reaching as far as Florida.

Accidental
in GA and NC

Buff-bellied hummingbird (sexes are similar).

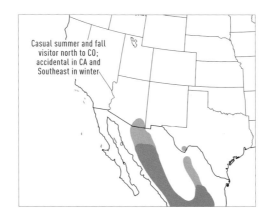

Casual summer and fall visitor north to CO; accidental in CA and Southeast in winter.

Adult male

Blue-throated Hummingbird

Lampornis clemenciae   SIZE: 5"

DESCRIPTION
A large and aggressive hummingbird found in summer in limited parts of southwest Texas, southwest New Mexico, and southeastern Arizona. This large hummingbird appears long-tailed and short-billed.

FIELD MARKS
The male's bright blue gorget can be hard to see in poor light. Better field marks are this species' large size, white eye stripe, and dark tail with outer feathers broadly tipped in white. The upper back is green, the lower black greenish bronze. The female is identical to the male but with a plain gray throat.

SOUNDS
Highly vocal, making a variety of sounds. Calls include a sharp *seet* note and buzzy trills. Song of male includes a long series of notes on a similar tone given from a perch.

BEHAVIOR
Highly aggressive and territorial, attacking other hummingbirds, hawks, and owls. Flicks tail while flying or foraging.

HABITAT
Rarely found outside its preferred habitat of thickly forested mountain streams and moist canyons.

Adult female

Magnificent Hummingbird

Eugenes fulgens   SIZE: 5¼"

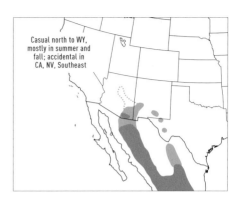

Casual north to WY, mostly in summer and fall; accidental in CA, NV, Southeast

DESCRIPTION
The adult male is stunning when seen in direct light. This large hummingbird is not aggressive, despite its size. It is fairly uncommon in the southwestern mountains along the Mexican border.

FIELD MARKS
The adult male has a purple crown, turquoise gorget, and black chest and belly. A small white spot behind the eye contrasts with the black face. Females are drab by comparison but share the white spot behind the eye, as well as a white eye line. Both sexes are dark green above.

SOUNDS
Calls include harsh *cheep* notes, sometimes in pairs, plus sputters and whistles. Song is a mixture of hisses, sputters, chips, and gurgles.

BEHAVIOR
Mainly an insect-eater, the magnificent is what's known as a "trapline" forager. It moves along a regular route, foraging for insects and some flower nectar, but does not claim and defend a territory based on food sources.

HABITAT
Found in "sky island" habitat in Arizona, New Mexico, and Texas: mixed pine-oak and riparian forests in mountains above 5,000 feet.

Adult female

Adult male

Adult male

Adult female

White-eared Hummingbird

Hylocharis leucotis
SIZE: 3¾"

DESCRIPTION
A medium-small species irregularly found north of the U.S.-Mexico border in the Southwest.

FIELD MARKS
The broad white eye stripe that gives the species its name is obvious in all ages and sexes. Males have a black face, short bill with black tip and red base, and a white central patch on the greenish breast. The greenish color of the gorget extends onto the upper sides and flanks.

SOUNDS
Call is a sharp metallic *chink!* Song is a series of call notes with occasional rising trills.

BEHAVIOR
Aggressive around nectar sources. Both sexes participate in courtship display flights, which involve chases.

HABITAT
Uncommon in mountains of southeastern Arizona, southwestern New Mexico, and western Texas in pine-oak woodlands between 4,500 and 10,000 feet. Moves to lower elevations in winter.

Very rare to casual summer visitor to NM, w. TX; accidental in n. TX, CO, MS

Lucifer Hummingbird

Calothorax lucifer

SIZE: 3½"

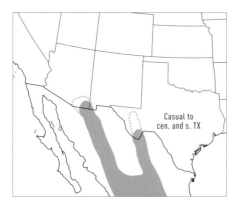

Casual to cen. and s. TX

DESCRIPTION
Named not for the devil but for the Greek word for "light-bearer," which refers to its large gorget. The Lucifer is small and slim with a long black decurved bill and a long tail. When perched, it gives a hunched appearance. It is one of the most difficult hummingbird species to see in the U.S.

FIELD MARKS
Adult males have a large purple-magenta gorget with a ragged lower edge, white breast, and greenish bronze back. Sides show light rufous. Females are greenish above and white below with varying amounts of light rufous on the breast and belly. The tail is long and forked.

SOUNDS
Calls are soft, dry *chip* notes. The male's song is a soft squeak given in territorial disputes. Tail and wing feathers make sounds during dive displays.

BEHAVIOR
Aggressively territorial. Rarely fans tail, even in flight. Males perform both shuttle and dive displays for females, often at their nest sites.

HABITAT
Shrubby foothills and canyons, wooded streams, and dry washes of southeastern Arizona, southwestern Texas, and southwestern New Mexico.

Adult female

Adult male

Butterflies

Chapter 8: What Is a Butterfly?

MENTION "INSECT," and many people think of mosquitoes, flies, and ants. Their instinct is to swat. Others reflect on honey and agricultural products, results of beneficial insects that pollinate and produce food. Butterflies fall somewhere in between; they won't bite us, but they don't produce many items valuable to commerce. Their real gift is the beauty they bring into our lives, via vibrant colors on their delicate wings and by pollinating flowers we enjoy around our homes and in our travels.

If you lure hummingbirds to your yard, it's a safe bet you will also host butterflies. Both are attracted to colorful, nectar-producing flowers, and perhaps by other enticements such as a reliable source of moisture, shelter, and conditions that encourage reproduction. As our human lives become more hurried and focused on technology, opportunities to watch hummingbirds and butterflies at close range are increasingly special. Spending even a few moments observing these creatures in the wild is an enriching and worthwhile experience.

Butterfly Biology

Butterflies have certain signature characteristics. Adult butterfly bodies are neatly divided into three segments: head, thorax (midsection), and abdomen. The head contains two prominent compound eyes; slender paired antennae; and the proboscis, a tubular mouthpart that remains coiled while the butterfly is in flight or at rest. Two pairs of wings—the forewings and hindwings—attach to the thorax; their color patterns provide the first clue to identification. Like all insects, butterflies have six legs; they are paired and attach to the lower thorax.

Butterflies belong to the second-largest order of insects. They are abundant in tropical habitats around the world but have dispersed to woodlands, fields, mountains, and wetlands in temperate regions. A few butterflies live in Arctic areas. Butterflies are cold-blooded, which means they rely on heat provided by their surroundings. The ambient temperature must reach 55°F to 60°F before most species take flight. On cool days, butterflies bask with their wings spread like solar panels, soaking up warmth in order to fly.

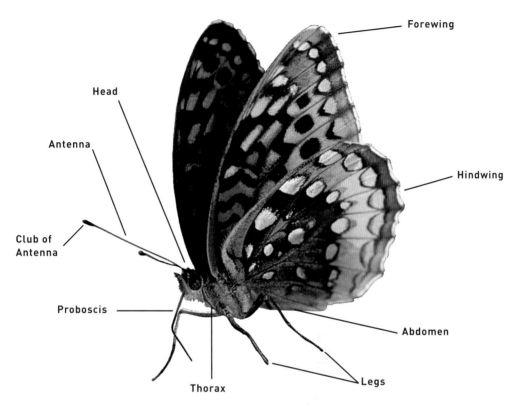

Forewing

Head

Antenna

Hindwing

Club of
Antenna

Proboscis

Abdomen

Legs

Thorax

PARTS OF *a butterfly.*

Butterflies fly very differently than hummingbirds. Spread your arms straight out from your shoulders with the palms of your hands facing down to simulate hummingbird flight. Now bring your arms forward, turning your palms up. Keeping palms up, move your arms farther back than their initial position, and flip your palms down. Return your arms to the starting position. Do this again and watch the tips of your fingers trace a figure eight in the air. Now repeat this routine 60 times per second, which (if you could do it) approximates how a hummingbird hovers.

To mimic butterfly flight, raise your arms directly over your head until your hands touch. Keeping your arms stiff, drop them to your side and repeat the process as briskly as you can. Butterflies travel at "flutter speed"—much slower and less controlled than that of hum-

A BASKING *white peacock absorbs solar energy before taking flight on a cool morning.*

BLUE IRIDESCENT scales and regular pigmented scales on the hindwing of an eastern tiger swallowtail.

mingbirds—when moving between flowers. Butterflies have four wings: a pair of triangular-shaped structures close to the head—the forewings—and a pair of more rounded wings behind—the hindwings. Independent muscles control each wing, allowing butterflies to climb, soar, descend, and turn. But these movements are subtle, so it appears as though the wings work in tandem pairs.

If you've picked up a butterfly, you may have noticed a powdery substance remaining on your fingers. These are fragile scales that have rubbed loose from the wings. Butterflies and moths belong to the insect order Lepidoptera, derived from Greek words meaning "scale-wing." Indeed, the wings of butterflies and moths are covered with overlapping rows of tiny flat scales. Scales assist flight stability and add color to thin wing membranes. Certain hues (especially gray, brown, yellow, and orange) come from pigments in the scales. Iridescence on some butterfly wings (typically green, blue, purple, or silver) comes from the scale's structure, which like a prism, bends light into individual color components. This is essentially the same process that creates the glowing sheen of hummingbird feathers.

BUTTERFLIES ARE best distinguished from moths by their antennae with club-shaped tips.

BUTTERFLY OR MOTH?

Can a quick glance at a scaly-winged insect determine whether it's a butterfly or a moth? In general, butterflies fly during the day, and most moths are active at night. Butterflies tend to fly gracefully, whereas most moths have rigid wingbeats and more erratic flight patterns. At rest, most butterflies bring their wings together, upright over their backs. Moths tend to rest with their wings folded around them or stretched out at their sides. Most butterfly bodies are slim and relatively hairless; moths tend to be plump and hairy. Unfortunately, there are exceptions to each of these examples. The best identifying characteristic is the insect's sensory receptor. Butterfly antennae are thin, with a clublike tip. Moths have feathery antennae that taper to narrow outer ends. So at first glance, look at the antennae to identify what kind of scaly-winged insect you're viewing.

Approximately 20,000 species of butterflies and 150,000 species of moths have been discovered worldwide. In some of the world's remote habitats, additional species await detection. One reason that butterflies and moths remain mysterious is that their caterpillars look completely different from adults. There is no easy way to tell the difference between butterfly and moth caterpillars.

MOTH ANTENNAE have a distinctive feathery shape.

Butterfly Life History

A huge distinction between humans and insects is how their bodies are supported. Humans (as well as other mammals, birds, reptiles, amphibians, and fishes) have a skeletal framework of strong bones within their bodies. Insects have an *exoskeleton,* a rigid outer shell that encases and supports the creature. Because exoskeletons are not as pliable as human skin, when the insect eats and grows it becomes too large for its outer covering. At certain stages of life, a new exoskeleton forms underneath, and the insect crawls out of its too-small surroundings. The shedding process is called a molt, and growth time between molts is referred to as the instar period. Typical insects undergo 4 to 8 molts; some molt up to 20 times. Insects usually stop molting when they reach adulthood.

The process of change from insect egg to adult is called *metamorphosis*. In species such as crickets, the baby that hatches from the egg resembles an adult. Each molt reveals a larger, but similar, version. This is *simple metamorphosis*. Butterflies and moths go through four very different stages: egg, caterpillar, pupa, and adult. This maturing process is called *complete metamorphosis.*

Let's follow a monarch through its life cycle. Adult males and females of this familiar orange and black species are nearly identical in size and appearance, except that males have a small black scent gland positioned along a vein on the inner surface of each hindwing. Pairs mate by uniting their abdomens. Soon after, the female begins depositing single pale eggs on milkweed plants. Before she dies, the female will lay about 200 eggs, each slightly thicker than a pencil lead.

THE HATCHLING caterpillar of a monarch eating its egg-shell before dining on the leaf of host plant butterfly milkweed.

Depending on air temperatures, the eggs hatch in four days to a week. Tiny caterpillars devour the ribbed eggshell and begin eating the surrounding milkweed leaves. The white sap of these plants contains toxins that are transferred to the caterpillars and eventually to adult butterflies, giving them a bitter taste that is repulsive to predators. Over the next two or three weeks, the ravenous caterpillars will eat, grow, rest, and shed their skins four times. Mature caterpillars measure

A MONARCH caterpillar hanging in a J.

THE MONARCH caterpillar pupating one day later. Actual transformation takes just a few minutes.

2 inches long and weigh a thousand times more than their egg.

When the caterpillar has finally finished eating, it spins a silken pad on a stem or sturdy leaf and attaches its hindlegs. It hangs quietly in a J shape for about a day and then begins motions that resemble pull-ups. This frees the outer covering from the new exoskeleton underneath. Once the old covering is loose, the shedding process takes just a few minutes. A split opens behind the head, and the creature inside swells at the bottom. It wriggles with circular motions, forcing the old skin upward. The resulting chrysalis is the perfect shade of green to hang unnoticed amid surrounding plants.

During the next two weeks, the former caterpillar tranforms inside the chrysalis into a butterfly with wings and six legs. A day before hatching, the outer layer of the chrysalis becomes clear, revealing the tightly curled monarch inside. Finally, the emerging creature gulps air to expand and split the chrysalis. When the adult crawls out, its abdomen is swollen with fluid that will pump through its unfurling wings. In a few hours, the new butterfly is thoroughly dry and strong enough to fly. Often it flutters to the nearest flower for a big drink of nectar.

Other butterflies have similar life cycles, but each kind targets one (or a few) preferred plant species for egg laying. Most butterfly eggs

From Caterpillar to Butterfly

On several occasions, I've been fortunate to discover and photograph caterpillars as they pupate. The process is always fascinating, and it happens faster than you might expect. It amazes me how rapidly monarch caterpillars wiggle out of their yellow-and-black-striped skins. It reminds me of pulling a sweatshirt off over your head. Once the remnants of old skin are pushed to the top, the new green chrysalis shimmers with flecks of gold. —*CT*

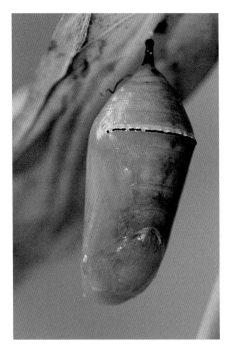

THE MONARCH *chrysalis hangs for about two weeks.*

AN ADULT *monarch emerging from its chrysalis.*

hatch within a week, and caterpillars are genetically programmed to feast on these host plants. Butterflies such as checkerspots and mourning cloaks lay clusters of eggs, but the majority of butterflies deposit one or several eggs per plant, usually on new growth to give each caterpillar plenty of potential food. The spring azure is a widespread butterfly that lays its eggs on flower buds. Butterflies in the white and sulphur family also lay their bright orange, pink, and red eggs in conspicuous places. Caterpillars in this family are cannibals on smaller instars. If an adult female senses that an egg has already been deposited, she will place her spawn elsewhere.

Egg colors and shapes are very distinctive. Zebra heliconian (formerly known as zebra longwing) eggs look like miniature ears of sweet corn. Spicebush swallowtail eggs resemble tiny Ping Pong balls; atala eggs are turban-shaped. There is also much variation in the chrysalis. Monarchs, anglewings, ladies, and fritillaries pupate while hanging upside down. Falcate orangetips and many swallowtails support themselves upright, using a silken belt to connect their midsection to a plant stem. Most chrysalises are very well camouflaged.

THROUGH THE SEASONS

Butterflies have something akin to antifreeze in their cells to endure frigid temperatures in northern climates. Some coppers and hairstreaks spend the winter as eggs attached to sturdy perennial stems or twigs. Great-spangled fritillaries and other fritillary species overwinter as tiny caterpillars. So do tiny eastern tailed-blues, which curl up inside bean and pea pods. The majority of butterflies native to cold climates spend the winter snug in their chrysalis, attached to a plant or on the ground amid insulating leaf litter.

Only a few species brave temperate winters as adults. Best known are mourning cloaks, question marks, commas, and tortoiseshells. With autumn's chilly days, these butterflies seek shelter in tree crevices or between overlapping boards in barns and sheds. They will even squeeze into gaps around residential foundations and porches—anywhere that offers protection from penetrating cold, freezing winds, and deep snow. Occasionally during a prolonged midwinter warm spell, hardy individuals emerge to bask in the sun or search for equally robust flowers. In mild southern regions, sleepy orange (named for hibernating through cold spells), variegated fritillary, and red admiral butterflies also overwinter as adults.

In the North, resident butterflies typically devote a year to the reproductive cycle. The somberly colored mourning cloak provides a good example. Each spring the previous year's adults emerge from hibernation to lay eggs on early-leafing trees such as willow or elm. Eggs hatch, and caterpillars require several weeks to develop. Caterpillars pupate, and later in summer new adults appear. These adults overwinter and renew the cycle by laying their eggs the following spring.

In warmer climates, mourning cloaks have two broods: eggs laid in the spring go through metamorphosis quickly enough for emerging adults to reproduce in early summer. From that second generation of adults come eggs, caterpillars, and the overwintering adults. Interestingly, you can guess how old a mourning cloak is by looking at the edges of its wings. In freshly emerged adults, the edging bands are creamy yellow; adults that have hibernated display white wing margins.

While all butterflies go through four life stages, the time required for this process varies greatly. During hot summers, some species can complete the entire metamorphosis in about a month, while other species require a full year. On average, adult butterflies survive about three weeks. This varies, however, from about a week's life expectancy in the adult stage of many blues to nine months for overwintering commas and mourning cloaks.

A MOURNING cloak, which overwinters as an adult, basks in the sun on a warm spring day.

BUTTERFLY MIGRATION

Most butterflies are stay-at-homes rather than long-distance migrants. Those with specific food and habitat requirements often live within small ranges that provide precise conditions. For example, the veined blue inhabits a few dry, mid-elevation mountain slopes in southern California where its host plant, wild buckwheat, grows. Even though hoary saltbush, the host plant of the San Emigdio blue, has a much wider distribution, this rare butterfly lives only along a few streams and riverbeds that provide adequate moisture in the San Joaquin Valley and Mojave Desert in California. Neither species strays far from its preferred surroundings.

Winter Caterpillars

Most butterflies do their egg laying when host plants are plentiful. Where I live in western North Carolina, the great spangled fritillary is a common species, but females don't lay eggs when host plants are in prime condition. Instead, they deposit as many as 2,000 eggs in late summer while their host plants, wild violets, are waning. Tiny fritillary caterpillars hatch in two or three weeks and imbibe some moisture, but they remain dormant until perennial violets appear the following spring. Many die, but a few caterpillars that have lived seven months without food finally feast. We seldom see them because they are active at night and live on the ground. Survivors pupate, and usually by the first week in June, adults flock to nectar plants in our butterfly garden. Butterfly milkweed and purple coneflower are among their favorites. —CT

THE SAN emigdio blue lives only in south-central California, where its hoary saltbush host and specific habitat conditions occur.

By contrast, butterflies with less specific requirements sometimes fly great distances. Noted travelers include the red admiral, painted lady, common buckeye, gulf fritillary, great southern white, cloudless sulphur, dainty sulphur, and sachem. These species reside year-round in the southern U.S. or northern Mexico. As the weather across the continent warms each spring, some of the adults begin fluttering north, laying eggs that become new generations in more northerly places. Unlike migratory birds, many of these summer wanderers do not return south. Instead, they perish when flowers freeze.

Only a few species make southward flights. During the summer, common buckeyes range through much of the U.S. and southern Canada. In September and October, thousands of common buckeyes are sometimes observed streaming south through seashore preserves along the New York and New Jersey coasts. Smoky purple eyespots on their wings make them readily identifiable. Mourning cloaks, red admirals, and question marks are often observed with them but in smaller numbers. Where these creatures go and whether they overwinter are questions not yet fully answered.

Ladies on the Move

A PAINTED lady rests during migration, Lava Beds National Monument, California.

Two decades ago my husband, Pat, and I lived at Lava Beds National Monument, east of the Cascade Mountains on the California-Oregon border. As we sat outside eating lunch on a fine early spring day, we noticed painted lady butterflies coursing north, flying parallel to the mountain ridges. Not just a few butterflies, but hundreds of them—all resolutely headed . . . where?

A bit of research revealed that painted ladies were formerly known as cosmopolite butterflies, because they are found throughout temperate areas of North America, Europe, Asia, and Africa and on numerous islands. Yet they are not year-round residents in all these places. North American painted ladies overwinter in the Sonoran Desert. They reproduce abundantly, using thistles, mallows, and plants in the daisy family as hosts. Plentiful adults emigrate north and east through a wide range of habitats, spawning several generations during the summer. We also learned there would be no return passage in autumn. After painted ladies reach their ultimate destination, they perish with winter's freezing temperatures. —CT

MONARCHS CLUSTER *in winter roosts such as this one at Pismo Beach, California.*

The monarch is the only butterfly species that has mastered birdlike patterns of north–south migration. Very few individuals make the entire roundtrip; innate knowledge of where and when to travel is passed genetically to succeeding generations. Let's look at the longest-lived group of monarchs—adults maturing from the late-summer brood. They will survive for the next eight months, if they're lucky.

West of the Rocky Mountains, most monarchs fly to the California coast. Airplane pilots have reported them fluttering as high as 10,000 feet. Eleven major overwintering colonies occur in mild seaside locations from Fremont to San Diego, where Monterey pine, Monterey cypress, and eucalyptus trees swaddled in occasional fog make perfect roosts. Among the largest colonies are those in Pacific Grove, Morro Bay, and Pismo Beach, collectively sheltering tens of thousands of monarchs each winter.

Monarchs east of the Rockies follow landforms such as the eastern coastline, the Appalachian Mountains, and the Mississippi basin. Along the way, single butterflies gather into groups, flying south or southwest toward a few special forests in central Mexico. Monarchs originating south of Hudson Bay in Canada travel farthest, covering nearly 2,400 miles. They advance 25 to 30 miles a day, reaching the Gulf Coast by late September and central Mexico by late October. Finally, some 150 miles west of Mexico City, some 10,000 feet high in the Transvolcanic Range of Mexico's Sierra Madre, they gather and rest in oyamel fir trees whose dense boughs offer protection from chilling winter rain and occasional snow.

Despite a 1986 decree to protect Mexico's dozen major butterfly colonies, local logging continued and several important groves dwindled in size. Since 2007, enforcement has been more effective. Ecotourism to several colonies within the Monarch Butterfly Biosphere Reserve boosts local economies. In years of abundance, 400 million monarchs have clustered amid the firs, their weight causing branches to sag. In midwinter, they hang listlessly; when the sun warms the cool mountain air, monarchs take short flights to search for nearby sources of moisture.

By February, monarchs sense the call of procreation and the air swirls with copulating pairs. Looking up through masses of lilting

black and orange wings against deep blue sky is one of nature's breath-
taking spectacles. By late March, winter survivors begin to stream
northward, but eight months of life on the wing have taken their toll.
These monarchs flutter on frayed, faded wings, beating to a biological clock whose time has almost run out. As they return north, gravid
females pause to deposit eggs on whatever milkweed plants they pass.
Each ensures that her offspring can continue, even if her wings won't
carry her back where the journey began.

From these eggs, three or four fast-maturing broods spread fresh
monarchs farther north and east. The intermediate generations live
about a month, but they expand the population. Adult monarchs
emerging late in the summer are likely to be great-great-grandchil-
dren of adults that left here last year. Unlike the fast-maturing broods
that preceded them, the ultimate generation will not become sexually
mature until winter. Their first task is to gather as much floral nectar

as possible to fuel their southward journey and accumulate winter fat reserves.

For each million butterflies that rest in the sheltering Mexican groves, perhaps only one individual will actually find its way back to North America's midsection. If you see it, you will recognize its tattered appearance and labored flight. Take a moment to reflect on its journey—from pale egg to glistening chrysalis to lustrous adult, from midwestern roadside to Gulf bayou to Mexican mountaintop, back again through rain and wind, past speeding cars and fields sprayed with herbicides—to the milkweed plant in your garden that welcomes and bids it to pass its marvelous genetic message to succeeding generations. Monarchs are one of nature's miracles!

Did You Know?

A MALE diana fritillary on butterfly milkweed. Its coloration is typical for the fritillary group.

A FEMALE diana fritillary on butterfly milkweed. These females have evolved with color patterns that mimic distasteful pipevine swallowtails.

1. BUTTERFLIES SEE DIFFERENTLY THAN HUMANS DO. Butterflies have large eyes composed of thousands of individual lenses, so they detect motion acutely. Butterflies see colors and patterns differently than humans do, because their eyes perceive more wavelengths of light, including ultraviolet frequencies, and they can see polarized light. Some flowers have prominent ultraviolet patterns that direct butterflies to the nectar within them.

2. BUTTERFLIES EAT STRANGE THINGS. Although most caterpillars feed on specific host plants, harvester caterpillars eat live insects called woolly aphids. Even weirder, mature harvester caterpillars bury themselves among the bodies of their dead prey to pupate. When adult harvesters emerge, they sip aphids' sweet honeydew secretions. Question mark butterflies consume tree sap and rotting fruit rather than flower nectar. They actually get drunk when they imbibe too many fruits that have fermented.

3. MOST SPECIES OF BUTTERFLIES EXHIBIT SUBTLE DIFFERENCES BETWEEN MALES AND FEMALES. Diana fritillaries are very different. These unusual creatures live along wooded, violet-lined streams in southeastern forests. Males are marked typically for the fritillary group—in shades of

brilliant orange and dark brownish black. Females, however, look nothing like males. They are black with delicate blue and white dapples on the outer wing edges, mimicking pipevine swallowtails.

4. BUTTERFLIES NAVIGATE OVER VAST EXPANSES OF WATER. Little yellow butterflies are residents of the southeastern U.S., West Indies, and South America. In some years their populations swell, and huge numbers emigrate throughout the Caribbean islands. Christopher Columbus experienced one of these mass flights as he sailed through it on the *Santa Maria*.

5. TINY VS. TITAN. The world's largest butterfly is the Queen Alexandra's birdwing, native to Papua New Guinea. Its wingspan is 11 inches. Giant, Thoas, and Appalachian tiger swallowtails tie (with 5¼-inch wingspans) as North America's largest species. (The Appalachian tiger swallowtail is thought by some scientists to be a subspecies of the eastern tiger swallowtail.) The world's smallest butterfly is *Tongeia minima*, a Chinese species with a ½-inch wingspan.

Myths Debunked

Myth: *Caterpillars can't sing.*
Reality: We might guess the only noise a caterpillar can make is the sound of chewing. Wrong! Some hairstreak, blue, copper, and metalmark caterpillars can move body parts known as files or scrapers against the plants they rest on, creating a buzzing vibration, or "song." Why? They summon specialized ants, which eat a sugary substance the caterpillars excrete. Some ants even carry caterpillars to their nests, dine on the sugars, and return the caterpillars to their food plants! What do the caterpillars get in return? Ants protect them from predators, such as parasitic wasps.

Myth: *Butterflies have eyes on their wings.*
Reality: Like many butterflies, common, mangrove, and tropical buckeyes have attention-grabbing eyespots on their wings. Neo-

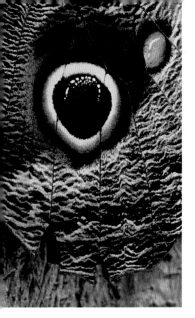

A CLOSE-UP of an eyespot on a Neotropical owl butterfly. The pattern may deceive predators into thinking the butterfly is a much larger bird.

tropical owl butterflies have a large eye design on each hindwing that is so realistic it even includes tiny highlights in the dark pupil area. But none of these are eyes that can see. Instead, they mimic the appearance of a large creature, such as an owl, and thus protect the butterfly by fooling predators into thinking it is dangerous.

Myth: *All butterflies need flowers to survive.*
Reality: Many North American butterflies rely on flowers to provide nectar for adults but there is always an exception. The northern pearly-eye, a 2-inch brown creature that lives in shady hardwood forests in the eastern U.S., does not use flowers. It gets nutritious sugars from willow and poplar tree sap. Northern pearly-eyes, white admirals, and red-spotted purples also dine on carrion.

Myth: *A butterfly landed on me because my bright clothing looked like a flower.*
Reality: Butterflies do sometimes land on humans, but the truth is, they want to eat our sweat. Yuck! Butterfly diets lack the mineral sodium, an ingredient in salt. Butterflies taste with their feet. If they land on our skin and taste salt, they usually stay to eat some. Don't be afraid—they won't bite! Simply hold still while they use their long, thin proboscis to gently suck up the tiny particles. While they vacuum our sweat, they give us a very special opportunity to observe them up close.

Myth: *Butterflies spend the winter in cute little houses.*
Reality: Do you have one of those attractive butterfly roosting boxes in your yard? Have you ever seen a butterfly using it? Probably not. In much of North America, winters are too cold for butterflies to survive as adults. Most endure winter as eggs or pupa. A few species do hibernate, but adults crawl into nooks and crannies, under shingles and siding, or into tree cavities. Ambient heat from the building or the tree's mass helps warm them. Cold air inside an empty box with slits in the front isn't very enticing to mourning cloaks, commas, question marks, and other northern overwintering species. If you have one of these boxes, enjoy it for the exterior design (they are often beautifully painted), or place

sheets of corrugated cardboard vertically inside to loosely fill the empty space. Who knows, a homeless butterfly might think that looks like layered tree bark and stick around for a snooze.

SOMETIMES HUMANS *are visited by a butterfly intent on eating sweat from our skin.*

Chapter 9: Watching Butterflies

A CENTURY AGO, people interested in birds were more likely to carry a shotgun and study specimens in hand than to watch birds through binoculars. Our outlook on butterflies has also changed. Nearly all butterfly identification books published before 1980 began with detailed instructions on how to net, kill, and mount these fragile insects for personal collections. Then environmentally aware writers and butterfly conservation organizations such as the Xerces Society, the North American Butterfly Association, and Monarch Watch began promoting nondestructive observation. They also popularized gardening for butterflies, encouraging us to watch the progression from egg to caterpillar to adult in our own backyards.

Finding Butterflies

If you haven't seen butterflies in your neighborhood, where should you search for them? Looking carefully, you may find several dozen species in natural habitats close to your home. On a grander scale, only a few places in the world don't have butterflies. So except for Antarctica, there are countless possibilities to travel and add to your checklist.

As delicate as they appear, butterflies are very adaptive. Some butterflies are at home in deserts, while others spend their lives on the tundra, in mountain meadows, or in vine-draped rain forests. Fossils indicate that ancestral butterflies developed during the Cretaceous period some 120 million years ago, about the same time diverse flowering plants evolved. Gossamer wings have carried these insects across continents and large expanses of water to colonize new lands. Painted ladies that emerge in North Africa, for instance, fly through Europe into Scandinavia and navigate to Iceland.

The greatest butterfly diversity occurs in Central and South America, where many topographical and ecological zones lie in close proximity. From sandy shores and swamp forests to snowcapped Andean peaks, South America hosts more than one-third of the world's butterfly species. The Indian subcontinent and tropical regions of Southeast Asia also have remarkably beautiful and distinctive butterflies.

About 725 species have been identified north of the Mexican bor-

A CLIPPER, native to forests of southeastern Asia.

der. Texas claims the largest state checklist with more than 425 species. The Rio Grande Valley, home to the National Butterfly Center near Mission and a string of preserves stretching from Brownsville to Falcon, offers some of the best year-round opportunities for butterfly observation. About 40 percent of all species seen in North America reside in or have passed through this area. Demonstrating how diversity decreases as one travels north, approximately 2,000 species occur in Mexico, about 575 species have been tallied in the contiguous U.S., and 275 species are recorded on Canada's national checklist.

In northern areas, butterfly activity starts on warm spring days and continues through autumn's frosts. The most productive observation times are in summer, especially from early July into mid-August. In warmer regions, butterflies are active year-round. Unlike birders, butterfly watchers don't need to be in the field before sunrise. Cold-blooded butterflies spend time absorbing solar heat before taking wing. They tend to be most active between midmorning and late afternoon.

If you are new to butterfly watching, it makes sense to begin near home. Key requirements include nectar-bearing flowers, ample sunshine, and little or no wind. A botanical garden will attract butterflies in a city because it offers a long season of blooms and masses of color that butterflies notice from a distance. Wild habitats provide diverse nectar sources and enticing host plants. So visit nature preserves and parks, looking especially in areas where two or more habitat types meet—in streamside meadows or where a pond laps against a brushy hillside. Follow trails, bike paths, river walks, and greenways, pausing now and then to scan for the flash of colorful wings. You should be amply rewarded with butterfly sightings.

As your skills and interests grow, you may wish to travel farther and encounter new species. Since butterfly abundance is governed by food and habitat requirements, a successful viewing trip hinges on being in the right place at the right time. For instance, glimpsing the Schaus' swallowtail necessitates a trip to Biscayne National Park or Key Largo in southern Florida, where host wild lime and torchwood trees grow. The cranberry blue takes wing for just a few weeks during its life cycle. Although this species has a huge range—from Canada's Hudson Bay through Alaska's Yukon Valley—adults appear only in boggy areas in July. Another reason for butterfly-related travel is to experience peak migration along a major flyway. Cape May, at the southern tip of New

THE MALACHITE *ranges from Brazil to southern Florida and Texas, and highlights the dazzling butterfly diversity of the Neotropics.*

Tips for Watching

The key to finding butterflies is to be quietly observant. Train your eyes to pick up color patterns and movements, especially of well-camouflaged species. If you spot a distant butterfly, inch slowly toward it. Since a butterfly can detect contrasting light levels, don't let your shadow sweep across it. When a butterfly repeatedly feeds at certain flowers, move nearer by stalking like a cat. Then remain motionless. Patience often brings you eye to eye with your quarry. Frequently the butterfly will disregard you and just eat. —CT

Jersey, is a funneling point where thousands of monarchs and other migrant butterflies stream south in September and October.

DESCRIBING WHAT YOU SEE

As you become more aware of butterflies, you'll want to describe their appearance to others and will undoubtedly consult identification guides. It's important to know some standard descriptive terms and names of body parts. While most serious *butterfliers* (those who watch and appreciate butterflies) study adults, they identify common caterpillars as well. We'll spend a few moments becoming familiar with both.

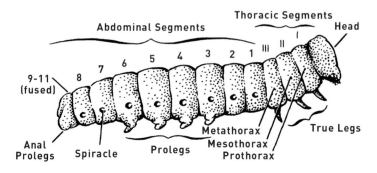

PARTS OF a caterpillar.

Most caterpillars are long and cylindrical, with three major body regions: head, thorax, and abdomen. Hairstreak, blue, copper, and azure larvae are flat, resembling a slug in shape, with small legs hidden beneath. The distinction between body regions is less apparent in caterpillars than in adults.

A caterpillar's head is the first segment at the front of its body. Heads are rounded or button-shaped, smaller, and often harder than the other segments. Even though most caterpillars have six pairs of simple eyes, or *ocelli,* they do not see well. They also have a short pair of sensory antennae. Because the caterpillar's primary job is to eat, the most prominent part of the head is a well-developed mouth. Between the caterpillar's upper and lower lips are two curved *mandibles* (jaws), which in many species are equipped with sharp edges for shearing off plant bits. Sensitive *maxillary palps* guide food into the mandibles. A silk-spinning organ on the lower lip can anchor the creature as needed to a leaf, stem, or other surface.

The next three segments compose the thorax. At the bottom of each segment is a pair of jointed true legs that later will become the adult butterfly's legs. Swallowtails have an *osmeterium,* a Y-shaped appendage that thrusts from the caterpillar's thorax and excretes a smelly substance to repel predators.

The remaining 11 segments form the abdominal region. Five of them, usually the third, fourth, fifth, sixth, and tenth segments, have a pair of false legs (*prolegs*) attached. These legs are cylindrical rather than jointed, and they end in small gripping hooks. Their function is the same as that of true legs, to support and move the caterpillar. The last pair, called *anal prolegs* or claspers, is employed when caterpillars hang to begin the transition to a chrysalis.

Caterpillar bodies may be completely hairless, smooth with a pair of fleshy filaments at each end (as on a monarch caterpillar), smooth with a rear horn, or hairless but covered with knobby bumps. Caterpillars may also be completely hairy, tufted, bristled, or covered with branched spines. Textured coverings may hide the circular openings on the side of a caterpillar, called *spiracles,* through which the creature breathes.

While the caterpillar's function is to eat, the adult butterfly is responsible for reproduction and dispersal. Although divided into head, thoracic, and abdominal regions, the adult's appearance is very different from that of its caterpillar. Atop a butterfly's head are two slender, club-tipped antennae that receive information about smell. The butterfly's mouth is a flexible, tubelike proboscis. It can be extended to suck nectar from flowers (like drinking through a straw) or compactly rolled when not in use. Two scale-covered *palpi* extend tusklike from either side of the proboscis.

The compound eyes that dominate a butterfly's head are each made of some 6,000 sight receptors with lenses (*ommatidia*). Butterflies apparently see a mosaic pattern rather than a sharply focused image, but their vision is good enough to realize when something around them moves or when a predator approaches too close. Butterflies detect a wider range of colors in the ultraviolet spectrum than humans see and can also perceive polarized light. Many male and female butterflies are differently marked with ultraviolet patterns on their wings. While humans can't see the difference, butterflies can instantly recognize a potential mate or a competitor.

The butterfly's midsection, or thorax, has three segments, each with a pair of legs attached. Members of the brush-footed butterfly family (including fritillaries, ladies, and anglewings) have tiny, curled front legs, making them appear to have only four instead of six walking legs.

A MATURE black swallow-tail caterpillar on parsley, its host plant.

THE JULIA heliconian is a brush-footed butterfly. It has four normally developed legs and two very tiny front legs.

Butterfly legs consist of slender, hard-shelled sections that bend at their joints like a suit of armor. On the outer end of each leg is a claw-like *tarsus* used to grasp plants or perches. Inside the tarsi are sensory receptors that "taste" the chemical composition of surfaces they contact. With a momentary touch, a female butterfly knows whether the plant she has encountered is the correct host for her eggs.

Two forewings and two hindwings attach to the thorax. Opposing sets of interior muscles draw the wings up and down. Butterflies also influence wing movement by changing the shape of their thorax. Prominent veins, which are strong tubes within the wing membranes, contain nerves and a place for *hemolymph* (butterfly blood) to circulate. Pegged to the wings in neat overlapping rows are up to 1.5 million colorful scales. Some butterflies also have specialized scent scales used in courtship.

Remaining body segments form the slender abdomen. Together, the abdomen and thorax contain spiracles that allow air into the respiratory system. The abdomen also houses testes in males and ovaries in female butterflies. Some males extend bristles, called hair pencils, from their abdomen to disperse powerful scent pheromones. These chemical communicators are used to woo mates and repel competitors. At the end of the male's abdomen are paired claspers used to grasp the female during mating.

Identifying Butterflies

You won't need much equipment to begin butterfly watching. An identification guide to carry into the field is helpful. Take a few moments to thumb through it prior to your first outing, becoming familiar with how it is organized. It's also helpful to know what distinctive features define major butterfly families (see Chapter 14).

Guidebooks describe shapes and colors on upper and lower surfaces of the wings. They highlight life-cycle information, flight patterns, and unique body characteristics. The most helpful guides also include notes about habitat, range, and preferred foods. Some guides are illustrated with color photos, while others have color art. Compare them at a good bookstore and choose the style you prefer.

Field guides illustrate butterflies in fresh condition. Remember that colors will fade with age; delicate features such as swallowtail tails may be missing. Males and females of the same species may look different, and females are often larger. Appearance of the same spe-

A FIELD guide or regional guidebook with color illustrations is a great help in identifying butterflies.

cies may vary slightly from region to region. Beginners often benefit by watching butterflies with someone more experienced. Take advantage of local parks that offer guided nature walks or special butterfly programs.

Enthusiastic butterfliers use close-focusing binoculars for detailed looks at their quarry. Within the past decade, optics manufacturers have introduced hybrid birding/butterfly-watching choices, and at least one company makes dedicated butterfly binoculars. To be useful, optics for butterflies should have magnification within the 6- to 8-power range and focus as close as 6 feet (dedicated models focus to less than 2 feet). Take a small notebook to record sketches and observations, or a checklist to track dates and places you see new species.

You'll begin to instantly recognize general sizes, shapes, and colors that identify related groups, such as whites and sulphurs or milkweed

BUTTERFLY WATCHERS with binoculars.

butterflies. Using a field guide, and paying particular attention to range maps that narrow choices to species from your area, you can sort through illustrations of wing patterns to figure out what you're seeing. It's helpful to have a trip companion. One person can describe what the live butterfly looks like; the other can check written descriptions in the guide. Butterfly watching provides a wonderful opportunity to include children or grandchildren in an outdoor activity.

If your winged subject flies, don't give up. As it moves, you will see both upper and lower surfaces of the wings. Also note the flight style. Skippers move reactively, with jerky wing motions. Whirlabouts have fast, spiraling flights. Admirals, like many of the brush-foots, have a characteristic flap-and-glide wing cadence. Blues stay low, and monarchs sail above most of the plants in a meadow.

With experience, you'll associate butterfly appearances in your yard with the emergence of host plants or nectar sources. When something new flutters by, you may not instantly know what it is, but the shape, color, flight pattern, or behavior will alert you to look more closely. For many people, learning about butterflies leads to a broader understanding of plants and of other animals in the "big picture" scientists refer to as ecology.

Flight Patterns

A SPICEBUSH swallowtail in a blur of motion.

As you become more practiced, you will differentiate between similar species on the wing. For instance, in western North Carolina we have an abundance of pipevine and spicebush swallowtails. Both are large black insects with blue markings. The pipevine is slightly smaller and more compact, and its wings have a lustrous sheen like coal. It often flies low, stopping frequently around the edges of puddles. Spicebush swallowtails are larger and typically visit tall flowers, such as phlox, ironweed, and joe pye weed. They seldom stop flapping their elegant wings, even while gathering nectar. —*CT*

A PAINTED lady basking on a warm paving stone.

JULIA HELICONIAN butter-flies mating.

A FEMALE giant swallow-tail laying eggs on its host plant.

Butterfly Behavior

As you pay more attention to butterflies, you will witness interesting daily and seasonal activities. Even when you (or scientists) can't explain why butterflies do something, encounters that provide insight into behavior are always fascinating.

BASKING

In order to absorb maximum solar radiation when it's cold, butterflies visit sun-splashed rocks, tree trunks, patio railings, and paving stones. If the habitat has only a few good sunning points, individuals may fight over prime spots. Sunbathers typically orient with abdomens facing the heat and wings spread wide to soak up sunlight. Black is very efficient at absorbing solar radiation. White butterflies often sit with their light-colored wings raised at an angle, which deflects and concentrates solar rays onto the black thorax and abdomen, warming them more quickly than if the wings were flat. Cold butterflies may bask a long time, repositioning every few minutes as the sun moves across the sky.

HILLTOPPING

In regions that have prominent high terrain, male butterflies venture to open areas around steep slopes. Unmated female butterflies also head for these "butterfly malls," and both sexes spend time fluttering around, checking each other out. They often mate, then females return to habitats suitable for laying their eggs.

MATING

When male and female butterflies approach each other, they often move together and begin an upward, spiraling courtship display. The process is not completely understood, but wings may briefly touch and pheromone scents may be involved. Copulation occurs while the pair is perched. After the male engages the female's abdomen with claspers on the tip of his abdomen, they can fly away together if disturbed.

EGG LAYING

Gravid female butterflies deposit eggs by briefly touching the tip of their abdomen to the host plant. Swallowtails flutter back to revisit the same host several times, but they spread eggs widely enough so each caterpillar will find plenty to eat. Julia heliconians and zebra heliconians deposit multiple eggs on sprawling passion vine hosts. Monarch females perform a precise touch-and-go on milkweed, scattering their eggs if enough host plants are available. When you notice a butterfly depositing eggs, watch through binoculars to pinpoint the exact leaf or stem she visits. Then approach the plant for a close look at the fresh eggs.

FIGHTING

Male butterflies often select a favorite perch from which they can sun while keeping watch over their territory. Some regularly leave the perch to patrol, chase intruders, feed, and search for mates. Others occupy less prominent perches and use them as bases for spirited attacks on intruding butterflies or birds. Hackberry emperors, red admirals, and red-spotted purples all brazenly buzz humans and pets.

PUDDLING EASTERN tiger swallowtails.

PUDDLING

Groups of butterflies sometimes congregate along sandy creek edges and muddy riverbanks, or line the edges of temporary mud puddles. They imbibe moisture and dissolved mineral salts, which supply nutrients lacking in a nectar diet. Dozens or sometimes hundreds of individuals—many of them recently hatched male swallowtails, sulphurs, or blues—gather in favorite puddling places. Some butterflies also visit animal excrement and decaying animal carcasses to ingest minerals.

ROOSTING

Where do butterflies spend the night? Many rest on bark or twigs sheltered by tree canopies or sleep under wide leaves. Zebra heliconians, which reside from the Gulf Coast into South America and the West Indies, are known for communal roosting. They return nightly to twigs of a favorite shrub or vine, protected under the canopy of an overarching forest. These conditions are common in the hammocks of southern Florida. Sometimes by asking a park naturalist for directions, you may be able to see a flock of zebras going to roost at dusk.

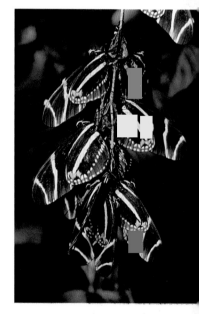

ROOSTING ZEBRA heliconians.

Watching butterflies is a way to rekindle our childlike curiosity and the excitement of discovery deep within us. Butterfly watching often rewards participants with glimpses of intense beauty and a renewed appreciation of nature. Try it!

Chapter 10: Attracting and Feeding Butterflies

Do you have a flower or herb garden? If so, is it something you started, or did you inherit it from previous owners? Maybe you have a new home—and great intentions—but you've only been able to plant a tree here, a shrub there, or a few perennials the neighbor gave you. Don't feel bad, because many folks landscape their yards over time. The point is, few people plan their landscapes with butterfly observation in mind. Yet lots of us love to watch butterflies. If we realized how simple it is to attract them, and that butterfly gardens often require less maintenance than traditional landscapes, more of us might try it. The next few chapters walk you through the process step-by-step. Let's begin by thinking about what surroundings, or habitat, butterflies need to survive.

WITH A bit of planning, a backyard garden can provide the food, water, shelter, and protected sites butterflies need for their life stages.

Habitat Requirements

As we've already learned, butterflies transform through four life stages: egg, caterpillar, pupa, and adult. During each interval, their requirements are slightly different, but you can make everything they need available in a small butterfly garden. Every bountiful wildlife habitat provides food, water, shelter, and protected nesting sites. We'll consider how each of the butterfly life stages interacts with these components.

EGGS AND CATERPILLARS

Pregnant female butterflies are genetically programmed to lay eggs on specific host plants. Butterfly caterpillars are picky eaters, perhaps like your own children. Most caterpillars rely on just one or two favorite foods, and mother butterflies must select the correct host. Unlike birds, butterfly parents do not make a nest, care for their eggs, or tend their babies. Relationships perfected during eons of plant-butterfly evolution ensure that host plants provide food and shelter essential for nurturing eggs and caterpillars.

That's right—host plants not only offer shelter from weather and predators, but they sacrifice their own cells to supply food and moisture to caterpillars! This is a vital concept to understand when gardening for new generations of butterflies. Think of host plants as babysitters, giving eggs and caterpillars what they need in the absence of parents. Planting appropriate hosts will definitely bring butterflies to your yard.

Once caterpillars appear, they eat as ravenously as human teenagers. Between hatching and pupating, monarch caterpillars increase their mass 2,000 times in only two weeks! If sufficient butterfly eggs are laid in a small area, lots of host plants will be devoured. Gardening for caterpillars won't make your yard look like Martha Stewart's. Expect successful host plants in your butterfly garden to look like Swiss cheese—or worse—after caterpillars finish chewing on them. Baby butterflies are like the guests who came to dinner and stayed and stayed. . . .

But that's okay—you want to grow butterflies, not perfect host plant specimens! Scatter hosts throughout the garden so females will find many places to lay eggs. Plant hosts abundantly so there will be lots for caterpillars to eat. Interspersing hosts with shrubs or other sturdy plants gives caterpillars hiding places. Maturing caterpillars molt several times, and prior to molting, they hide among leaves or branches to rest while their new exoskeleton forms under their old one.

QUEEN CATERPILLARS *eating their milkweed host plant.*

Guess Who Came to Dinner?

Some years ago, Pat and I landscaped our suburban yard in Martinsburg, West Virginia, for birds and butterflies. No tuliptrees grew near us, and we wanted one because they host eastern tiger swallowtails. A few miles away, we noticed young tuliptrees growing like weeds in a friend's flower bed. She generously gave us a little tree for our backyard. Within days, we found swallowtail eggs on it. Half a dozen caterpillars hatched, and as they grew, they devoured leaf after leaf. We kept the largest caterpillar on the tuliptree, where it pupated. Before the rest starved, we moved them to an alternate host, wild cherry. Despite being completely denuded, the tuliptree unfurled reserve leaves and survived. When we moved away a few years later, the nearly devoured tree was 15 feet tall. —CT

A SPICEBUSH swallowtail caterpillar ready to pupate in a crevice in a rock wall.

PUPA

After caterpillars satisfy their hunger, they transform into a pupa (or chrysalis). Caterpillars often rest on a sturdy twig or perennial plant stem or snuggle into a cracked rock before entering this phase. Some remain in the pupa for a few weeks; others endure half a year within their camouflaged casing. Since the pupa is immobile, its outer covering is tough enough to withstand temperature and humidity changes and obscured enough to avoid discovery by predators. Pupas are self-contained; they neither eat nor drink. So don't worry about providing food for this stage, but be careful as you prune and remove old vegetation from your garden. Don't accidentally toss the pupas out with the compost!

ADULTS

When adult butterflies emerge from the chrysalis, their immediate need is for something sturdy to hold onto while they pump fluid from their swollen abdomen into their expanding wings. If adults can't inflate their wings properly, they won't be able to fly. By design, caterpillars select a durable plant stem for attaching their chrysalis. Later, the emerging adult clings to the same stem, sitting quietly for a few hours until its wings dry. This is a critical time for protection from predators. Make certain your butterfly garden has enough shrubby plants to accommodate pupating caterpillars and emerging adults.

Just as hosts are essential for growing caterpillars, nectar-producing flowers are important for attracting adults—so important, in fact, that we devote a section in the next chapter to choosing food-producing plants and integrating them into your backyard habitat. Chapter 12 contains lists of nectar plants that will feed butterflies in your backyard.

FEEDERS VERSUS FLOWERS

Several manufacturers make cute saucer-shaped feeders promoted to attract butterflies. These typically have a reservoir that holds sugar-water "nectar" and small openings through which butterflies can drink. In conservatories, where live butterflies are housed in glassed or screened enclosures, you may see monarchs and painted ladies at sugar-water dispensers, but in backyard settings nectar feeders don't work very well. Most nectar-consuming butterflies prefer gathering the sweet stuff naturally.

That said, you can attract certain butterflies with natural foods other than flower nectar. Satyrs (earth-toned creatures with eyespots on their wings) and commas feed on tree sap. Red-spotted purples, white admirals, and common wood-nymphs are among many species that dine on dung, carrion, and rotting fruits. To bring them into your garden, serve something they'll recognize. Planting fruit trees is one approach. Woodpeckers called sapsuckers visit orchards, drill-

A CAMOUFLAGED zebra heliconian chrysalis on passionvine.

The Recipe

When I was a kid, a folksy show called *The Waltons* was popular on TV. Two sweet old ladies, the Baldwin sisters, had minor roles in many episodes because neighbors were always stopping by for a sip of "the recipe." The shy sisters were bootleggers, and their beverage lured connoisseurs from far and wide.

When it comes to feeding butterflies, the Baldwin sisters would have said, "Nix the nectar, bring on the beer!" They're right—red admirals, Compton tortoiseshells, question marks, viceroys, and red-spotted purples are much more likely to sample a brew of fermented fruit sloshing in stale beer than come out of the woods for plain sugar water.

Numerous recipes for this heady concoction are traded among butterfly enthusiasts. Here's the recipe our local nature center swears by: 1 large can beer, 1 cup molasses, ½ cup brown sugar, 3–4 mashed overripe bananas. Mix all ingredients and let them ferment several days. Serve in feeders; excess may be refrigerated. Cheers! —CT

A RED-SPOTTED purple eating a rotting peach.

ing many shallow holes into the bark of fruit trees so the wounds will weep. Sapsuckers return to eat sap and the insects it attracts. Butterflies slurp fruit-tree sap and feed on fallen, rotting fruits such as crab apples, peaches, nectarines, and cherries.

To dispense butterfly food, such as "the recipe" (see page 149), here's a butterfly feeder project simple enough for kids to make. You'll need a 10-inch plastic plant saucer and seven plastic mesh dish scrubbers (use the puffy, round kind, and select blue and yellow if available). Arrange them so they cover the bottom of the saucer, with shoulders touching. The scrubbers serve as dry landing platforms, so butterflies can perch and drink without submerging in the brew, even if they get tipsy. Add an inch of the recipe to the bottom of the saucer. Place the feeder on a flat surface within easy view—perhaps at the edge of your patio or on a decorative concrete block that raises it off the ground in your garden. For windy days, add a flat rock in the bottom to keep the dish from blowing away.

Warning: Like the Baldwin sisters, you may attract a large group of admirers, which in this case will be mostly insects. If ants become a problem, retrofit the saucer to hang by drilling three holes at evenly spaced intervals just below the saucer's rim. Attach one end of a 15-inch piece of flexible wire or heavy fishing line through each hole and secure the opposite ends together above the feeder. Select a shepherd's crook or other suitable hook to suspend the saucer as you would a hanging flower basket. Also purchase an ant moat (typically used to ant-proof hummingbird feeders) and two S hooks. To finish ant-proofing, fill the moat with water and hang it from the crook with an S hook. Attach another S hook below the moat to suspend the feeder's harness. Voilà!

If bees and yellow jackets raid the feeder, forgo the scrubbers and cover the saucer with fiberglass window screening, held tautly in place by a large rubber band or half a dozen binder clips. Adjust the fill level for your feeder so butterflies can land on the screen and insert their proboscis through the mesh for a drink, but so bees' and wasps' smaller mouthparts can't reach the liquid. Take the feeder inside at night if raccoons patter about your neighborhood, or be prepared for a rowdy late-night bar scene.

Feeder maintenance is easy. If hot summer temperatures evaporate the liquid, rehydrate the solution with beer. If rain dilutes the brew or when the feeder is empty, wash the saucer and scrubbers in the dishwasher, or sanitize them with a solution of 10 percent bleach in hot water. Rinse thoroughly before refilling.

Another nearly effortless approach is to offer rotting fruit on a plant saucer or atop a mound of freshly turned earth in a flower bed. Putrid pears, peaches, mangos, nectarines, cantaloupes, watermelons, and even strawberries and grapes supply sugars, nutrients, and moisture in an all-natural form. If you don't have slimy fruit hiding in the refrigerator, introduce yourself to your grocery store's produce manager or folks at your local farm stand, who might make you a great deal on past-their-prime items.

One more sure-fire feeder strategy is to purchase overripe bananas on sale, peel, and freeze them whole. When needed, thaw one and blend with ¼ cup of wine. (Plain banana works okay too.) Slather on a saucer and serve to your butterflies.

Feeders are fun, but when they go empty or linger with moldy, unfit food, it will be "flutter-bye" instead of butterfly. Feeders are good supplemental tools, but to enhance your backyard's natural qualities, nectar-producing plants have the most appeal. Even if you're limited to a deck or apartment balcony, it's possible to offer a few container-grown plants that will attract butterflies.

A *SIMPLE* butterfly feeder will attract numerous species to a fermented mixture of fruit and sugar.

WATER

Butterfly eggs are sealed inside a waxy coating, and caterpillars naturally ingest moisture as they graze on plants. The pupa rests within a leathery shell. So providing water for butterflies during their early life stages is not necessary. Adults are adept at finding water too. Nectar-eaters slurp sugar water; fruit-eaters consume moisture in the slurry of softened plant tissue. Some adults drink the morning dew, and many more love a shallow puddle.

Not all butterflies flock to wet places, but certain species can't resist. Perhaps you have seen a cluster of butterflies taking flight as you drive a puddle-pocked dirt road after rain. Around the world, sulphurs are habitual puddlers; some African species boldly rest on the heads of Nile crocodiles along river edges. They are probably gleaning minerals from the crocodiles' nasal and tear-duct secretions. (Yes, butterflies eat crocodile tears!) In North America, swallowtails are highly visible puddlers, especially in sunny places. California sisters, Florida purplewings, skippers, blues, and whites visit soggy soil in forest habitats.

A *QUESTION* mark butterfly dines on watermelon.

PIPEVINE SWALLOWTAILS
puddling, or drinking moisture, at moist gravel.

Why are certain butterflies particularly attracted to damp soil? Scientific research reveals that leaf-eating caterpillars lack sodium in their diets. While they're munching away, they should be saying "Please pass the salt." But sodium is scarce in some habitats, and if you were to put salt directly on the plants in your garden, it would probably kill them. So what's a butterfly to do? Puddle!

Nearly all puddlers are males. They find moist places where salts are concentrated—often where an animal previously relieved its bladder or bowels, or perhaps died and decomposed. Often this is along a stream or around a puddle, but sometimes butterflies land on human skin or on other creatures that expel sweat. Apparently, when one or two butterflies discover a good puddling spot, their posture signals others of their species—and sometimes different species—to join the club. One study found that yellow tiger swallowtails almost exclusively join other tiger swallowtails, whereas dark-colored pipevine swallowtails sometimes gather with tiger and spicebush swallowtails in mixed groups. Puddlers typically stay in the same place for long periods without much movement. They sit very close together, sometimes opening their wingtips at a slight angle or pumping their wings slowly. If you look carefully, you may see drops of moisture on the butterflies' abdomens. Their bodies concentrate salts internally and expel excess water.

Here's the coolest part of the story: Males process the salt into love offerings. When they mate, males transfer a *spermatophore,* or reproductive packet, to females. The packet contains salts and amino acids that allow the female to lay more eggs. Some of this very necessary sodium is also passed to the next generation through the female's eggs.

A down-to-earth project that will improve your backyard butterfly refuge is a puddling station. Look for a sunny spot visible from a favorite window or sitting area, ideally near an outdoor water spigot. A quiet, open location within sight of flowers is better than someplace busy. You'll want fluttery visitors to stick around rather than be disturbed every few minutes. Grab a shovel and remove the grass from a circle 12 to 18 inches in diameter, fashioning a central depression. If you have clumpy, claylike soil, ask the kids for some sand from their sandbox and mix it in. Place a nice-looking flat rock toward the rear of the soil depression, and water the soil often enough so that it stays moist.

In dry climates or where water conservation is a concern, select a site the same way, but after taking out the grass, remove the dirt onto

a large sheet of cardboard or plastic. You'll want to bury a garbage-can lid or large plant saucer so the rim is slightly above soil level and the curve of the container forms a shallow bowl. Wiggle the lid back and forth until it seats and is level. Mix clean sand with the dirt you removed, so the result is half sand, half soil. Shovel this mixture into the container, building it to the lip but keeping the soil 1–2 inches lower in the center. If you removed rocks, return a few around the depression. With a garden hose, spray the area gently until the soil becomes spongy. Repeat as necessary to keep the area damp. Butterflies of all sizes and stripes will thank you.

EVEN IF you don't intentionally offer excrement, butterflies will consume nutrients from bird droppings in your yard. This silver-spotted skipper is sampling phoebe droppings.

Oh, Poo!

Skip this section if you are squeamish. Read on if you want to increase the attractiveness (to a butterfly) of your puddle project by adding piddle or poo to provide scarce minerals.

One summer day I was sitting on the porch with our neighbor, Grace, who was nearly 90 at the time and had lived on the farm next to ours all her life. Grace was a great observer of nature and full of commonsense wisdom. "Look," she said, pointing to a small brown butterfly with silver blotches on its wings. "There's a chickenshit butterfly."

A bit surprised, I asked her why she used that name. "Well, we always had 'em around our chicken house, and that's what they ate." So I carefully watched the creatures I call silver-spotted skippers. Grace was exactly right! Silver-spotted skippers are among hundreds of butterfly species that munch minerals from sources humans consider unthinkable to eat, including excrement and rotting flesh.

Actually, the largest, most beautiful concentrations of swallowtails, skippers, blues, and sulphurs I've seen near our home occurred after another neighbor's cows got loose and trotted up and down our dirt road all day, making deposits. More butterflies than I knew existed in these hills covered the pancake-shaped piles until they dried out. Butterflies came again after rains, until the do-do finally disintegrated. So if you're not squeamish—and if you don't have small children who might wander into something you'd prefer they don't—you can enhance your puddling area with the occasional cow pie, horse hockey, pet piddle, or fish guts. Scientists tell us many butterflies have an excellent sense of smell to detect odors from dung and carrion, smells that lead them to a protein-based meal. Bon appétit! —CT

NUMEROUS BUTTERFLIES, including a boldly striped zebra swallowtail, gather to eat pet poop.

A MALACHITE taking shelter under a leaf.

SHELTER

Stormy weather can damage a butterfly's fragile wings. Driving rain, hail, sudden snowstorms, high winds, and unexpected cold are all butterfly killers. A well-rounded backyard habitat should provide shelter from these extremes. In the tropics, where both butterflies and rainfall are prolific, delicate creatures hide under large leaves during downpours. You can provide natural umbrellas by planting wide-leafed shrubs and trees. Sunflower, viburnum, spicebush, pawpaw, rhododendron, magnolia, catalpa, and sycamore become natural umbrellas on rainy days.

Seashores, mountains, and prairies are all places where fierce winds blow. Butterflies need windbreaks, such as hedges and clusters of evergreen trees, to escape buffeting that will otherwise destroy their wings. In most areas, severe storms typically come from one direction. If you aren't certain what that is, contact a local TV weather forecaster or ask your county extension agent. Consider planting a group of trees and shrubs that will provide a place sheltered from the prevailing wind.

Butterfly houses, which look like bird nest boxes with narrow entrance slits, are sold to provide shelter, but they seldom entice butterflies inside. Your habitat will be much homier to butterflies if you are fortunate enough to have a sturdy dead tree in your yard. Butterflies crawl into crevices in the wood and hide under peeling bark to spend cold periods in torpor. If you don't have an appropriate tree or large stump, incorporate a fallen log into your yard design. As a bonus, various fungi will grow on the dead wood. Mourning cloaks, hackberry emperors, and red admirals all nibble on mushrooms and slime mold.

Wood piles are another source of shelter, primarily for overwintering caterpillars. If you carry an armload of firewood inside, inspect it before chucking logs into the wood stove or fireplace. Any listless caterpillars curled into a ball should be returned outside to the pile or to a similar refuge in a stump or fallen log.

Finally, interspersed with sheltering trees and windbreaks, you'll want open, sunny places where butterflies have room to fly back and forth to nectar plants. Since chilly butterflies perch in the sun to warm themselves, and males keep watch from their perches for potential mates, basking stations will be popular with your winged visitors. They will also be handy spots for you to view the butterflies. Place a few flat, dark rocks where the sun will warm them each morning. Put a comfortable chair nearby, and enjoy the peaceful ambiance of butterflies quietly basking in a sun-dappled yard.

*A **DEAD** tree with peeling bark offers crevices where butterflies can spend the winter.*

Chapter 11: Plants for Butterflies

IMAGINE AN IDYLLIC DAY in your butterfly garden: Beautiful little caterpillars munch on the leafy food you've provided. Adult butterflies busily feed on nectar. Females pause at specific host plants to lay eggs. Males hang out on prominent perches, watching for potential mates and chasing less macho competitors. Some flit off to happy hour, joining other guys sipping mineral cocktails or noshing tasty tidbits. On sunny days your guests relax on exposed rocks, logs, even deck railings. When it rains, they crawl under leafy shrubs; at night some may gather in a group slumber party. During prolonged cold, trees with deep crevices protect your delicate treasures until warmth returns.

The secret to providing well-rounded butterfly habitat is to offer an insecticide-free diverse combination of host plants, nectar-producing plants, sheltering vegetation, and reliable moisture. The more varied your host and nectar offerings, the more kinds of butterflies you'll entertain. In this chapter we'll learn how to arrange all of these elements in a garden design that pleases both butterflies and homeowners.

Planning Your Butterfly Habitat

In Chapter 4 we learned how to design backyard habitats for hummingbirds. If you already have hummers outside your windows, enticing butterflies will be easy, because these creatures share favorite food plants. If you haven't read Chapter 4, don't worry. In the next few paragraphs we'll highlight important steps to make a specific plan for your backyard garden and choose plants that butterflies can't resist. But before you rush off to purchase flowers, let's invest a few moments with pencil and paper to create a physical plan to ensure your success.

INVENTORY YOUR ASSETS

Most residential yards have something that wildlife will find attractive. Decide which favorite windows or outdoor relaxing areas will be the viewpoints for enjoying your butterfly garden. From each of these portals, take a few moments to list the natural assets your yard already offers. These may include:

ENTICE BUTTERFLIES to a colorful garden that offers a variety of host and nectar-producing plants, as well as shelter and a source of moisture.

- established trees, shrubs, or vines

- flower beds with perennials or annuals

- arbors with flowering vines or shrubs

- a birdbath, small pond, or other source of water

- hedges, windbreaks, or brush piles to provide shelter

- any of these elements in neighboring yards, or nearby, that attract butterflies

Habitats surrounding your home will shape your guest list, since butterflies occupy a wider range than what your yard can provide. If you live in a city or the suburbs, expect cosmopolitan butterflies such as painted ladies, sulphurs, and skippers that feast on abundant thistles, legumes, and grasses. You will count more individuals in late summer and early autumn than any other season. If your home is situated near natural meadows or woodlands, expect a more diverse list of winged visitors. They will appear at varying intervals depending on life cycles of each species.

SKETCH YOUR YARD

On a blank sheet of paper, sketch your yard. Your diagram doesn't have to win an art award, but it does need to show the general arrangement of your surroundings. Make your yard map as though you were hovering above your house, looking straight down. Begin by filling the page with the boundaries of your property. Now add shapes of your house, deck or patio, outbuildings, walkways, driveway, and fences in proportion to their sizes. Write *EAST* on the side of the map where the sun rises and *WEST* where it sets, then mark *NORTH* and *SOUTH*.

Looking from favorite places inside the house, on the deck, or from the patio, use ★ to show the views you want to develop. Then draw natural assets you already have. Mark large trees using squiggly circles with T in the center. Use smaller squiggly circles with S to indicate shrubs and V for vines. Sketch your flower beds, marking P where perennials grow, A for annuals, and G for garden vegetables. If you have a creek, mark its path with →'s pointing downstream. Place an F for

Why Garden for Butterflies?

No matter how small your garden is, you can grow plants that benefit butterflies. . . . Most people employ butterfly gardening to create movement and drama in their gardens and to experience the beauty of butterflies at home. Done correctly, butterfly gardening can also help increase butterfly populations.
—*Jeffrey Glassberg, author of* Enjoying Butterflies More

each bird or butterfly feeder you already have; use a W to show water, such as a birdbath or small pond. Draw a ▼ wherever there is an outdoor faucet. Add additional assets, such as a brush pile or dead tree. (Refer to page 47 for a sample yard map.)

ANSWERING QUESTIONS about frost dates, soil type, and sun exposure before purchasing plants or seeds will make your gardening efforts much more successful.

FIVE QUESTIONS

Next, answer these questions:

1. HOW MUCH SUNLIGHT DOES MY YARD RECEIVE? Butterfly plants thrive in intense light. On a sunny day, keep track of areas you want to develop for butterfly gardening. If they receive at least six cumulative hours of direct light, sun-loving plants should survive there. Mark these areas with ☀. On the north side of your home and beneath established trees and shrubs, it may be too shady for full-sun plants. Use the ◉ symbol to indicate these places. Some butterflies visit shade-tolerant flowers. Check plant lists in Chapter 12 for the same symbol, identifying choices that don't need as much light.

2. HOW WINDY IS MY YARD? Certain places always seem windy, and that's bad for butterflies whose fragile wings easily become tattered. If you live near the seashore, on the prairie, or where mountain winds howl, use clustered evergreen trees, hedges, walls, or privacy fencing to provide relief. Inquire at your county extension office to learn which direction prevailing winds come from. Use ➞ to show that direction. Locate some food-producing flowers and host plants in wind-sheltered beds.

3. WHAT ARE THE AVERAGE DATES OF SPRING AND AUTUMN FROST? County extension agents or local master gardeners can advise when it's warm enough to plant tender annuals. Catalog descriptions and tags on nursery stock usually indicate plants best suited for certain zones.

4. WHAT IS MY YARD'S SOIL LIKE? Take a few minutes to really look at the soil in your yard. Is it loose and dry, sandy, moist enough to hold together if you squeeze some in your hand, or does it contain so much clay it forms a bricklike mass? Local factors—such as minerals present or lacking in your soil—or special challenges like swampy or desert conditions require specific gardening techniques. Mark areas of concern—such as perpetual wet spots, dry rocky areas, or places you prefer not to mow—on your map. See page 49 for advice on testing your soil.

5. WILL KIDS OR NEIGHBORS AFFECT MY BUTTERFLY GARDEN? Lots of activity has the potential to disturb butterflies, so situate your garden in a quiet place. Also remember that butterfly gardens and street traffic don't mix! Make an X on your map over busy places, such as where kids or pets play. Children love outdoor projects involving wildlife, so invite your kids or the neighbors' to help with the garden. Encourage them to be gentle with caterpillars and butterflies. Neighbors may initially have concerns about no-mow areas as sources of weed seed. Tell them about your plans to attract butterflies before you abandon the mower, and perhaps adjacent property owners will join your efforts. Backyard habitats are gaining popularity, but always check community "weed laws" so you don't violate homeowner covenants.

Butterfly-friendly Plants

After putting your plan on paper, consult Chapters 12 and 14 to decide what "magnet" plants to add to your garden. Your choices will determine which butterflies seek nectar and lay eggs in your backyard. If planting space is limited, or if you don't want to invest lots of time and money, select double-duty plants that serve as caterpillar hosts while providing nectar for adult butterflies, or that attract butterflies and hummingbirds. Butterfly milkweed is a great example. It's actually a triple treat: a host plant for monarchs, a nectar source for many butterflies, and food for hummingbirds. Other bonus plants that lure hummingbirds and butterflies include blazing star, phlox, anise hyssop, Mexican sunflower, verbena, zinnia, butterfly bush, and wild lilac or ceanothus.

If there are certain butterflies you want to entice to your yard, create a planting list tailored to those specific goals. Using the species profiles in Chapter 14, with additional input from a butterfly field guide or the Internet, you can identify favorite nectar and host plants for each species you wish to attract. Record these plants on "butterfly recipe cards" similar to the template below. Merge these plant selections into your garden plan and refer to the cards, or a shopping list derived from them, when you begin to acquire planting stock.

Target Butterfly: **Spring Azure**

Plant Type	Host plants	Nectar plants
Annual		Hyssop
Perennial	Black snakeroot	Chives, Milkweed, Violet
Shrub	Meadowsweet, viburnum	Escallonia, Blackberry
Vine		
Tree	Flowering or Silky dogwood	Holly, Willow

USING THIS book, other field guides, and the Internet, identify host and nectar plants for butterflies you wish to attract. Record these on index cards to compile a shopping list for nursery visits.

Don't overestimate the time and energy you have available for your butterfly gardening project. Start with one bed or area rather than the whole yard. Pace yourself by clearing the site, removing the sod, and amending the soil for this specific area before purchasing plants. Make cardboard labels with names of desired plants and place them at intervals visualizing plant growth. Moving labels to perfect the arrangement is much easier than digging multiple holes to shift the plants! Once you are pleased with the design, it's time to visit a local garden center or submit your catalog order form.

TWO QUEENS *seeking nectar at a Mexican sunflower.*

WHAT MAKES PLANTS IRRESISTIBLE?

Like hummingbirds, butterflies have evolved mutually beneficial relationships with certain plants. Many plants advertise with fragrance. They also welcome butterflies by providing convenient landing platforms and offering nectar, which is best known as the raw material from which bees make honey. Some flower structures encourage butterflies to brush against pollen while they probe for nectar. Flowers are rewarded when the winged guests move pollen from female to male organs, completing fertilization. The resulting seeds create new plants.

To imagine an ideal flower for a butterfly, picture a zinnia. Butterflies are not as agile in flight as hummingbirds. Flat petals on the zinnia's outer perimeter provide space for the butterfly to land. Multiple florets in the center offer abundant food, so a butterfly can linger and drink from many little nectar pockets. The zinnia design is repeated in many members of the daisy family: sunflower, blanketflower, coneflower, cupflower, cosmos, and arnica, to name a few. Large butterflies, including swallowtails, monarchs, and queens, need sturdy landing pads, so frequently seek nectar on big flat flowers.

Flowers that attract butterflies come in many other shapes and sizes. Flower clusters with flat or gently rounded tops provide support while butterflies sip from individual florets. Examples include milkweed, phlox, joe pye weed, sulphur-flower, mistflower, heliotrope, and lantana. Butterflies also visit flowers with spikes, such as blazing star, goldenrod, hyssop, and salvia. Spiraling up and down these plumes, they extract food from each blossom. Clustered and spiked arrangements are convenient because butterflies can gather nectar from many individual sources in one stop, rather than expending energy flying between flowers. Lupine, Virginia bluebells, and many mints have trumpet-shaped blooms appropriately sized for butterflies' mouthparts and stems strong enough to bear a winged visitor's weight.

Butterflies see in the visible light spectrum and also in the ultraviolet range, so blue, lavender, and purple flowers definitely attract them. The vivid purple-magenta of blazing star, joe pye weed, purple coneflower, and phlox is a prominent theme in alluring butterfly flowers. Some orange, yellow, pink, and white flowers also catch butterflies' attention. Many blossoms exhibit ultraviolet patterns that humans cannot see but butterflies can. It's common for butterfly-luring flowers to have inward-leading UV lines that guide the insects to internal nectar rewards.

Nectar is a water-based mixture of natural sugars—including fructose, glucose, and sucrose—plus amino acids, traces of salts, proteins, and essential oils. While hummingbirds target many flowers that produce nectar of about 25 percent sugar content (one part sugar to four parts water), butterflies visit a wide variety of food sources with less sweet, similar, or sweeter nectar than hummingbirds eat. Butterflies often select nectar containing supplemental amino acids.

Nectar production varies with environmental conditions in which the flowers grow. For instance, a newly opened blossom produces more nectar than a several-day-old flower. More nectar is manufactured by a plant on a sunny day than on an overcast day or at night. During the day, a plant growing in the sun will produce more nectar than the same species growing in the shade. Thus, a specific nectar plant may be very attractive to butterflies in one backyard setting and not as attractive in another yard.

Host plants don't provide salts or nitrogen-based compounds to caterpillars, so adult butterflies make up for these deficiencies through food and flower choices. Many butterflies "puddle" to drink dissolved minerals, or feed on rotting fruits, dung, or dead animals for extra protein. Plants growing in certain types of soil absorb trace elements through their roots, and these compounds become nectar components. Butterflies consume nectar at these flowers in much the same way that humans take vitamin supplements. Male queen butterflies, for example, flock to Gregg's mistflower to drink nectar containing nutrients they process into sex pheromones. Male butterflies

BLACKEYED SUSAN viewed in normal light.

BLACKEYED SUSAN photographed to simulate the ultraviolet light seen by butterflies. The patterns that butterflies detect in UV light are not normally visible to humans.

often concentrate essential nutrients into *spermatophores* (packets of sperm, plus salts and proteins necessary for egg development) that are presented to females during mating. These spermatophore gifts sometimes account for half the male butterfly's weight!

NATIVE PLANTS

From a butterfly's perspective, native plants are preferable to plants imported from halfway around the globe. Natives are plants that would have grown within 50 miles of your yard when Europeans arrived in North America. They produce flowers and fruits of useful sizes at proper times to satisfy wildlife needs. Many native plants have important evolutionary ties with butterflies. Their flowers offer nectar of the perfect sweetness and are sometimes pollinated during the process. Natives are adjusted to local soils and climates, are more drought-tolerant, and are usually more disease resistant than exotics.

Here's another reason to include as many native plants as possible in your butterfly garden. The nursery industry breeds new plant varieties for large blossom size, prolific blooms, or specific colors. But these cultivars may lack the nectar-producing capacity of their ancestral stock. That's often the reason butterfly gardeners complain that no butterflies visit a blazing star or blackeyed Susan they've planted. It's likely they purchased nectar-deficient cultivated varieties rather than true natives. When selecting plants, go to your local nursery on a sunny day and watch which flowers butterflies land on. If they stay briefly and don't unfurl their tongues, the flower is not offering nectar. Adult butterflies taste with receptors on their feet to select food. When they detect sweetness, they will uncoil their proboscis and stay for dinner.

To successfully blend native plants and cultivars into the same garden space, arrange plants with similar requirements (such as their need for water or shade) near one another. Remember that native plants may have a more sprawling form, in contrast to bedding plants that are bred for their shapeliness. Natives may also have a shorter, more intense bloom time and then slip into a period of less attractive spent blossoms and ragged foliage. When beyond-their-prime natives fade, add fast-blooming annuals—such as marigolds for sun or impatiens for shade—to brighten these spaces. You can also add instant color in the spring or brighten bare spots throughout the season by moving a few potted annuals into strategic locations in your butterfly garden.

DESIGNING FOR BUTTERFLIES

Chapter 4 contains suggestions for designing an aesthetically pleasing backyard that is inviting to wildlife. Here are some additional techniques that attract butterflies.

- Create flower beds with long oval or crescent shapes, providing lots of edge effect where you can see butterflies and caterpillars. If lawn or paths surround these beds, you'll have easy access for spreading mulch, pruning, weeding, thinning plants, and performing other garden chores.

- Place tall species at the back of beds adjoining property lines, windbreaks, or fences, and place lanky plants in the center of circular or island beds. Use successively shorter species toward the front or outer edges. This will create a sweeping effect and ensure that none of the plantings is blocked from view.

- Put host plants along paths or front edges of beds if you want a ringside seat to watch caterpillar development. If you are not interested in studying caterpillars as they devour foliage and transform into adults, locate host plants in less noticeable parts of your garden where chewed leaves won't be distracting.

- Concentrate several nectar plants together to draw butterflies' attention to bright patches of color. Allow enough room in your design for individual plants to grow and spread to full height and width.

- Arrange compatible trees, shrubs, and flowers by their needs for moisture/dryness, sun/shade, or other growing requirements. Group these plants as you might find them in the wild—with shade-loving perennials or shrubs under spreading tree canopies, for instance. By mimicking nature's designs, you will provide a living refuge for caterpillars and butterflies that offers shade, shelter, and wind protection.

- To create a garden that is relatively stable once established, choose perennials, which come back every year from overwintering roots, and annuals such as blanketflower that self-sow seeds for the next year's plants. You'll still need to thin and weed in such gardens, but little new planting will be required. Deadheading (removing old blossoms before they go to seed) will stimulate new flushes of blooms.

- If you have never transplanted potted stock into the ground, review the steps outlined on page 52.

SUCCESSFUL BUTTERFLY gardens appeal to butterflies and people. Blend plant hues and textures in tasteful arrangements, and plant enough of each offering to create a large splash of color.

For your butterfly habitat to be accepted by friends and neighbors, it should have visual appeal. Humans expect gardens to display a seasonal sequence of blooms and at times provide masses of color. Creating organized beds and patterns within plantings or defining borders shows that the effort is planned instead of haphazard. Paths invite visitors to wander through this outdoor space. Coordinating nectar flower colors with similar accent colors will call attention to humanizing features in the garden, such as benches, feeders, nest boxes, or rustic sculptures.

If your garden is large enough, why not create a meadow where rowdier natives can proliferate? For example, Indian hemp resembles milkweed but sprawls ungracefully and has less showy flowers. The blossoms attract a wide range of pollinators, so it's a valuable addition if you have room. Purple milkweed presents a dilemma because its leaves are too tough for monarch caterpillars to chew, and it doesn't bloom every year. When it does, great spangled fritillaries and many other species mob the spectacular flowers. Both are good meadow candidates. So are native bur marigolds (also called sticktights or beggarticks), which produce annoying little seeds that cling to clothing and pet fur.

Few gardeners intentionally plant red or white clover, but these plants offer plentiful nectar, plus the latter hosts orange sulphur caterpillars. Although we seldom welcome lawn weeds, English and common plantain feed common buckeye, variegated fritillary, and checkerspot caterpillars. Ground ivy, purple dead nettle, and self-heal satisfy numerous adult butterflies, yet we eradicate these exotics from most gardens. Try to propagate as many natives as possible, but weeds will sneak into your meadow, adding to its diversity. If your wild corner becomes too exuberant, occasional mowing or burning may restore balance. Advertise butterfly-hosting intentions with signs that identify your wildlife habitat.

Healthy Backyard Ecosystems

It's also possible to make your butterfly garden too tidy. In cold climates, most butterflies overwinter as caterpillars or pupas. A few hibernate as adults; several pass the winter as eggs. Eggs are frequently laid in bark crevices, on twigs, or hidden among leaf litter, where natural surroundings provide insulation. White admiral caterpillars aren't finished growing when it gets cold in their northern habitats, so they wrap themselves in a rolled leaf base until spring. Many other over-wintering caterpillars remain dormant, protected by leaf litter, hidden among rocks, or in crannies that shield them from winter storms. Don't make your garden too neat. A few rocks, logs, large shrubs, tree bark, and loose leaves create just the shelter these tiny creatures need.

Healthy natural ecosystems retain lots of organic debris. Fallen leaves, twigs, and old logs provide food and shelter for the important workers that enrich and aerate your soil. These "forgotten" creatures include tiny invertebrates, earthworms, millipedes, and microbes that digest, decompose, and recycle old plant material into a rich growing medium. Decaying leaves, bits of bark, twigs, and other plant debris covering your garden soil also provide food, moisture, and cover for these essential garden helpers. To encourage decomposers in your butterfly garden, use shredded leaves, pine needles, or chipped wood mulch to cover the soil, if nature doesn't already supply these materials. As a bonus, mulch will prevent many weeds from growing and will make it easier to pull those that do sprout.

AN EASTERN tiger swallowtail pupa attached to a leaf, where it will spend the winter. Removing accumulated leaves and natural debris in the fall can result in the accidental destruction of overwintering butterfly eggs, caterpillars, and pupa.

Container Gardens

The traditional vision of a butterfly garden involves a plot of ground with a variety of host and nectar plants. What if your "yard" is a deck, apartment balcony, rooftop, or window box? There's good news! Even if your gardening space is tiny, you can indeed foster caterpillars and adult butterflies.

The best approach is to prepare a window box or a few appropriately sized containers for your deck or patio. (See page 53 for details on growing plants in containers.) Your potted garden will thrive in at least six hours of sunlight per day. To attract as many species as possible, offer host plants for caterpillars as well as nectar sources for adults.

You'll increase your success if you do some pre-planting research to discover which butterflies are common in your neighborhood. Contact a local nature center and ask which 10 butterfly species are most likely to be seen there. Or simply stroll through your neighborhood and nearby parks, identifying butterflies you see. Select annual plants that host or provide nectar for these species from the lists in Chapters 12 and 14. If you have room in your containers, plant enough annuals to keep a progression of blooms through the frost-free season.

Making a Difference

Although an army of butterfly gardeners cannot quite compensate for the extensive loss of butterfly habitats, we can definitely have a positive effect. With suburbia covering an ever greater percentage of the land, a transition from lawns and exotic plants to a more butterfly-friendly environment will keep at least some species from declining precipitously. In fact, I predict that a number of butterfly species will increase in number and expand their ranges due to the efforts of butterfly gardeners. —*Jeffrey Glassberg*, *author of* Enjoying Butterflies More

As host plants do their job, you'll have a ringside seat for the fascinating life cycle from egg to caterpillar to chrysalis to adult, all within inches of your window or a few steps from your door.

With a bit of planning and persistence, you can establish a butterfly garden almost anywhere. Invest some time in creating attractive habitats around your home. Soon you'll be welcoming wildlife into your neighborhood and your life. You won't regret it!

HELIOTROPE GROWS *well in container gardens and attracts many varieties of butterflies with its fragrant purple flowers.*

Chapter 12: A Butterfly Garden Plan

IN THIS CHAPTER you will find three generic plans for butterfly habitats. The design for a typical quarter- to half-acre residential backyard can be tailored for different sizes and shapes of yards by deleting or adding plants. If you have sufficient space, install clusters of perennials or annuals to offer butterflies ample nectar sources. If your yard has a different directional orientation from the generic plan, determine which places are sunny or shady, then select appropriate plant species from the lists below. Place them in island or crescent-shaped beds to maximize sun exposure and to allow access as you tend them.

The second plan typifies a view from a favorite window or patio. It envisions the vertical spaces that trees, shrubs, vines, and other features will occupy, as well as offering an overhead perspective of the layout. Varying the heights of plants in your garden creates pleasing aesthetic views, as well as shady or moist microclimates that certain butterflies need. The third plan takes a similar approach for a container garden on a deck or small patio. Or you may prefer to develop a customized plan following the steps in Chapter 11.

Butterflies use many categories of plants: lawn grasses, annual and perennial flowers, vines, shrubs, trees, garden vegetables, even weeds. To develop your landscape, select one of the generic plans or draw a personalized version, then incorporate host and nectar plants from your regional list into the design. Imagine your yard as a butterfly cafeteria. The plan you create provides an opportunity to "set the table" with plant delicacies that will attract butterflies. Use the symbols on spaces in the generic plan to identify the category (tree, shrub, etc.), then choose appropriate species for your yard. If your yard is already well landscaped, you can incorporate butterfly-luring plants into open spaces in your garden.

Key for All Plans

T—Tree	**A**—Annual	☀ —Sun
S—Shrub	**G**—Garden plants	◉ —Shade*
V—Vine	**W**—Water	
P—Perennial	**F**—Feeder	

Nectar plants attract butterflies most effectively when planted in full sun.

WITH A *well–planned offering of nectar and host plants, even small gardens can attract butterflies.*

Regional Plant Lists

The following plant lists are based on average climatic conditions in the eight regions shown on the accompanying map. Bold entries highlight universally successful host and nectar plants for each area. As you plan your butterfly garden, include several of the boldfaced selections in your design. If your backyard space allows, experiment with a few additional native host and nectar-producers. You may wish to consult the species profiles in Chapter 14 to learn which plants have the best potential to attract local butterflies. If the choices seem overwhelming, seek advice from experienced native plant or butterfly gardeners, master gardeners, naturalists at local nature centers, or staff members at area native plant nurseries, all of whom can offer valuable expertise.

Many of the boldfaced entries should be in stock at local garden centers. Whenever there is a choice between an unenhanced native plant and a cultivated version, choose the "unimproved" native. Why? Plants often lose their nectar-producing ability when they are hybridized. In the Midwest, for instance, native blackeyed Susans (*Rudbeckia fulgida* and *R. hirta*) grow in prairies, meadows, and along roadsides where they attract pearl crescents, sulphurs, and many types of skippers with their nectar. *R. fulgida* has a widespread cultivar, 'Goldsturm', that is sold at many chain stores. *R. hirta* has been hybridized to include a huge number of 'Gloriosa Daisy' strains promoted in nursery catalogs. These cultivars don't provide adequate nectar. If you plant them instead of natives, you and your butterflies will be disappointed.

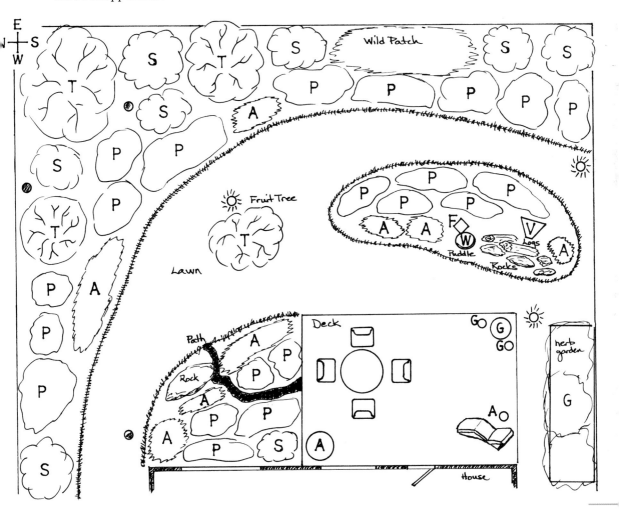

THIS GENERIC plan for a backyard butterfly habitat will guide you in selecting plants appropriate for your yard.

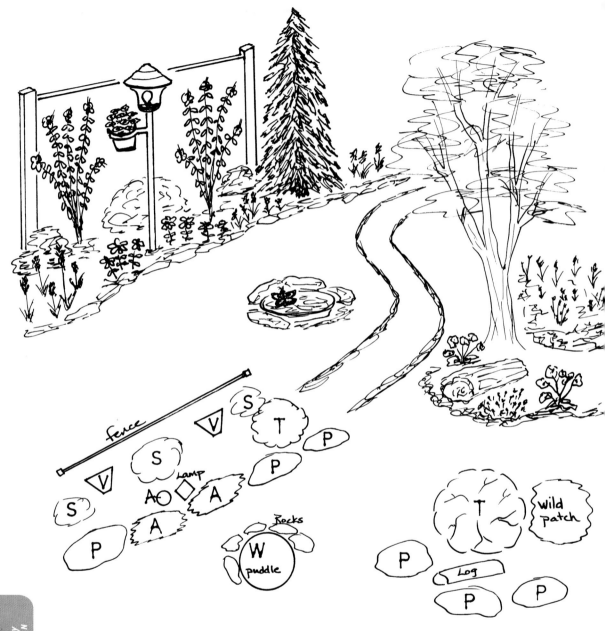

fence

S

V

V

S

S

T

A ○ Lamp

A

P

A

P

Rocks

W
puddle

P

T

wild
patch

P

Log

P

P

THIS GENERIC butterfly habitat plan will help you make efficient use of vertical spaces.

USE THIS generic plan for a container-based butterfly garden if your yard is small or you wish to attract butterflies to a deck or rooftop.

HORTICULTURAL CULTIVARS *often lose their nectar-producing capacity in the plant-breeding process. Whenever possible, select native varieties. These pearl crescents are feeding on a blackeyed Susan.*

NATIVE PLANT *societies and similar groups occasionally sponsor sales of responsibly grown wildflowers that are seldom found in traditional garden centers. These cardinal flowers will attract butterflies and hummingbirds.*

Some of the listed plants may be available only from native plant nurseries or online sources. Always purchase responsibly grown nursery stock rather than plants dug from the wild. If you are new to gardening, take this book to the nursery or garden center. Show your regional list to a staff member who specializes in wildlife habitats and who can help you select a good combination of plants to anchor your garden.

Plan nursery visits at midday on warm, sunny days, and walk among the plants in open-air settings, watching for butterflies. When one lands on a flower, see if its proboscis unrolls. When butterflies linger and sip nectar, the plant will provide satisfying nectar in your backyard. Grab the pot and rush to the checkout counter!

Beginning butterfly gardeners often start with proven varieties, such as *Verbena* 'Homestead Purple' or *Lavender* 'Goodwin Creek Grey', plus natives like milkweed that attract common butterflies with general requirements. As your interest in butterfly gardening grows, you may want more diversity. Visit regional parks, natural areas, and botanical reserves to see native plants used by less common butterflies. To obtain varied host plants and nectar flowers, watch for native plant sales sponsored by butterfly organizations or park friends' groups. Check with authorities in natural areas to see if limited seed collecting is possible. If so, you may be able to grow some of these plants yourself.

You will also recognize common "weeds" on these lists. Thistles and mustards thrive in untended places, but butterflies visit them regularly for nectar and caterpillar food. Depending on how formal you want your butterfly garden to appear, you can include a few of these in an unobtrusive corner of the yard to take advantage of their superior butterfly-attracting properties, or you can depend on vacant lots in your neighborhood to provide the weedy flora.

Plants on the regional lists have proven their ability to attract butterflies, but some work best in specific conditions, such as near the ocean, in high elevations, in boggy places, or where it is dry. Remember to read any notes about growing conditions. Each region is large, so there are many choices to address diverse microclimates. As you gain butterfly gardening experience, you'll discover which plants work well and which are less effective. Your results may differ from those of nearby butterfly gardeners, based on differences in soils, sun exposure, or what habitats surround your yard. You may want to experiment with popular plants suggested for a nearby region. When you discover outstanding butterfly plants, add more (as your space allows) to send fluttery visitors a bold invitation. While red is vital for attracting hummingbirds, blue, lavender, purple, orange, and yellow flowers usually summon butterflies.

Encouraging Natural Diversity

In recent years I have become an advocate for native plant species. After watching for the last 30 years our loss of natural diversity—what I call the "Mid-Atlantic Meltdown"—I feel we can no longer afford the luxury of planting everything we may want in our gardens. We need to be responsible gardeners and use natives whenever possible. I have learned that most non-native species can easily be replaced with a native that works just as well attracting pollinators. My experience is based on growing and field-testing plants—recording species and numbers of visiting butterflies—before making plants available (or not) to my customers.

Years ago Pat Sutton, a retired naturalist at Cape May Bird Observatory, author, and butterfly expert, and I compared our yard butterfly plant lists. We were both surprised to see that (to use a phrase she attributes to butterfly gardener Jane Ruffin) some of the "chocolate cake" butterfly plants in New Jersey were very different from those in Maryland. For example, one of her best nectar sources was globe amaranth. When I grew the same species and color here, the flowers were ignored by most butterflies. There are regional differences in butterfly preference, even between states so close to one another. So your butterfly gardening experiences could be quite different from mine. —*Denise Gibbs, contributing author,* Butterfly Gardens: Luring Nature's Loveliest Pollinators to Your Yard (Brooklyn Botanic Garden)

Each plant on the list requires at least six hours of daily sun unless noted by the ◉ symbol. Even though some nectar-producing plants will tolerate shade, it's best to grow them in full sun to stimulate nectar production. Host plants are less critically affected by sun or shade, but passionflower is a notable exception. Gulf fritillaries lay eggs on these vines in full sun, while zebra heliconians deposit their eggs on passionflower in the shade.

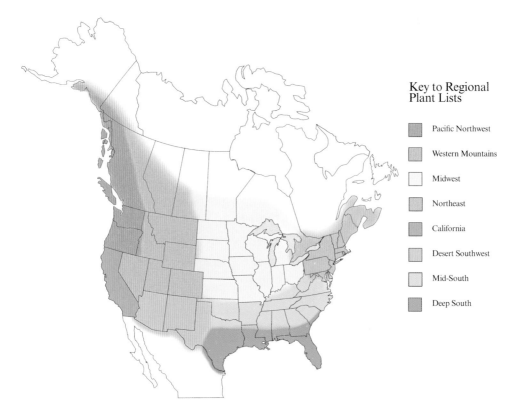

Key to Regional Plant Lists

- Pacific Northwest
- Western Mountains
- Midwest
- Northeast
- California
- Desert Southwest
- Mid-South
- Deep South

LOCATE YOUR regions on this map, then check the plant list for suggested butterfly host and nectar-producing species.

The common and scientific names in these lists are based on the U.S. Department of Agriculture Plant Database. You may encounter several common names used for the same plants, but scientific (Latin) names will define them precisely to nursery and garden center employees.

Key to Plant List Symbols

N—Native to region

*—Attracts hummers and butterflies

ω—Nectar source for adult butterflies

§—Host plant for caterpillars

◉—Tolerates shade

!—Use caution

Boldface—One of the most effective host or nectar plants for the region

GLOBE AMARANTH.

PACIFIC NORTHWEST

ANNUALS

Winged everlasting (*Ammobium alatum*) ω
Bloodflower, or tropical milkweed (*Asclepias curassavica*) * ω §
Bachelor's buttons (*Centaurea cyanus*) ω
Cosmos (*Cosmos bipinnatus, C. sulphureus*) ω
Globe amaranth (*Gomphrena globosa*) ω
Annual statice, or sea lavender (*Limonium sinuatum*) ω
High mallow (*Malva sylvestris*) §
Pincushion plant (*Scabiosa columbaria*) ω
Marigold (*Tagetes patula*) ω
Mexican sunflower (*Tithonia rotundifolia*) * ω
Brazilian verbena (*Verbena bonariensis*) * ω
Garden verbena (*Verbena* 'Homestead Purple', *Verbena* × *hybrida*) ω
Zinnia (*Zinnia angustifolia, Z. elegans*) * ω

PERENNIALS

Hollyhock (*Alcea rosea*) * § ◉
Marsh mallow (*Althaea officinalis*) ω §
Pearly everlasting (*Anaphalis margaritacea*) **N** ω §
Golden marguerite (*Anthemis tinctoria*) ω

Swamp milkweed (*Asclepias incarnata*) * ω § (for damp areas)

Showy milkweed (*Asclepias speciosa*) N * ω §

Butterfly milkweed (*Asclepias tuberosa*) * ω § (for dry areas)

Winter cress, or American yellow rocket (*Barbarea orthoceras*) N ω § (biennial)

Bur marigold, or sticktights (*Bidens cernua*) N ω

Jupiter's beard, or red valerian (*Centranthus ruber*) ω ●

Thistle (*Cirsium brevistylum, C. edule*) N ω § (biennial)

Yerba buena (*Clinopodium douglasii*) N ω ●

Sweet William (*Dianthus barbatus*) ω (biennial)

Western bleeding heart (*Dicentra formosa*) N * § ●

Purple coneflower (*Echinacea purpurea*) * ω

Globe thistle (*Echinops exaltatus, E. ritro*) §

Fleabane (*Erigeron philadelphicus, E. peregrinus*) N ω

Sulfur flower (*Eriogonom umbellatum*) N ω §

Idaho fescue grass (*Festuca idahoensis*) N §

Oregon gumweed (*Grindelia stricta*) N ω

Cow parsnip (*Heracleum maximum*) N § ! (causes skin irritation)

Showy stonecrop, or sedum (*Hylotelephium spectabile*) ω

Elecampane (*Inula helenium*) ω

Lavender (*Lavandula angustifolia, Lavandula × intermedia*) ω

Cheeseweed mallow (*Malva parviflora*) §

Finetooth beardtonuge (*Penstemon subserratus*) N §

Spreading phlox (*Phlox diffusa*) N ω

Plantain (*Plantago major* 'rubrifolia') §

Western bistort (*Polygonum bistortoides*) N §

Douglas's knotweed (*Polygonum douglasii*) N §

Curly dock (*Rumex crispus*) § (biennial) (spreads easily)

Stonecrop (*Sedum lanceolatum, S. oreganum, S. spathulifolium*) N ω §

Goldenrod (*Solidago canadensis, S. multiradiata*) N ω §

Aster (*Symphyotrichum lateriflorum, S. spathulatum, S.* spp.) N ω §

Stinging nettle (*Urtica dioica*) N § ● ! (causes skin irritation) (spreads easily)

Blue vervain, or swamp verbena (*Verbena hastata*) N ω

Violet (*Viola adunca, V. nuttallii*) N §

Mule-ears (*Wyethia angustifolia, W.* spp.) N ω

VINES

Common hop (*Humilis lupulus*) § (spreads easily)
Orange honeysuckle (*Lonicera ciliosa*) **N** * ⍵ §

SHRUBS

White sagebrush, or silver king artemisia (*Artemisia ludoviciana*) **N** §
Butterfly bush (*Buddleja davidii*) * ⍵ ◉
Wild lilac, or ceanothus, or blue blossom (*Ceanothus sanguineus, C. thyrsiflorus, C. velutinus*) **N** ⍵ §
Mountain mahogany (*Cercocarpus betuloides, C. ledifolius*) **N** §
Redosier dogwood (*Cornus stolonifera*) **N** §
Rabbitbrush (*Chrysothamnus nauseosus*) **N** ⍵
Wild buckwheat (*Eriogonum microthecum, E. nudum*) **N** ⍵ §
Salal (*Gaultheria shallon*) **N** §
Ocean spray (*Holodiscus discolor*) **N** ⍵ §
Western mock orange (*Philadelphus lewisii*) ⍵
Chokecherry (*Prunus virginiana*) **N** §
Coffeeberry (*Rhamnus californica*) **N** ⍵ § ◉
Squaw current (*Ribes cereum*) **N** §
Blackberry (*Rubus arcitcus, R.* spp.) **N** ⍵
Lilac (*Syringa vulgaris*) * ⍵ § (provides tree sap)
Evergreen huckleberry (*Vaccinium ovatum*) **N** ⍵ §
Chastetree (*Vitex agnus-castus*) * ⍵

TREES

California buckeye (*Aesculus californica*) * ⍵ §
Alder (*Alnus oregona, A. rhombifolia, A. sinuata*) **N** §
Serviceberry (*Amelanchier alnifolia*) **N** §
Pacific madrone (*Arbutus menziesii*) **N** §
Common juniper (*Juniperus communis*) **N** §
Black cottonwood (*Populus trichocarpa*) **N** §
Douglas-fir (*Pseudotsuga menziesii*) **N** §
Oregon white oak (*Quercus garryana*) **N** §
Black locust (*Robinia pseudoacacia*) §
Willow (*Salix* spp.) **N** ⍵ §
Western redcedar (*Thuja plicata*) **N** §

Key to Plant List Symbols

N—Native to region

*—Attracts hummers and butterflies

⍵—Nectar source for adult butterflies

§—Host plant for caterpillars

◉—Tolerates shade

!—Use caution

Boldface—One of the most effective host or nectar plants for the region

GREAT SPANGLED *fritillary on Brazilian verbena.*

Invasive Species

In response to the human desire for showy new plants in our gardens, explorers from the horticultural trades have roamed far and wide searching for wild stock. During centuries past, foreign flowers, trees, and shrubs were imported with little thought about diseases and destructive insects that rode along as hidden passengers. Prime examples include the Asian blight that wiped out magnificent American chestnut trees a century ago and the invasive woolly adelgid that has recently destroyed eastern hemlock trees.

Sometimes an imported landscape plant becomes an invader when there are no native predators or diseases to keep it in check or it multiplies too rapidly. Many exotic plants have spread out of control, displacing natural North American vegetation. Some of these exotics used by butterflies include Canada thistle (*Cirsium arvense*), many non-native *Centaureas*, dame's rocket (*Hesperis matronalis*), dyer's woad (*Isatis tinctoria*), broad-leaved peppergrass (*Lepidium latifolium*), privet (*Ligustrum vulgare*), purple loosestrife (*Lythrum salicaria*), pellitory (*Parietaria judaica*), and wisteria (*Wisteria floribunda, W. sinensis*). These are not recommended in our plant lists because of their potential to escape from gardens.

We have recommended a few non-native plants that could escape from backyard habitats, but responsible culture should not create problems. These include mimosa (*Albizia julibrissin*), queen's wreath (*Antigonon leptopus*), butterfly bush (*Buddleja davidii*), annual bachelor's buttons (*Centaurea cyanus*), fennel (*Foeniculum vulgare*), common hop (*Humilis lupulus*), and Brazilian verbena (*Verbena bonariensis*). If you discover any of your non-native plants beginning to spread aggressively, remove them before they become a problem.

A good way to prevent unintentional dispersal of exuberant plants from your garden is to collect and destroy seed pods or seed heads before they ripen. Make certain these seeds are *not* added to leaves and garden wastes collected for community mulching depots. Most states and some communities keep watch lists of banned plants. Check with your county extension agent or consult the national invasive plant list on the Internet (www .invasive.org). If certain plants are identified as invaders in your area, do not plant them. —*CT*

CHECKERED WHITE on rabbitbrush.

CALIFORNIA

ANNUALS

Blood flower, or tropical milkweed (*Asclepias curassavica*) * ⓦ §

Bur marigold, or sticktights (*Bidens cernua, B. laevis*) **N** ⓦ

Purple everlasting, or cudweed (*Gamochaeta purpurea*) **N** ⓦ §

Heliotrope (*Heliotropium arborescens*) ⓦ ⊙ ! (poisonous if eaten)
     (choose fragrant varieties only)

Impatiens (*Impatiens walleriana*) * ⊙

Spanish clover (*Lotus purshianus*) **N** ⓦ §

Tansy phacelia (*Phacelia tanacetifolia*) **N** ⓦ

Dwarf plantain, or California plantain (*Plantago erecta*) **N** §

Pincushion plant (*Scabiosa columbaria*) ⓦ

Marigold (*Tagetes patula*) ⓦ

Dandelion (*Taraxacum officinale*) ⓦ (spreads easily)

Mexican sunflower (*Tithonia rotundifolia*) * ⓦ

Garden verbena (*Verbena* 'Homestead Purple', *Verbena* × *hybrida*) ⓦ

Zinnia (*Zinnia angustifolia, Z. elegans*) * ⓦ

PERENNIALS

Yarrow (*Achillea millefolium*) **N** ⒲

Lily-of-the-Nile (*Agapanthus orientalis*) ***** ⒲ ●

Nettleleaf giant hyssop, or horse-mint (*Agastache urticifolia*) **N** ⒲

Hollyhock (*Alcea rosea*) ***** ⒲ §

Dogbane (*Apocynum androsaemifolium*) **N** ⒲ § (spreads easily)

Indian hemp (*Apocynum cannabinum*) **N** ⒲ (spreads easily)

Milkweed (*Asclepias californica, A. speciosa, A.* spp.) **N** ⒲ §

Narrowleaf milkweed (*Asclepias fascicularis*) **N** ⒲ §
(spreads easily)

Butterfly milkweed (*Asclepias tuberosa*) ***** ⒲ §

Winter cress, or American yellow rocket (*Barbarea orthoceras*) **N** ⒲ §
(biennial)

Elegant brodiaea (*Brodiaea elegans, B.* spp.) **N** ⒲

Purple reedgrass (*Calamagrostis purpurascens*) **N** §

Pussypaws (*Calyptridium umbellatum*) **N** ⒲

Thistle (*Cirsium occidentale*) **N *** ⒲ (biennial)

Jupiter's beard, or red valerian (*Centranthus ruber*) ⒲ ●

California aster, or California corethrogyne
(*Corethrogyne filaginifolia*) **N** ⒲ §

Western bleeding heart (*Dicentra formosa*) **N *** § ●

Blue dicks (*Dichelostema capitatum*) **N** ⒲

Globe thistle (*Echinops exaltatus, E. ritro*) §

Hummingbird trumpet, or California fuchsia
(*Epilobium canum*) **N *** ⒲

Seaside buckwheat (*Eriogonum latifolium*) **N** ⒲ §

Wright's buckwheat (*Eriogonum wrightii*) **N** ⒲ §

Western wallflower (*Erysimum capitatum*) **N** ⒲ § (biennial)

Western goldenrod (*Euthamia occidentalis*) **N** ⒲

Idaho fescue grass (*Festuca idahoensis*) **N** §

Salt heliotrope (*Heliotropium curassavicum*) **N** ⒲

Junegrass (*Koeleria macrantha*) **N** §

California goldfields (*Lasthenia californica*) **N** ⒲

Wild pea (*Lathyrus jepsonii, L. lanszwertii, L. polyphyllus*) **N** §

Lavender (*Lavandula angustifolia, Lavandula* 'Goodwin Creek Grey') ⒲

Deerweed (*Lotus scoparius*) **N** ⒲ §

Lupine (*Lupinus bicolor, L. excubitus*) **N** §

Cheeseweed mallow (*Malva parviflora*) §

Monkeyflower (*Mimulus aurantiacus *, M. guttatus*) **N** §

Coyote mint (*Monardella villosa*) **N** ⑭

Plantain (*Plantago hirtella, P. lanceolata*) §

Sweetscent, or salt marsh fleabane (*Pluchea odorata*) **N** ⑭

Cudweed, or everlasting (*Pseudognaphalium bicolor, P. canescens*) **N** ⑭ §

California figwort, or California bee plant (*Scrophularia californica*) **N** §

Stonecrop, or sedum (*Sedum lanceolatum, S. obtusatum, S. spathulifolium*) **N** ⑭ §

Checkerbloom, or checker mallow (*Sidalcea malviflora*) **N** §

Goldenrod (*Solidago californica, S. multiradiata*) **N** ⑭ §

Western needlegrass (*Stipa occidentalis*) **N** §

Cow clover (*Trifolium wormskioldii*) **N** §

Stinging nettle (*Urtica dioica*) **N** § ◉ ! (causes skin irritation)

Vervain (*Verbena hastata, V. lasiostachys, V. lilacina*) **N** ⑭

Violet (*Viola adunca, V. glabella, V. purpurea*) **N** §

VINES

California Dutchman's pipe (*Aristolochia californica*) **N** §

Climbing milkweed, or fringed twinevine (*Funastrum cynanchoides*) **N** ⑭ §

Bluecrown passionflower (*Passiflora caerulea*) ⑭ §

Lily of the valley vine (*Salpichroa origanifolia*) §

SHRUBS

California wild indigo, or leadplant (*Amorpha californica*) **N** ⑭ §

Glossy abelia (*Abelia × grandiflora*) * ⑭

Coyote brush (*Baccharis pilularis*) **N** ⑭

Mule fat (*Baccharis salicifolia*) **N** ⑭ §

Indian broom (*Baccharis sarothroides*) **N** ⑭

Butterfly bush (*Buddleja davidii, B. globosa*) * ⑭ ◉

Wild lilac, or buckbrush, or ceanothus, or blueblossom (*Ceanothus cuneatus, C. sanguineus, C. thyrsiflorus*) **N** * ⑭ §

Buttonbush (*Cephalanthus occidentalis*) **N** * ⑭ ◉

Blue leadwort, or Burmese plumbago (*Cerastostigma griffithii*) * ⑭

Fernbush (*Chamaebatiaria millefolium*) **N** ⑭ §

Rabbitbrush (*Chrysothamnus nauseosus, C. parryi*) **N** ⑭

Pride of Madeira (*Echium candicans*) * ⑭

Yerba santa (*Eriodictyon californicum, E. crassifolium, E. trichocalyx*) **N** ⑭

Longstem buckwheat (*Eriogonum elongatum*) **N** ω §

California buckwheat, or Mojave buckwheat
(*Eriogonum fasciculatum*) **N** ω §

Naked buckwheat (*Eriogonum nudum*) **N** ω §

Escallonia (*Escallonia bifida*) **N** ω ○

Toyon (*Heteromeles arbutifolia*) **N** ω

Chinese hibiscus (*Hibiscus rosa-sinensis*) * ω

Lantana (*Lantana camara, L. montevidensis*) * ω

Beach lupine (*Lupinus arboreus*) **N** §

Mahonia, or grape holly (*Mahonia aquifolium, M. nervosa,*
M. pinnata) **N** * ω ○

Bitter cherry (*Prunus emarginata*) **N** ω §

Desert apricot (*Prunus fremontii*) **N** ω

Chokecherry (*Prunus virginiana*) **N** ω §

Coffeeberry (*Rhamnus californica*) **N** ω § ○

Western azalea (*Rhododendron occidentale*) **N** ω § ○

Lilac (*Syringa vulgaris*) * ω § (provides tree sap)

Chastetree (*Vitex agnus-castus*) * ω

TREES

California buckeye (*Aesculus californica*) **N** * ω §

Madrone (*Arbutus menziesii*) **N** * §

Orange, lemon, grapefruit (*Citrus* spp.) * §

California sycamore (*Platanus racemosa*) **N** §

Cottonwood (*Populus balsamifera, P. fremontii*) **N** §

Hollyleaf cherry (*Prunus ilicifolia*) **N** ω §

Hoptree (*Ptelea crenulata*) **N** ω §

Coast live oak (*Quercus agrifolia*) **N** §

Canyon live oak (*Quercus chrysolepsis*) **N** §

Willow (*Salix exigua, S. lasiolepis, S. scouleriana*) **N** ω §

SPIDER FLOWER.

DESERT SOUTHWEST

ANNUALS

Spider flower (*Cleome hasslerana*) * ⍵ §

Cosmos (*Cosmos bipinatus, C. sulphureus*) ⍵

Clasping yellowtops (*Flaveria chlorifolia*) **N** ⍵

Firewheel, or blanketflower (*Gaillardia pulchella*) **N** ⍵

South American mock vervain, or moss verbena (*Glandularia pulchella*) ⍵ (perennial in Zone 7 and warmer)

Sunflower (*Helianthus annuus*) **N** ⍵ §

Lupine (*Lupinus arizonicus, L. bicolor, L. concinnus, L. sparsiflorus*) **N** § (best in wild patches)

Pony beebalm (*Monarda pectinata*) **N** ⍵

Spanish needle (*Palafoxia arida*) **N** ⍵ §

Lacy phacelia (*Phacelia tanacetifolia*) ⍵ ! (causes skin irritation)

Annual phlox (*Phlox drummondii*) * ⍵

Marigold (*Tagetes patula*) ⍵

Mexican sunflower (*Tithonia rotundifolia, T.* spp.) * ⍵

Zinnia (*Zinnia angustifolia, Z. elegans*) * ⍵

Mexican zinnia (*Zinnia haageana*) ⍵

PERENNIALS

Threadleaf giant hyssop, or sunset hyssop, or licorice mint
(*Agastache rupestris*) **N** * ω

Stiff-arm rock cress (*Arabis perennans*) **N** §

Arizona milkweed, or slender milkweed
(*Asclepias angustifolia*) **N** * ω §

Antelope horn milkweed (*Asclepias asperula*) **N** ω §

Broad-leaf milkweed (*Asclepias latifolia*) **N** ω §

Zizotes milkweed (*Asclepias oenotheroides*) **N** ω §

Showy milkweed (*Asclepias speciosa*) **N** * ω §

Butterfly milkweed (*Asclepias tuberosa*) **N** * ω §
(**N** to mountains, needs water elsewhere)

Desert marigold (*Baileya multiradiata*) **N** ω

Willow ragwort (*Barkleyanthus salicifolius*) **N** ω

Grama grass (*Bouteloua curtipendula, B. gracilis*) **N** §

Southwestern paintbrush, or squawfeather (*Castilleja integra*) **N** * §
(plant with grama grass)

Jupiter's beard, or red valerian (*Centranthus ruber*) ω ◉

Scruffy prairie clover (*Dalea albiflora*) **N** ω

Twin seed (*Dicliptera resupinata*) **N** §

Wright's buckwheat (*Eriogonum wrightii*) **N** ω §

California goldfields (*Lasthenia californica*) **N** ω

Cardinal flower (*Lobelia cardinalis*) **N** * ω **!** (poisonous if eaten)

Deerweed (*Lotus scoparius*) **N** ω §

Great Basin lupine (*Lupinus* × *alpestris*) **N** §

Mallow, or musk mallow (*Malva alcea, M. moschata, M. sylvestris*) ω §

White sweetclover (*Melilotus albus*) ω

Monkeyflower (*Mimulus guttatus*) **N** §

Pincushion plant (*Scabiosa columbaria*) ω

Threadleaf ragwort (*Senecio flaccidus*) **N** ω

Senna (*Senna leptocarpa*) §

Goldenrod (*Solidago canadensis, S. multiradiata*) **N** ω §

Common dogweed (*Thymophylla pentachaeta*) **N** §

Blue vervain, or swamp verbena (*Verbena hastata*) **N** ω

Cowpen daisy, or golden crownbeard (*Verbesina enceliodies*) **N** ω §

Goldeneye (*Viguiera deltoidea, V. multiflora*) **N** §

VINES

Climbing milkweed vine, or fringed twinevine (*Funastrum cynanchoides)* **N** ω §

Common hop (*Humilis lupulus*) § (spreads easily)
Passionflower (*Passiflora bryonioides, P. foetida*) **N** * ω

SHRUBS

Agave (*Agave parryi*) **N** §
White mistflower, or white boneset (*Ageratina wrightii*) **N** ω
False indigo (*Amorpha fruticosa*) **N** §
Saltbush (*Atriplex canescens*) **N** §
Sweetbush (*Bebbia juncea* var. *aspera*) **N** ω §
Bouvardia (*Bouvardia glaberrima*) **N** ω
Butterfly bush (*Buddleja davidii*) * ω ◉ (plant lantana underneath
    to shade roots; needs water)
Woolly butterfly bush (*Buddleja marrubiifolia*) **N** ω
Bird-of-paradise, or Mexican holdback
    (*Caesalpinia mexicana*) * ω
Baja fairy duster (*Calliandra californica*) **N** * §
Blue mist shrub (*Caryopteris* × *clandonensis*) ω
Rabbitbrush (*Chrysothamnus nauseosus*) **N** ω ! (causes allergies)
    (best in wild patches)
Brittlebush (*Encelia farinosa*) **N** ω §
California buckwheat, or Mojave buckwheat
    (*Eriogonum fasciculatum*) **N** ω §
Desert lavender (*Hyptis emoryi*) **N** ω §
Lantana (*Lantana camara, L. montevidensis*) * ω
Desert senna, or Coues' cassia (*Senna covesii*) **N** §
Chastetree (*Vitex agnus-castus*) ω

TREES

Hackberry (*Celtis laevegata* var. *reticulata*) **N** §
Orange, lemon, grapefruit (*Citrus* spp.) * §
Coral bean (*Erythrina flabelliformis*) **N** * ω
Alligator juniper (*Juniperus deppeana*) **N** §
Canyon live oak (*Quercus chrysolepsis*) **N** §
Gambel oak (*Quercus gambellii*) **N** §
Arizona sycamore (*Platanus wrightii*) §
Cottonwood (*Populus angustifolia, P. fremontii*) **N** §
Honey mesquite (*Prosopis glandulosa*) **N** ω §
Willow (*Salix* spp.) ω §

Key to Plant List Symbols

N—Native to region
*****—Attracts hummers and butterflies
ω—Nectar source for adult butterflies
§—Host plant for caterpillars
◉—Tolerates shade
!—Use caution
Boldface—One of the most effective host or nectar plants for the region

BLUE MIST shrub.

WESTERN MOUNTAINS

ANNUALS

Rock cress (*Arabis drummondii, A. glabra*) **N** ω § ◉

Spider flower (*Cleome hasslerana*) * ω §

Lemon beebalm (*Monarda citriodora*) * ω

Pony beebalm (*Monarda pectinata*) **N** ω

Cleft-leaf wild heliotrope, or notchleaf phacelia
  (*Phacelia crenulata*) **N** ω

Pincushion flower (*Scabiosa caucasica, S. columbaria*) ω

Marigold (*Tagetes patula*) ω

Mexican sunflower (*Tithonia rotundifolia*) * ω

Brazilian, or tall, verbena (*Verbena bonariensis*) * ω (spreads easily)

Garden verbena (*Verbena* 'Homestead Purple', *Verbena* × *hybrida*) ω

Pansy (*Viola whittrockiana*) §

Zinnia (*Zinnia angustifolia, Z. elegans*) * ω

PERENNIALS

Threadleaf giant hyssop, or sunset hyssop, or licorice mint
  (*Agastache rupestris*) * ω

Hollyhock (*Alcea rosea*) ω
Swamp milkweed (*Asclepias incarnata*) * ω § (in damp conditions)
Butterfly milkweed (*Asclepias tuberosa*) * ω § (in dry conditions)
Winter cress, or American yellow rocket (*Barbarea orthoceras*) **N** ω §
  (biennial)
Bur marigold, or sticktights (*Bidens cernua*) **N** ω
False nettle (*Boehmeria cylindrica*) **N** §
Grama grass (*Bouteloua curtipendula, B. gracilis*) **N** §
Thistle (*Cirsium drummondii, C.* spp.) **N** § ω
Sulphur-flower (*Eriogonum flavum, E. umbellatum*) **N** ω §
Spotted joe pye weed (*Eupatoriadelphus maculatus*) **N** ω ◒
Common gaillardia, or blanketflower (*Gaillardia aristata*) **N** ω
Wild licorice (*Glycyrrhiza lepidota*) **N** §
Western sneezeweed (*Helenium autumnale*) **N** § ! (poisonous if eaten)
Western sunflower (*Helianthus occidentalis*) **N** ω
Blue flax (*Linum perenne*) **N** §
Lupine (*Lupinus × alpestris, Lupinus* spp.) **N** ω §
Cheeseweed (*Mallow parviflora*) §
Alfalfa (*Medicago sativa*) ω §
Scarlet monkeyflower (*Mimulus cardinalis*) **N** * ω
Wild bergamot (*Monarda fistulosa*) **N** * ω
Mountain sorrel (*Oxyria digyna*) **N** §
Broadleaf plantain (*Plantago major*) §
Desert rhubarb, or canaigre (*Rumex hymenosepalus*) **N** §
Lanceleaf sedum (*Sedum lanceolatum*) **N** §
Goldenrod (*Solidago canadensis, S. multiradiata*) **N** ω §
Golden prince's plume (*Stanleya pinnata*) **N** §
Aster (*Symphyotrichum laeve, S.* spp.) **N** ω
Clover (*Trifolium dasyphyllum, T. longipes, T. parryi*) **N** ω §
White clover (*Trifolium repens*) ω §
Stinging nettle (*Urtica dioica*) **N** § ◒ ! (causes skin irritation)
Blue vervain, or swamp verbena (*Verbena hastata*) **N** ω
Goldeneye (*Viguiera multiflora*) **N** §
Violet (*Viola adunca, V. nuttallii, V.* spp.) **N** §

VINES
Common hop (*Humilis lupulus*) §
Orange honeysuckle (*Lonicera ciliosa*) **N** * ω
Scarlet runner bean (*Phaseolus vulgaris*) §

Key to Plant List Symbols

N—Native to region

*****—Attracts hummers and butterflies

ω—Nectar source for adult butterflies

§—Host plant for caterpillars

◒—Tolerates shade

!—Use caution

Boldface—One of the most effective host or nectar plants for the region

SHRUBS

Bearberry, or kinnikinnick (*Arctostaphylos uva-ursi*) **N** * §
Butterfly bush (*Buddleja davidii*) * ⱳ ○ (Zone 5 and warmer)
Blue mist shrub (*Caryopteris* × *clandonensis*) ⱳ
Buckbrush (*Ceanothus fendleri*) **N** * ⱳ
Jersey tea (*Ceanothus herbaceus*) **N** ⱳ
Rabbitbrush (*Chrysothamnus nauseosus, C. viscidiflorus*) **N** ⱳ §
Shrubby cinquefoil (*Dasiphora fruticosa*) **N** §
Wild buckwheat (*Eriogonum microthecum, E.* spp.) **N** ⱳ §
Currant (*Ribes cereum, Ribes* spp.) **N** ⱳ § ○
Snowberry (*Symphoricarpus albus, S. vaccinoides*) **N** §
Lilac (*Syringa vulgaris*) * ⱳ (provides tree sap)

TREES

Serviceberry (*Amelanchier alnifolia*) **N** §
Hackberry (*Celtis laevegata* var. *reticulata, C. occidentalis*) **N** § ○
Ash (*Fraxinus anomala, F. pennsylvanica*) **N** §
Juniper (*Juniperus scopulorum*) **N** §
Lodgepole pine (*Pinus contorta*) **N** §
Ponderosa pine (*Pinus ponderosa*) **N** §
Cottonwood (*Populus angustifolia*) **N** §
Quaking aspen (*Populus tremuloides*) **N** §
Plum (*Prunus domestica*) ⱳ §
Chokecherry (*Prunus virginiana*) **N** * §
Gambel oak (*Quercus gambelii*) **N** §
Black locust (*Robinia pseudoacacia*) * §

Shade-gardening Tip

Is your garden shady? Discover the places where beams of midmorning sunlight penetrate to the ground. Move a decorative rock or small log into several of these sunlit areas so butterflies will perch and warm them themselves. —*CT*

BLACKEYED SUSAN *and butterfly milkweed.*

MIDWEST

ANNUALS

Snapdragon (*Antirrhinum majus*) §
Bur marigold, or sticktights (*Bidens cernua*) **N** ⱳ
Partridge pea (*Chamaecrista fasciculata*) **N** §
Cosmos (*Cosmos bipinatus, C. sulphureus*) ⱳ
Globe amaranth (*Gomphrena globosa*) ⱳ
Annual mallow (*Lavatera trimestris*) ⱳ §
Marigold (*Tagetes patula*) ⱳ
Mexican sunflower (*Tithonia rotundifolia*) * ⱳ
Zinnia (*Zinnia angustifolia, Z. elegans*) * ⱳ

PERENNIALS

Anise hyssop (*Agastache foeniculum*) ⱳ
Pearly everlasting (*Anaphalis margaritacea*) **N** ⱳ §
Big bluestem grass (*Andropogon gerardi*) **N** §
Pussy toes (*Antennaria neglecta*) **N** ⱳ (spreads easily)

Swamp milkweed (*Asclepias incarnata*) **N** * ⍵ §

Purple milkweed (*Asclepias purpurascens*) **N** * ⍵

Common milkweed (*Asclepias syrica*) **N** * ⍵ §

Butterfly milkweed (*Asclepias tuberosa*) **N** * ⍵ §

Whorled milkweed (*Asclepias verticillata*) **N** * ⍵

White turtlehead (*Chelone glabra*) **N** § ! (pink or red varieties
 are toxic to Baltimore caterpillars)

Thistle (*Cirsium altissimum, Cirsium* spp.) **N** ⍵ § (biennial)

Purple prairie clover (*Dalea purpurea*) **N** ⍵

Pale coneflower (*Echinacea pallida*) **N** ⍵

Purple coneflower (*Echinacea purpurea*) **N** ⍵ § ⊙

Daisy fleabane (*Erigeron annuus*) **N** ⍵

Joe pye weed (*Eupatoriadelphus fistulosus, E. maculatus, Eupatorium
 purpureum*) **N** ⍵ ⊙

Mock vervain, or verbena (*Glandularia canadensis*) **N** ⍵

Sunflower (*Helianthus decapetalus, H. grosseserratus, H. maximiliani, H.
 mollis*) **N** ⍵

False sunflower (*Heliopsis helianthoides*) **N** ⍵

Showy stonecrop, or sedum (*Hylotelephium spectabile*) ⍵

Blazing star, or gayfeather (*Liatris aspera, L. pycnostachya,
 L. spicata*) **N** * ⍵

Lupine (*Lupinus perennis*) **N** ⍵ §

Alfalfa (*Medicago sativa*) ⍵ §

Beebalm (*Monarda didyma*) **N** * ⍵

Wild bergamot (*Monarda fistulosa*) **N** * ⍵

Dotted mint, or spotted beebalm (*Monarda punctata*) **N** * ⍵

Stiff goldenrod (*Oligoneuron rigidum*) **N** ⍵

Russian sage (*Perovskia atriplicifolia*) ⍵

Phlox (*Phlox divaricata, P. paniculata, P. pilosa*) **N** ⍵ ⊙

Plantain (*Plantago lanceolata, P. major*) §

Mountainmint (*Pycnanthemum tenuifolium, P. virginianum*)
 N ⍵

Orange coneflower, or blackeyed Susan
 (*Rudbeckia fulgida, R. hirta*) **N** ⍵

Sheep, or common, sorrel (*Rumex acetosella*) §

Little bluestem grass (*Schizachyrium scoparium*) **N** §

Cup plant (*Silphium perfoliatum*) **N** ⍵

Goldenrod (*Solidago canadensis, S. nemoralis, S. speciosa*) **N** ⍵

Aster (*Symphyotrichum laevis, S. lanceolatum, S. novae-angliae, S.
 pilosum*) **N** ⍵ § ⊙

Red clover (*Trifolium pretense*) ω
White clover (*Trifolium repens*) ω §
Stinging nettle (*Urtica dioica*) **N** § ◉ ! (causes skin rash)
Vervain (*Verbena hastata, V. stricta*) **N** ω
Ironweed (*Vernonia fasciculata, V. gigantea*) **N** ω ◉
Violet (*Viola hirsutula, V. palmata, V. pedata, V. sororia, V.* spp.) **N** § ◉

VINES

Dutchman's pipe (*Aristolochia macrophylla*) § ◉
Common hop (*Humilis lupulus*) § (spreads easily)
Maypop, or passionflower (*Passiflora incarnata*) * ω § ◉
   (spreads easily)

SHRUBS

Leadplant (*Amorpha canescens*) **N** ω §
False indigo (*Amorpha fruticosa*) **N** §
Bearberry, or kinnikinnick (*Arctostaphylos uva-ursi*) **N** * §
Butterfly bush (*Buddleja davidii*) * ω ◉ (Zone 5 and warmer)
New Jersey tea (*Ceanothus americanus*) **N** * ω
Buttonbush (*Cephalanthus occidentalis*) **N** * ω
Lantana (*Lantana camara*) * ω
Labrador tea (*Ledum groenlandicum*) **N** ω
Spicebush (*Lindera benzoin*) **N** § ◉
Steeplebush (*Spiraea tomentosa*) **N** ω
Blueberry, huckleberry (*Vaccinium* spp.) **N** §
Pricklyash (*Zanthoxylum americium*) **N** §

TREES

Hackberry (*Celtis occidentalis, C. tenuifolia*) **N** § ◉
Redbud (*Cercis canadensis*) **N** * ω § ◉
Hawthorn (*Crataegus mollis*) **N** ω §
White ash (*Fraxinus americana*) **N** §
Eastern redcedar (*Juniperus virginiana*) **N** §
Tuliptree (*Liriodendron tuliperifa*) **N** §
Jack pine (*Pinus banksiana*) **N** §
Aspen (*Populus grandidentata, P. tremuloides*) **N** §
American plum (*Prunus americana*) **N** ω §
Wild cherry (*Prunus serotina*) **N** ω §
Common hoptree (*Ptelea trifoliata*) **N** §
Oak (*Quercus alba, Q. rubra, Q. velutina*) **N** §

Key to Plant List Symbols

N—Native to region
*****—Attracts hummers and butterflies
ω—Nectar source for adult butterflies
§—Host plant for caterpillars
◉—Tolerates shade
!—Use caution
Boldface—One of the most effective host or nectar plants for the region

Willow (*Salix interior, S. nigra*) **N** ⍵ §

Sassafras (*Sassafras albidum*) **N** §

Elm (*Ulmus americana, U. rubra, U. thomasii*) **N** §

A **MONARCH** *feeding on swamp milkweed in the Illinois butterfly habitat created by Richard and Susan Day.*

Illinois Butterfly Hotspot

Since 1990 Richard and Susan Day have based Daybreak Imagery, the couple's nature photography business, at their 63-acre farm near Alma, Illinois. Richard loves to photograph birds, butterflies, and dragonflies, and Susan describes herself as a "plant person." The Days have labored for two decades to create a bountiful 3-acre backyard wildlife habitat. They have also rehabilitated 5 acres of prairie on the property, renewed 18 acres of shallow wetlands, and preserved 20 acres of woods. In the process, they have lured 71 species of butterflies to the farm.

"We are an oasis in an agricultural desert," Richard observed. For miles in every direction around the Days' home are monoculture fields of corn and soybeans. "Each of our natural habitats hosts different butterflies," Susan continued. Skippers use grasses in the prairie, and naturally occurring sedges and several types of dock in the wetlands lure earth-toned coppers. Eastern tailed-blues, painted ladies, eastern tiger swallowtails, and pearl crescents flutter in colorful flower beds.

"We began by researching what butterflies occurred here and planting hosts they needed," Susan recalled. "If you don't have hosts, you won't have butterflies. We still try to add new plants every year." Experience has shown that locally grown native species survive best, attracting both butterflies and hummingbirds.

The Days supplement their perennials, shrubs, trees, and vines with numerous annuals in eye-catching containers. They also install masses of nectar plants to create bold swaths of color in backyard island beds. Tops among their nectar-producers are butterfly bush, Brazilian verbena, and *Lantana camara* 'Red Spread', as well as native butterfly milkweed and swamp milkweed. "Once while Richard was photographing in the wetland, he counted 14 butterfly species nectaring on swamp milkweed," Susan remembered. That remarkable scene underscored the value of native habitat and makes all the work that Richard and Susan have invested in their wildlife sanctuary extremely satisfying. —*CT*

A COMMON buckeye on blue mistflower.

MID-SOUTH

ANNUALS

Snapdragon (*Antirrhinum majus*) §

Large bur marigold, or sticktights (*Bidens laevis*) **N** ω

Partridge pea (*Chamaecrista fasciculata*) **N** §

Firewheel, or blanketflower (*Gaillardia pulchella*) **N** ω

Heliotrope (*Heliotropium arborescens*) ω ◉ **!** (poisonous if eaten)
    (choose fragrant varieties only)

Lantana (*Lantana camara*) ✲ ω

Lemon beebalm (*Monarda citriodora*) **N** ω

Egyptian star cluster (*Pentas lanceolata*) ✲ ω (old-fashioned varieties
    with dark throats)

Drummond phlox (*Phlox drummondii*) ω ◉

Rabbit-tobacco, or sweet everlasting (*Pseudognaphalium
    obtusifolium*) **N** §

Pincushion flower (*Scabiosa caucasica, S. columbaria*) ω
Marigold (*Tagetes patula, T. tenuifolia*) ω
Mexican sunflower (*Tithonia rotundifolia*) * ω
Zinnia (*Zinnia angustifolia, Z. elegans, Zinnia* 'Profusion Orange', *Zinnia* 'Profusion Fire') * ω

PERENNIALS

Black cohosh, or bugbane (*Actaea racemosa*) **N** § ○
Pearly everlasting (*Anaphalis margaritacea*) **N** § ○
Pussy toes (*Antennaria plantaginifolia*) **N** § (spreads easily)
Indian hemp (*Apocynum cannabinum*) **N** ω ! (poisonous if eaten) (spreads easily)
Smooth rock cress (*Arabis laevigata*) **N** §
Poke milkweed (*Asclepias exaltata*) **N** ω § ○
Swamp milkweed (*Asclepias incarnata*) **N** * ω §
Purple milkweed (*Asclepias purpurascens*) **N** * ω (for western areas)
Common milkweed (*Asclepias syrica*) **N** * ω §
Butterfly milkweed (*Asclepias tuberosa*) **N** * ω §
Wild indigo (*Baptisia tinctoria*) **N** §
False nettle (*Boehmeria cylindrica*) **N** §
Crinkleroot, or two-leaved toothwort (*Cardamine diphylla*) **N** ω § ○
White turtlehead (*Chelone glabra*) **N** § ! (pink or red varieties are toxic to Baltimore caterpillars)
Field thistle (*Cirsium altissimum, C. discolor, C.* spp.) **N** §
Spring beauty (*Claytonia caroliniana, C. virginica*) **N** ω
Blue mistflower (*Conoclinum coelestinum*) **N** ω (spreads easily) (for wet areas)
Sweet William (*Dianthus barbatus*) ω (biennial)
Purple coneflower (*Echinacea purpurea*) **N** * ω ○
Globe thistle (*Echinops ritro*) §
Joe pye weed (*Eupatoriadelphus fistulosus, Eupatorium purpureum*) **N** ω ○
Boneset (*Eupatorium hyssopifolium, E. perfoliatum, E. sessilifolium*) **N** ω
Grass-leaved goldenrod (*Euthamia graminifolia*) **N** ω (spreads easily)
Mock vervain, or verbena (*Glandularia canadensis*) **N** ω
Swamp sunflower (*Helianthus angustifolius*) **N** ω ○ (for wet areas)
Woodland sunflower (*Helianthus divaricatus*) **N** ω ○ (for dry areas)

Blazing star (*Liatris aspera, L. pilosa, L. pycnostachya, L. scariosa,
    L. spicata*) **N** * ധ (*Liatris* cultivars have no nectar)
Virginia bluebells (*Mertensia virginica*) **N** ധ ◉
Beebalm (*Monarda didyma*) **N** * ധ
Wild bergamot (*Monarda fistulosa*) **N** * ധ
Dotted mint, or spotted beebalm (*Monarda punctata*) **N** * ധ
    (biennial)
Stiff goldenrod (*Oligoneuron rigidum*) **N** ധ
Phlox (*Phlox divaricata, P. maculata, P. paniculata, P. subulata*) **N** ധ
Mountain mint (*Pycnanthemum icanum, P. muticum,*
    P. virginianum) **N** ധ ◉
Orange coneflower (*Rudbeckia fulgida*) **N** ധ
Browneyed Susan, or thin-leaved coneflower (*Rudbeckia triloba*) **N** ധ
Lyre-leaved sage (*Salvia lyrata*) **N** * ധ ◉
Little bluestem grass (*Schizachyrium scoparium*) **N** §
Wild senna (*Senna hebecarpa, S. marilandica*) **N** ധ §
Goldenrod (*Solidago juncea, S. sempervirens, S. speciosa*) **N** ധ
Indiangrass (*Sorghastrum nutans*) **N** §
Aster (*Symphyotrichum laeve, S. novae-angliae, S. oolentangiense,*
    S. pilosum) **N** ധ
Meadow parsnip (*Thaspium trifoliatum*) **N** §
Stinging nettle (*Urtica dioica*) **N** § ◉ ! (causes skin rash)
Swamp verbena, or blue vervain (*Verbena hastata*) **N** ധ
Ironweed (*Vernonia fasciculata, V. gigantea, V. noveboracensis*) **N** ധ
Violet (*Viola hirsutula, V. palmata, V. pedata, V. sagittata,*
    V. sororia) **N** § ◉

VINES

Dutchman's pipe (*Aristolochia macrophylla, A. tomentosa*) **N** § ◉
    (spreads easily)
Coral, or trumpet, honeysuckle (*Lonicera sempervirens*) **N** * ധ § ◉
Climbing hempvine, or climbing boneset (*Mikania scandens*) **N** ധ
Maypop, or passionflower (*Passiflora incarnata*) **N** * ധ § ◉ (spreads
    easily)

SHRUBS

Leadplant (*Amorpha canescens*) **N** ധ §
Groundsel-tree (*Baccharis halimifolia*) **N** ധ (for coastal areas)
New Jersey tea (*Ceanothus americanus*) **N** ധ

Key to Plant List Symbols

N—Native to region

*****—Attracts hummers and
butterflies

ധ—Nectar source for adult
butterflies

§—Host plant for caterpillars

◉—Tolerates shade

!—Use caution

Boldface—One of the most
effective host or nectar plants
for the region

Buttonbush (*Cephalanthus occidentalis*) **N** * ധ

Summersweet, or sweet pepperbush (*Clethra acuminata, C. alnifolia*) **N** ധ

Spicebush (*Lindera benzoin*) **N** § ◉

Azalea (*Rhododendron arborescens*) **N** ധ

Blackberry (*Rubus allegheniensis*) **N** ധ

Meadowsweet (*Spiraea latifolia*) **N** ധ

Blueberry, huckleberry (*Vaccinium corymbosum, V.* spp.) **N** ധ §

Pricklyash (*Zanthoxylum americium*) **N** §

TREES

Pawpaw (*Asimina triloba*) **N** § ◉

Hackberry (*Celtis occidentalis, C. tenuifolia*) **N** §

Redbud (*Cercis canadensis*) **N** * ധ § ◉

Ash (*Fraxanus americana*) **N** §

Eastern redcedar (*Juniperus virginiana*) **N** §

Tuliptree (*Liriodendron tuliperifa*) **N** §

Sweet bay (*Magnolia virginiana*) **N** § ◉

Crab apple (*Malus angustifolia, M. coronaria*) ധ §

Pine (*Pinus rigida, P. virginiana*) **N** §

Cottonwood (*Populus deltoides, P. heterophylla*) **N** §

American plum (*Prunus americana*) **N** ധ §

Black cherry (*Prunus serotina*) **N** § ◉

Common hoptree (*Ptelea trifoliata*) **N** §

Oak (*Quercus alba, Q. rubra, Q. velutina*) **N** §

Black locust (*Robinia pseudoacacia*) **N** §

Willow (*Salix caroliniana, S. nigra*) **N** ധ §

Sassafras (*Sassafras albidum*) **N** § ◉

Elm (*Ulmus alata*) **N** §

A ZEBRA heliconian on lantana.

DEEP SOUTH

ANNUALS

Spanish needles, or beggarticks (*Bidens alba, B. pilosa*) **N** ⍵ § ⊙
    (perennial in Zones 7–10)

Browne's blechum, or green shrimp-plant (*Blechum pyramidatum*) §
    (perennial in Zones 9–10)

Partridge pea (*Chamaecrista fasciculata*) **N** §

Yellowtops (*Flaveria floridana, F. linearis*) **N** ⍵ (perennial in Zones
    9–10)

Blanketflower, or firewheel (*Gaillardia aestivalis, G. pulchella*) **N** ⍵

Impatiens (*Impatiens wallerana*) * ⍵ ⊙

Star cluster (*Pentas lanceolata*) * ⍵ (choose old-fashioned varieties
    with dark throats)

Drummond phlox (*Phlox drummondii*) **N** * ⍵

PERENNIALS

Huisache daisy, or butterfly daisy (*Amblyolepis setigera*) **N** ⍵ (for
    western areas)

Virginia snakeroot (*Aristolochia serpentaria, A. virginiana*) **N** § ⊙

Swamp milkweed (*Asclepias incarnata*) **N** * ⍵ §

White-flowered milkweed, or aquatic milkweed
    (*Asclepias perennis*) **N** ⍵ §

Butterfly milkweed (*Asclepias tuberosa*) **N** * ⍵ § (for dry areas)

Green milkweed (*Asclepias viridis*) **N** ⍵ §

Water hyssop, or herb of grace (*Bacopa monnieri*) **N** §

False nettle (*Boehmeria cylindrica*) **N** §

Blue mistflower (*Conoclinum coelestinum*) **N** ⍵ (spreads easily)
(for wet areas)

Gregg's mistflower, or palm-leaf thoroughwort
(*Conoclinum greggii*) ⍵ §

Goatweed (*Croton capitatus, C. cascarilla*) **N** §

Mexican heather (*Cuphea hyssopifolia*) ⍵

Beggarticks, or sticktights (*Desmodium frondosa*) **N** ⍵ §

Joe pye weed (*Eupatoriadelphus fistulosus*) **N** ⍵ ◉

Mock vervain, or verbena (*Glandularia bipinnatifida,
G. canadensis*) **N** ⍵

South American mock vervain, or moss verbena (*Glandularia
pulchella*) ⍵ (perennial in Zone 7 or warmer)

Dotted mint, or spotted beebalm (*Monarda punctata*) **N** * ⍵
(biennial)

Fogfruit (*Phyla nodiflora*) **N** §

Wild petunia (*Ruellia brittoniana*) * ⍵

Wild petunia (*Ruellia caroliniensis, R. nudiflora*) **N** * ⍵

Blood, or tropical, sage (*Salvia coccinea*) **N** * ⍵

Porterweed (*Stachytarphaeta jamaicensis, S. urticifolia*) ⍵

Stokes' aster (*Stokesia laevis*) **N** ⍵ ◉

Aster (*Symphyotrichum patens, S. urophyllum, S.* spp.) **N** ⍵

Stinging nettle (*Urtica dioica*) **N** § ◉ ! (causes skin rash)

Brazilian, or tall, verbena (*Verbena bonariensis*) * ⍵ (spreads easily)

Violets (*Viola missouriensis, V. sororia, V.* spp.) **N** § ◉

VINES

Coral vine, or queen's wreath (*Antigonon leptopus*) ⍵
(spreads easily)

Dutchman's pipe (*Aristolochia tomentosa*) **N** § ◉ (spreads easily)

White tubervine (*Funastrum clausum*) **N** ⍵ §

Maypop, or passionflower (*Passiflora incarnata*) **N** * ⍵ § ◉ (spreads
easily)

Yellow passionflower (*Passiflora lutea*) **N** § (spreads easily)

Corkystem passionflower (*Passiflora suberosa*) **N** §

Mexican flame vine (*Pseudogynoxys chenopodioides*) ⍵

SHRUBS

Glossy abelia (*Abelia × grandiflora*) * ⍵ ◉
Pawpaw (*Asimina angustifolia, A. triloba*) **N** § ◉
Groundsel-tree (*Baccharis halimifolia*) **N** ⍵ (for coastal areas)
Butterfly bush (*Buddleja davidii*) * ⍵ ◉
Pride-of-Barbados (*Caesalpinia pulcherrima*) * ⍵
Buttonbush (*Cephalanthus occidentalis*) **N** * ⍵
Summersweet, or sweet pepperbush (*Clethra alnifolia*) **N** ⍵
Sweet croton (*Croton argyranthemus*) **N** § ◉
Brazilian skyflower, or golden dewdrop (*Duranta repens*) ⍵
Firebush, or scarlet bush (*Hamelia patens*) **N** ⍵ ◉
Yaupon holly (*Ilex vomitoria*) **N** ⍵ ◉
Sweetspire (*Itea virginica*) **N** ⍵
Peregrina (*Jatropha integerrima*) * ⍵
Lantana (*Lantana camara, L. montevidensis*) * ⍵
Lantana, or West Indian shrub-verbena
    (*Lantana urticoides*) **N** * ⍵
Wax myrtle (*Myrica cerifera*) **N** § ◉
Plumbago (*Plumbago auriculata*) ⍵
Azalea (*Rhododendron canescens*) **N** ⍵
Cassia, or senna (*Senna alata, S. bicapsularis, S. corymbosa*) §
Blueberry (*Vaccinium ashei*) **N** ⍵ §
Chastetree (*Vitex agnus-castus*) ⍵
Coontie (*Zamia pumila*) **N** § ◉
Hercules' club (*Zanthoxylum clava-herculi*) **N** §

TREES

Mimosa (*Albizia julibrissin*) * ⍵
Torchwood (*Amyris elemifera*) **N** § (for Florida Keys)
Hackberry (*Celtis occidentalis, C. tenuifolia*) **N** § ◉
Redbud (*Cercis canadensis*) **N** * ⍵ § ◉
Orange, lemon, grapefruit (*Citrus* spp.) * §
Florida strangler fig (*Ficus aurea*) **N** § ◉
Sweet bay (*Magnolia virginiana*) **N** § ◉
Red bay (*Persea borbonia*) **N** § ◉
American plum (*Prunus americana*) **N** ⍵ §
Black cherry (*Prunus serotina*) **N** § ◉
Common hoptree (*Ptelea trifoliata*) **N** §
Coastal plain willow (*Salix caroliniana*) **N** ⍵ §
Sassafras (*Sassafras albidum*) **N** § ◉
Lime pricklyash (*Zanthoxylum fagara*) **N** §◉

AN EASTERN tiger swallowtail on wild bergamot.

NORTHEAST

ANNUALS

Snapdragon (*Antirrhinum majus*) §

Bloodflower, or tropical milkweed (*Asclepias curassavica*) * ⍵ §

Globe amaranth (*Gomphrena globosa*) ⍵ ◉

Lantana (*Lantana camara, L. montevidensis*) * ⍵

Sweet alyssum (*Lobularia maritima*) ⍵ ◉

Pincushion flower (*Scabiosa atropurpurea, S. grandiflora*) ⍵

Marigold (*Tagetes patula*) ⍵

Mexican sunflower (*Tithonia rotundifolia*) * ⍵

Brazilian, or tall verbena (*Verbena bonairensis*) * ⍵ (spreads easily)

Garden verbena (*Verbena* 'Homestead Purple', *Verbena* × *hybrida*) ⍵

Zinnia (*Zinnia angustifolia, Z. elegans, Zinnia* 'Profusion Orange',
   Zinnia 'Profusion Fire') * ω

PERENNIALS

Anise hyssop (*Agastache foeniculum*) ω
Bentgrass (*Agrostis perennans*) **N** §
Pearly everlasting (*Anaphalis margaritacea*) **N** ω §
Pussy toes (*Antennaria neglecta*) **N** ω (spreads easily)
Dogbane (*Apocynum androsaemifolium*) **N** ω (spreads easily)
Bristly sarsaparilla (*Aralia hispida*) **N** ω
Swamp milkweed (*Asclepias incarnata*) **N** * ω §
Common milkweed (*Asclepias syrica*) **N** * ω §
Butterfly milkweed (*Asclepias tuberosa*) **N** * ω §
Wild indigo (*Baptisia tinctoria*) **N** §
False nettle (*Boehmeria cylindrica*) **N** §
Crinkleroot, or two-leaved toothwort (*Cardamine diphylla*) **N** ω § ⊙
Pennsylvania bittercress (*Cardamine pratensis*) **N** ω §
Perennial bachelor's buttons (*Centaurea montana*) ω §
Dog mint, or wild basil (*Clinopodium vulgare*) ω
Blue mistflower (*Conoclinum caelestinum*) **N** ω
Shrubby cinquefoil (*Dasiphora fruticosa*) **N** §
Flat-topped white aster (*Doellingeria umbellata*) **N** ω
Purple coneflower (*Echinacea purpurea*) **N** ω ⊙
Joe pye weed (*Eupatoriadelphus maculatus*) **N** ω ⊙
Common boneset (*Eupatorium perfoliatum*) **N** ω
Grass-leaved goldenrod (*Euthamia graminifolia*) **N** ω
   (spreads easily)
Sneezeweed (*Helenium autumnale, H. tenuifolium*) **N** ω §
Cow parsnip (*Heracleum maximum*) **N** § ! (causes skin irritation)
Hawkweed (*Hieracium aurantiacum, H. caespitosum, H. lachenalii*) ω
Showy stonecrop, or sedum (*Hylotelephium spectabile*) ω
Candytuft (*Iberis sempervirens*) ω
English lavender (*Lavandula angustifolia*) ω
Blazing star, or gayfeather (*Liatris scariosa, L. spicata*) **N** * ω
Lupine (*Lupinus perennis*) **N** ω
Virginia bluebells (*Mertensia virginica*) **N** ω ⊙
Wild bergamot (*Monarda fistulosa*) **N** * ω
Phlox (*Phlox divaricata, P. maculata, P. paniculata, P. subulata*) **N** ω
Salt marsh fleabane (*Pluchea purpurascens*) **N** ω

Jacob's ladder (*Polemonium reptans*) **N** ⲱ ◉
Pickerelweed (*Pontederia cordata*) **N** ⲱ
Mountainmint (*Pycnanthemum multicum, P. tenuifolium,*
    P. virginianum) **N** ⲱ
Curly dock (*Rumex crispus*) § (biennial) (spreads easily)
Little bluestem (*Schizachyrium scoparium*) **N** §
Wild senna (*Senna hebecarpa*) **N** §
Goldenrod (*Solidago speciosa*) **N** ⲱ
Aster (*Symphyotrichum novae-angliae, S. novae-belgii, S. prenanthoides*)
    N ⲱ
Red clover (*Trifolium pratense*) ⲱ
Stinging nettle (*Urtica dioica*) **N** § ◉ ! (causes skin rash)
Ironweed (*Vernonia glauca, V. noveboracensis*) **N** ⲱ
Violet (*Viola fimbriatula, V. lanceolata , V. primulifolia, V. rotundifolia*)
    N § ◉

VINES

Dutchman's pipe (*Aristolochia macrophylla*) **N** § ◉ (spreads easily)
Common hop (*Humilis lupulus*) § (spreads easily)
Climbing hempvine, or climbing boneset (*Mikania scandens*) **N** ⲱ

SHRUBS

Speckled alder (*Alnus rugosa*) **N** § (hosts aphids for harvesters)
False indigo (*Amorpha fruticosa*) **N** §
Bearberry, or kinnikinnick (*Arctostaphylos uva-ursi*) **N** * §
Butterfly bush (*Buddleja davidii*) * ⲱ ◉
Blue mist shrub (*Caryopteris* × *clandonensis*) ⲱ
New Jersey tea (*Ceanothus americanus*) **N** ⲱ ◉
Buttonbush (*Cephalanthus occidentalis*) **N** * ⲱ
Summersweet, or sweet pepperbush (*Clethra alnifolia*) **N** ⲱ
Silky dogwood, redosier dogwood (*Cornus obliqua, C. stolonifera*)
    N ⲱ §
Spicebush (*Lindera benzoin*) **N** § ◉
Winged sumac (*Rhus copallinum*) **N** ⲱ §
Blackberry, dewberry (*Rubus allegheniensis, R. flagellaris*) **N** ⲱ
Meadowsweet, or steeplebush (*Spiraea latifolia, S. tomentosa*) **N** ⲱ §
Lilac (*Syringa vulgaris*) * ⲱ (provides tree sap)
Blueberry (*Vaccinium angustifolium*) **N** ⲱ §

TREES

Red maple (*Acer rubrum*) **N** ⍵

Pawpaw (*Asimina triloba*) **N** § ○

Birch (*Betula* spp.) **N** §

Hackberry, dwarf hackberry (*Celtis occidentalis, C. tenuifolia*) **N** § ○

Redbud (*Cercis canadensis*) **N** * ⍵ § ○

Eastern redcedar (*Juniperus virginiana*) **N** §

Tuliptree (*Liriodendron tulipifera*) **N** §

Pitchpine (*Pinus rigida*) **N** §

Aspen (*Populus grandidentata, P. tremuloides*) **N** §

American plum (*Prunus americana*) **N** ⍵ §

Black cherry (*Prunus serotina*) **N** § ○

Oak (*Quercus alba, Q. ilicifolia, Q. spp.*) **N** §

Willow (*Salix nigra, Salix* spp.) **N** ⍵ §

Sassafras (*Sassafras albidum*) **N** § ○

Elm (*Ulmus americana*) **N** §

Help Wanted: Weeds

Weeds are broadly defined as plants growing in places you don't want them. But many widespread weeds, such as plantain, thistle, and crabgrass, are butterfly hosts, and some offer nectar. If one of these weedy hosts is occupying a place in your garden where you really don't want it, check carefully for caterpillars before uprooting it. If caterpillars are present, allow them to finish eating, which may take a week or two. When they leave to pupate, you can remove or transplant the host to a more appropriate place. —*CT*

A VARIEGATED *fritillary on marigold in a container garden.*

CONTAINER GARDENS

The following list suggests plants that grow well in containers. If you live in mild climates, some will overwinter outdoors. Farther north, these plants will die without winter protection and will need to be restarted from seeds or bedding plants the following spring.

ANNUALS

Dill (*Anethum graveolens*) §

Snapdragon (*Antirrhinum majus*) §

Globe thistle (*Echinops ritro*) §

Fennel (*Foeniculum vulgare*) §

Annual sunflower (*Helianthus annuus*) ω

Heliotrope (*Heliotropium arborescens*) ω ◉ ! (poisonous if eaten)
   (choose fragrant varieties only)

Impatiens (*Impatiens wallerana*) * ω ◉

Lemon beebalm (*Monarda citriodora*) **N** ω

Marjoram (*Origanum dictamnus, O. majorana, Origanum* ×
   marjoricum) ω

Oregano (*Origanum vulgare*) ω

Egyptian starcluster (*Pentas lanceolata*) * ω (choose old-fashioned
    varieties with dark throats)
Parsley (*Petroselinum crispum, P. hortense*) §
Anise (*Pimpinella anisum*) ω §
Pincushion flower (*Scabiosa caucasica, S. columbaria*) ω
Marigold (*Tagetes patula, T. tenuifolia*) ω
Garden verbena (*Verbena* 'Homestead Purple', *Verbena* × *hybrida*) ω
Zinnia (*Zinnia angustifolia, Z. elegans, Zinnia* 'Profusion Orange',
    Zinnia 'Profusion Fire') * ω

ANNUAL VINES

Scarlet runner bean (*Phaseolus vulgaris*) §
Blackeyed Susan vine (*Thunbergia alata*) ω ◉

SMALL SHRUBS

Chinese hibiscus (*Hibiscus rosa-sinensis*) * ω
Lantana (*Lantana camara*) * ω

Assisting Nature

When we lose the common wildlife in our immediate surroundings, we run the risk of becoming inured to nature's absence, blind to delight, and, eventually, alienated from the land. This is where butterfly gardeners come in—they create and maintain diverse habitats for species that need not become endangered, bolster the numbers of species in our midst, and collectively engage themselves in the rewarding nearness of nature. —*Robert Michael Pyle, in* Butterfly Gardening

A DIVERSE hillside planting in a southern California backyard provides excellent butterfly habitat.

A LIGHT-COLORED *female orange sulphur on mint in an herb garden.*

HERB AND VEGETABLE GARDENS FOR BUTTERFLIES (ANY REGION)

ANNUALS

Dill (*Anethum graveolens*) §
Mustard greens (*Brassica juncea*) ω §
Broccoli, cabbage, cauliflower, collard (*Brassica oleracea*) §
Turnip (*Brassica septiceps*) §
Sea kale (*Crambe maritima*) §
Carrot (*Daucus carota sativus*) §
Annual sunflower (*Helianthus annuus*) ω
Garden cress (*Lepidium sativum*) § ●
Catmint (*Nepeta grandiflora, N. mussinii, N. racemosa*) ω
Marjoram (*Origanum dictamnus, O. majorana, Origanum × marjoricum*) ω
Oregano (*Origanum vulgare*) ω
Scarlet runner bean (*Phaseolus vulgaris*) §
Anise (*Pimpinella anisum*) ω §
Radish (*Raphanus sativus*) ω §
Lemon thyme (*Thymus × citriodorus*) ω

PERENNIALS

Chives (*Allium schoenoprasum*) ω
Borage (*Borago officinalis*) ω §
Fennel (*Foeniculum vulgare*) §

Strawberry (*Fragaria* spp.) **N** ω
Jerusalem artichoke (*Helianthus tuberosus*) ω
Lovage (*Levisticum officinale*) §
Spearmint (*Mentha spicata*) ω
Parsley (*Petroselinum crispum, P. hortense*) § (biennial)
Rhubarb (*Rheum* × *cultorum*) § ◉
Sheep sorrel (*Rumex acetosella*) §
Rue (*Ruta graveolens*) §
Tansy (*Tanacetum vulgare*) ω

VINES
Grape (*Vitus* spp.) ω (rotting fruit)

SHRUBS
Rosemary (*Rosmarinus officinalis*) ω
Blackberry (*Rubus* spp.) ω

TREES
Apple, crab apple (*Malus* spp.) ω (rotting fruit; tree sap)
Pear (*Pyrus* spp.) ω (rotting fruit; tree sap)

ON THE FARM
Field mustard (*Brassica rapa*) §
Soybean (*Glycine max*) §
Cotton (*Gossypium hirsutum*) §
Common hop (*Humilis lupulus*) §
Alfalfa (*Medicago sativa*) ω §
Corn (*Zea mays*) §

OTHER WILD FOOD SOURCES
Aphid honeydew:
  Alder (*Alnus* spp.)
  Beech (*Fagus grandiflora, F.* spp.) aphids for harvesters
Bird droppings
Carrion
Dung
Rotting fruit:
  Persimmon (*Diospyros virginiana*)
  Black cherry (*Prunus serotina*)
Tree sap

NORTHERN PEARLY-EYE *butterflies drinking tree sap.*

Seasonal Progression of Blossoms

In addition to incorporating a variety of plant sizes into your landscape, create a progression of blooming times, so something is always flowering from spring through autumn. Use your regional plant list to select nectar-producing annuals, perennials, shrubs, vines, and trees that provide food at different levels in your garden as well as during the changing seasons. A typical perennial progression might include spring phlox, midsummer milkweed, and autumn asters. Scatter appropriate host plants throughout your garden, and you'll have a procession of caterpillars too.

In climates with four seasons, late spring and autumn butterfly gardens often provide more nectar sources than butterflies will find in the wild. The following timetable suggests popular plant choices to create a continuous nectar buffet in the eastern U.S.

SPRING	EARLY SUMMER	LATE SUMMER
Creeping phlox *(Phlox subulata)*	Marigold *(Tagetes patula)*	Blue mistflower *(Conoclinum coelestinum)*
Sweet William *(Dianthus barbatus)*	Purple coneflower *(Echinacea purpurea)*	Joe pye weed *(Eupatorium purpureum)*
Violet *(Viola lanceolata)*	Butterfly milkweed *(Asclepias tuberosa)*	New England aster *(Symphyotrichum novae-angliae)*
Pearly everlasting *(Anaphalis margaritacea)*	Brazilian verbena *(Verbena bonariensis)*	Ironweed *(Vernonia gigantean)*
Red clover *(Trifolium pretense)*	Butterfly bush *(Buddleja davidii)*	Showy goldenrod *(Solidago speciosa)*

Chapter 13: Troubleshooting and FAQs

CONGRATULATIONS! You've planned and planted a butterfly garden, and now several types of host plants flourish in your backyard. Let's go outside and find some "baby butterflies."

Actually this may not be quite as easy as it sounds, because lots of predators are lurking out there. Many of the birds, spiders, wasps, praying mantises, assassin bugs, and specialized butterfly parasites in your backyard would love to discover and digest a juicy caterpillar or dine on an adult. That's why female butterflies lay so many eggs and often scatter them on numerous host plants. This ensures that from 200 to 400 eggs, at least a few will successfully complete the entire life cycle through the caterpillar, chrysalis, and adult stages to mate and lay more eggs for the next generation.

Predators

One of the most basic protections caterpillars have is their appearance. Many are green or earthy shades of brown, with striped patterns or spiky protrusions that blend into the caterpillars' surroundings. Lots of caterpillars display a countershading pattern, meaning caterpillar backs are darker than their sides. When caterpillars are in bright light, shadow falls on their light sides and bellies, creating the same color value all over and making the critters less visible from afar.

Eastern tiger swallowtail caterpillars are typical of many baby butterflies that rest between meals in a safe house made by pulling leaf edges of their host plant together with sticky strands of silk. Nymph and satyr caterpillars hide among host grasses by day, feeding at night to avoid being seen.

Many caterpillars have camouflage patterns that make them look like something predators fear or would never want to eat. For example, maturing spicebush swallowtail caterpillars have swollen thoracic areas with prominent "eye" markings, giving them the shape and appearance of a fearsome snake. Swallowtail caterpillars have an osmeterium, a red, orange, or yellow putrid-smelling organ usually kept in a fold behind the head, but flicked out like a snake's tongue when the caterpillar is alarmed. In their small instar stages, many swallowtail and admiral caterpillars employ shiny brown, black, and white cam-

LIKE MANY caterpillars, eastern tiger swallowtails display countershading that helps them blend with their surroundings. They rest between meals on silken pads and sometimes pull leaf edges together to hide within.

A *SPICEBUSH* swallow-tail caterpillar has a pattern that mimics that of a snake.

ouflage that looks exactly like freshly deposited bird droppings. What predator would eat that?

Some caterpillars taste horrible, so if a predator does grab them, they may be spit out. Distasteful caterpillars—such as the pipevine swallowtail and monarch—are often distinctively marked, so predators associate the color or pattern with an awful taste and won't eat anything that looks similar. Pipevine caterpillars derive their wretched taste from the host plant pipevine, black swallowtails concentrate astringent elements from parsley or fennel, and monarch and queen caterpillars are flavored by bitter glycosides ingested from milkweed sap. In many species, the pungent taste transfers from caterpillar to adult.

Ironically, the chemicals caterpillars concentrate in their bodies to deter predators were initially manufactured by the host plant to protect it from being eaten. During the process of evolution, certain butterflies have specialized by feeding on specific plants, overcoming their toxins, and turning toxins into distasteful protection. Female butterflies use antennae and receptors in their feet to seek and identify these plants when they are ready to lay eggs.

Pipevine butterflies are sometimes called "blue swallowtails" because of the shimmering, metallic upper surfaces on their hindwings. Where the pipevine's range overlaps with that of the eastern tiger swallowtail, which is normally yellow with black stripes, some female eastern tiger swallowtails are black with blue markings. They mimic the pipevine swallowtail's appearance for protection, without ingesting the noxious pipevine host plant. Pipevines taste so yucky that female Diana fritillaries and both sexes of the red-spotted purple also mimic pipevine swallowtails to avoid predators.

The ultimate master of mimicry is the viceroy, which has a clever costume for each life stage. Oval viceroy eggs blend in color and placement with galls (parasitic wasp casings) that infect willow hosts. Humped cream-and-brown viceroy caterpillars are bird dropping look-alikes. Between meals they rest in camouflaged shelters made of leaf bits attached to twigs. A viceroy chrysalis looks like a slimy bird dropping dripping off a plant stem. Yuck! And the bright orange-and-black-striped adults imitate monarchs.

Some adult butterflies take a direct, yet risky, approach against predators. Mourning cloaks burst into flight, making a clicking sound to repel intruders. White admirals in the North and closely related

Lorquin's and Weidemeyer's admirals in the West often perch on prominent twigs to bask and survey their territories. They curiously investigate, and sometimes persistently drive away, intruders such as dragonflies, other butterflies, and even small birds. Occasionally, however, a flycatcher will outmaneuver the pugnacious butterfly and end up with lunch.

THE WEB OF LIFE

Butterfly gardening can help restore the natural role of insects by balancing predator-prey relationships in your yard. It's not necessary to use chemicals to achieve showcase lawns or picture-perfect plant specimens. Only a tiny percentage of insects are seriously damaging; most go about their business without any detrimental effects on human lives or landscaping.

Indiscriminate use of insecticides or electronic bug zappers wipes out countless small creatures that are important because they actually prey on things we consider pests, or because they are in turn eaten by frogs, toads, lizards, songbirds, or other animals around us. The more your yard mimics the interactions of natural predators and prey, the healthier you and the environment will be. Conversely, if you apply a "systemic" pesticide, it will be absorbed into plant tissues and may broadly poison insects that feed on plants in the treated area. In some cases it's possible for poisons to be passed through the food chain to birds, frogs, and perhaps even you.

VICEROY CATERPILLARS and pupas resemble slimy bird droppings and thus are often overlooked by predators.

A GREAT crested flycatcher pauses before swallowing a comma butterfly it has captured in flight.

Home gardeners seeking mild forms of insect control often apply *Bacillus thuringiensis* to protect cabbage and broccoli plants from infestations of cabbage white larvae. "Bt" is a natural bacterial substance, which qualifies it as an organic insecticide, but it is lethal to all caterpillars. If you must use Bt to protect garden produce, don't use it on windy days or apply it to host plants, where it could wipe out hundreds of native caterpillars.

In general, keep backyard habitat plants as healthy as possible through very light applications of fertilizer (no fertilizer is needed for native plants) and thinning or weeding to reduce competition. Native plants can survive well without pampering, but during extended droughts, give them occasional generous waterings to let moisture soak deep to their roots. Healthy plants are less likely to invite insect attacks than plants stressed by lack of water or nutrients. If you notice a small infestation of undesirable insects, wait a few days to see if ladybugs or other predators dine on them. For larger infestations or disease, remove and destroy affected portions of the plant.

For tough cases, choose the least toxic remedy possible. Insecticidal soaps—which are biodegradable, organic options—will stop most harmful insect problems. Apply remedies to infected plants only, not widely throughout your garden. Remember that a few damaged leaves may signal where a healthy caterpillar dined. Nearby you may soon see a beautiful new butterfly in your garden.

Hazards

Butterflies face many hazards during their short life spans. One of the greatest risks is being eaten by a predatory bird, spider, wasp, or other insect. Severe weather, in the form of drenching rains, windstorms, or unexpected freezing temperatures, is another natural threat. But throughout evolutionary history, butterflies have found ways to cope with these dangers, such as female butterflies laying lots of eggs because fewer than 10 percent of the hatchling caterpillars typically reach adulthood.

Of more concern is our growing human population and related pressures on butterfly habitat. Nearly seven billion people inhabit Earth at present; United Nations population analysts project an increase to eight billion by 2025. Habitat destruction is the greatest overall threat to butterflies worldwide. For 35 years, professor Art Shapiro of the University of California, Davis has monitored 11 butterfly study plots

A CLOUDLESS sulphur being eaten by an ambush spider.

from San Francisco into the Sierra Nevada. He notes that butterfly diversity is declining rapidly at sites near sea level, in the Central Valley, and in the foothills. Cosmopolitan (weed-host) butterflies are also generally declining. According to the California Department of Fish and Game, 13 butterfly subspecies—all with small home ranges and specific environmental requirements—are currently on the state threatened or endangered list.

Butterflies such as the Karner blue, a rare subspecies that occurs in isolated colonies in the Northeast and Midwest, and Schaus' swallowtail of the Florida Keys are "good news" stories. Thanks to public awareness initiated by butterfly conservation groups, some vital habitat needed to support these rare butterflies is being preserved.

For species such as the dotted blue and square-spotted blue that have only one brood per year, climate change is a concern. Adult fe-

THE KARNER blue, a federally endangered subspecies of the Melissa blue, occurs in scattered specific habitats from New York to Minnesota. This female was photographed in Michigan's Lower Peninsula.

The Hairstreak Project

The coastal bramble hairstreak (formerly known as the costal green hair-streak), is a small butterfly nearly eliminated by development of dune and shoreline habitats around San Francisco Bay. It is currently found in only three isolated areas: on coastal dunes and bluffs of the Presidio and in the city neighborhoods of Hawk Hill and Rocky Outcrop in the Golden Gate Heights. The Hairstreak Project has inspired residents of the two city neighborhoods to grow deerweed and wild buckwheat host plants, and favorite nectar plants, in their yards. Residents are creating a corridor of food so the two isolated neighborhood populations can reach each other and interbreed, strengthening their genetic diversity. If the project is successful, much of the credit for thwarting extinction will go to backyard butterfly gardeners! —CT

males of both species emerge according to precise seasonal timing to lay eggs on unfurling wild buckwheat flower buds. Caterpillars feed on these host flowers during the brief blooming period. In laboratory experiments that simulate higher carbon dioxide levels (like those anticipated because of climate change), caterpillars have been shown to develop more slowly. If global warming disrupts precise seasonal cycles, some caterpillars may find little or nothing to eat. Another problem: as the climate warms, mountain-dwelling plants and their butterfly followers migrate to higher elevations. When plants reach mountaintops and can go no higher—and conditions are still warming—plants perish. If butterflies can't find similar plants elsewhere, they also expire.

Monarchs are the best-known butterflies in North America, thanks to their highly recognizable appearance and legendary migration. Common milkweed is a native monarch host plant that grows readily along roads and in farm fields throughout the eastern and midwestern U.S. and southern Canada. Many cornbelt farmers consider it a noxious weed and spray fields with herbicides, an indiscriminate process that also kills host and nectar plants for other butterflies.

The spraying of fields, roadsides, and other "weedy" places with herbicides is currently the most serious threat to North American monarchs because it eliminates host plants the caterpillars need to survive. Females lay each egg separately on a fresh milkweed leaf. About 100 million acres of milkweed have been destroyed since 1997. To compensate for lost habitat, several conservation groups are promoting Monarch Waystations, a program in which homeowners and butterfly gardeners plant a backyard patch of milkweed for monarchs.

Threats also await monarchs in the Mexican forests where they overwinter. During the past 15 years, more than 10 percent of the core groves in the Monarch Butterfly Biosphere Reserve have been lost to illegal logging. Monarchs hibernate there because the dense fir trees act as umbrella and blanket, protecting the fragile butterflies from rain, snow, and prolonged cold. When chunks of forest are cut, the canopy loses its thermal insulation. Twice in the early 2000s, extreme winter storms devastated the reserve, killing 70 to 80 percent of the monarchs hibernating there. Researchers reported walking through 4- to 6-inch-deep piles of dead butterflies.

Monarch populations fluctuate from year to year based on successful caterpillar development, factors influencing migration, and weather-related events at their Mexican and California coastal overwintering areas. Since counts began in Mexico during the winter of 1994–1995, monarch populations have generally declined. The winter of 2009–2010 produced the lowest count on record, with only 4¾ acres of forest inhabited by monarchs. In comparison, the largest count occurred in 1996–1997 when monarch numbers were 11 times greater.

A LONE milkweed plant growing in an agricultural field. Female monarch butterflies typically need at least 100 milkweed plants on which to lay their eggs.

A troubling question is raised by data from some 70,000 monarchs sampled since 1976. At the beginning of the study, slightly more than half of migrant monarchs were female. Female abundance dropped steadily during the past three decades. Sampling in several states through 2006 showed that females accounted for only 37 to 40 percent of local populations. Scientists do not know why the ratio has changed, but one possibility is an increasingly prevalent parasite *(Ophryocystis elektroscirrha)* that seems to infest female butterflies more than males. Obviously, the steadily decreasing number of females is bad news for the overall health of the monarch population.

Butterfly Conservation

Many places on this continent were once blanketed in meadows, creeks, verdant pastures, and woodlands where butterflies flew. Now they are covered with tract homes and chemically treated lawns. A study by Stanford University estimated that natural habitats in the U.S. shrink by 1.1 percent annually. "Generalist" butterflies survive—painted ladies, skippers, and swallowtails whose caterpillars willingly dine on thistles, lawn weeds, or shade-tree leaves, and who as adults sip nectar at marigolds and bachelor's buttons. Introduced cabbage whites are everywhere, but many natives are missing. When's the last time you noticed a viceroy? Have you ever seen a common wood-nymph or a great purple hairstreak? As suburban shrub-and-lawn landscaping replaces natural diversity, local host and nectar plants disappear, and so do the butterflies that rely on them.

The good news is that individuals *can* make a difference. More than 92 million acres in the U.S., an area nearly the size of California, are

WHY HOST butterflies? You'll have an opportunity to experience their fascinating life cycles up close, and you may also play a vital role in conserving species whose habitats are dwindling.

I Hear Butterflies

When one butterfly flies you do not hear it, but when thousands take to the sky at once you can hear their wings in the silence of the forest. —*Sharon Favorito, resident of San Miguel de Allende, Guanajuato, Mexico, after visiting Anganguao in the Monarch Butterfly Biosphere Reserve*

Planting for the Future

"Plant a tree" is a popular exhortation to those who are concerned about our environment, but significantly more tangible value can be had from planting a garden, a small forest, or a diverse native plant community to support an assemblage of native butterflies. Such local conservation efforts not only provide much-needed havens for the creatures themselves, but they also offer a promise that future generations will have the opportunity to experience the delight of watching a butterfly flutter about on a fresh spring morning. —*Dennis D. Murphy, in* Butterfly Gardening: Creating Summer Magic in Your Garden

tended by people like you and me. If you will surrender your water-guzzling, maintenance-requiring bluegrass and taxus shrubs for a butterfly-attracting wildscape, there's no reason you can't be surrounded by native beauties: admirals sailing around willow trees, gulf fritillaries and zebra heliconians visiting passionflower vines, monarchs munching milkweeds, and hairstreaks hovering near wild lilacs.

At the core of the decision to go native is the question "Why would you want to host wildlife in your backyard?" Granted, installing new plants can be tedious or a bit costly, depending on whether or not you do the work yourself and how extensive the project becomes. The most common incentive to go native is the personal pleasure of spending time outdoors in the midst of wildlife. The payoff is converting your yard into a diverse, welcoming home for native plants, butterflies, hummingbirds, and a wealth of other fascinating critters from insects to mammals. As concerned citizens of the planet, many people feel this is a morally correct thing to do. Others are inspired by the ability to share backyard moments of wonder with friends and family. Very few who have switched to native landscaping and now welcome butterflies and hummingbirds into their yards express regrets—except that they didn't start sooner.

Frequently Asked Questions

Q: *Where does the name "butterfly" come from?*
A: One explanation is that the common brimstone, a familiar butterfly in Europe, Asia, and North Africa, is among the first to appear in spring. Males are bright, buttery yellow and in medieval

England were known as the "butter-coloured fly." This was later shortened to "butterfly." Another explanation cites the old English pronunciation of "beautiful fly" being corrupted to our modern pronunciation of "butterfly."

Q: *What are the most common butterflies in North America?*
A: Across North America, north of the Mexico border, our most common *native* butterfly is the orange sulphur. Another resident species that's very common in the U.S. but only reaches southernmost Canada is the silver-spotted skipper.

Q: *Do male and female butterflies look alike?*
A: In most butterfly species, slight differences in patterns distinguish males and females. Some distinctions are not particularly visible to humans but are very apparent when viewed in ultraviolet light, which butterflies see well. In a few species, the sexes look very different. For instance, in southeastern Arizona female Chiricahua whites are orange with black veins, forewing cells, and edging. Males are stark white with black veins, forewing cells, and edging. An unusual situation in metalmarks and snouts is that females have six normal legs, whereas males have four normal and two reduced legs.

Q: *Why are certain butterflies called "sisters"?*
A: California and band-celled sister butterflies are stunning black insects with white wing patterns that supposedly remind viewers of a nun's habit. California sisters often gather along

European Immigrant—The Cabbage White

The cabbage white, accidentally introduced from Europe to Canada in 1860, is now found continentwide, from the Gulf of Mexico to the Arctic. Adults emerge from their chrysalis in early spring and immediately seek cabbage, broccoli, radishes, and related garden plants as hosts for their eggs. Generations reproduce rapidly, accounting for at least three broods annually, and even more in the South. This is probably the most prolific butterfly in North America, although its exotic heritage and crop-consuming habits don't always make it a welcome garden visitor. —*CT*

riverbanks to imbibe moisture, and they are frequently seen at vineyards, feeding on juice from overripe grapes.

THE CALIFORNIA *sister has a distinctive white wing pattern.*

Q: *Why are butterflies so colorful?*

A: Butterflies enjoy one of the broadest visible spectrums in the animal kingdom, being able to see ultraviolet frequencies humans cannot detect, as well as seeing violet, through all the colors we recognize, into red. Scientists believe they use visual cues to find nectar-bearing flowers and also to recognize other butterflies. Numerous butterflies defend territories, and colors may help identify competitors and potential mates. Colors may also be involved in mating rituals and mate selection. And some color patterns are actually designed to camouflage the butterfly, to protect it from detection by predators.

Q: *Do butterflies smell things?*

A: Adult butterflies use taste receptors on their feet to select food and larval hosts. They detect fragrance with their antennae.

Q: *Are butterflies pollinators?*

A: Yes. Some of the flowers that butterflies visit lack a way to transfer pollen from one reproductive part to another. By sticking to butterflies, pollen can be bumped a short distance within the same blossom or can hitchhike to another blossom. The deal is simple: plants offer food, which butterflies need, and butterflies transport pollen, which helps plants create the next generation.

Q: *How fast do butterflies fly?*

A: Flight speed has not been documented for most types of butterflies, but from monarch research, we can guess that top speed for a butterfly is about 12 miles an hour. Monarchs can exceed that in short bursts to escape danger, but in more normal situations—looking for host plants or searching for nectar—they fly at less than 10 miles per hour.

Q: *How long do butterflies live?*

A: Adults of many species live only a few weeks, but the entire reproductive cycle—from adult to egg to caterpillar to chrysalis to adult—can take a full year.

Q: *Are there butterflies in Hawaii?*

A: Yes, two species of butterflies are native there. Hawaiian blues, whose closest relatives live in the Bonin Islands (located several thousand miles west in the Pacific), use native koa trees as their host. Kamehameha ladies, similar to painted ladies but with fiery orange-red coloration, are found throughout Hawaii's largest islands. Monarchs and gulf fritillaries are among half a dozen species introduced to Hawaii that have naturalized there.

A GREAT spangled fritillary nectars on butterfly milkweed in a meadow planted to attract wildlife. These large butterflies have only one brood annually, so the reproductive cycle from adult to egg to caterpillar to chrysalis to adult consumes an entire year.

Chapter 14: Butterfly Species Profiles

Kindred Butterflies

A GREAT WAY TO LEARN about butterflies is to categorize them into kindred groups. If you are new to butterfly watching, knowing groups that have similar characteristics will help with identification. The approximately 725 butterfly species found north of Mexico are currently divided into six families. Since the brushfoot family is so diverse and contains many of North America's easily recognized butterflies, we further describe three familiar brushfoot subfamilies.

Depending on which identification guide you consult, certain butterflies have been given various common names, which can be very confusing. Throughout this book, common and scientific names follow the *Checklist of North American Butterflies Occurring North of Mexico,* second edition, compiled by the North American Butterfly Association.

- **Swallowtails**—large; many have fragile tails extending from hindwings.

  Of the approximately 600 species worldwide in this family, about 30 dwell in the U.S. and Canada. The swallowtails are graceful and widely distributed, making them favorites in butterfly gardens across the continent. Many of the tiny caterpillars mimic bird droppings; several mature caterpillars have snakelike eyespots to frighten predators.

- **Whites and sulphurs**—medium size; white or yellow color.

  More than 1,000 species of whites and sulphurs have been identified worldwide, with about 60 found north of the U.S.-Mexico border. Many of these have subtle differences in male-female patterns or colors. Caterpillars are often covered with fine hairs. Some species produce large numbers of adults that emigrate widely.

- **Gossamer-wings**—delicate, small features; intricate color patterns; erratic flight.

   This huge family includes about 6,000 species worldwide, but fewer than 150 occur in the U.S. and Canada. Caterpillars are slug-shaped; many eat buds and flowers. Some have honeydew glands attractive to ants. Adults display most colors of the rainbow; subfamilies include coppers, blues, hairstreaks, and harvesters.

- **Metalmarks**—most are tropical; U.S. species are small with metallic marks on wings.

   Nearly 90 percent of the world's metalmarks live in Central and South America. Fewer than two dozen species fly in the U.S. and just one reaches Canada. These butterflies are small, with earth-toned wings decorated in shimmering, jewel-like patterns. Caterpillars are plump but flattened. Most adults remain in their specific habitats rather than wandering.

- **Brush-foots**—medium to large size; many have orange and brown coloration.

   Are you a lumper or a splitter? For many years taxonomists considered snouts, satyrs, and milkweed butterflies as separate families. Now regarded as subfamilies, they are still distinctive enough to detail separately below. Excluding these creatures, the brush-foots are a large and diverse group, with more than 150 representatives in the U.S. and Canada. Caterpillars usually have spines. Chrysalises generally hang from silken attachments. Adults walk on four normally sized legs, but the first pair is reduced in size.

- **Snouts**—most are tropical; easily recognized by a beaklike projection on the head.

   These primitive-looking creatures have fewer than a dozen members of their subfamily worldwide, and only one species north of the U.S.-Mexico border. Ancestral snouts are found in ancient fossil layers with impressions of hackberry leaves, which is still their host plant.

- **Satyrs**—most are dull brown or gray, often with eyespots on wings.

  This subfamily includes about 50 U.S. and Canadian satyrs, wood-nymphs, browns, pearly-eyes, ringlets, alpines, and arctics. Most are gray or brown; on close inspection, many have intricate camouflage patterns. Caterpillars are usually green or tan and have distinctive paired tips at the rear. Most satyrs remain in their particular habitats or regions rather than wandering.

- **Milkweed butterflies**—the familiar monarch and queen belong to this mostly tropical subfamily.

  Most of the 150 milkweed species are native to tropical Asia. Only four venture north of Mexico, the most common of which is the wide-ranging monarch. Caterpillars are brightly banded, with long filaments on the head and rear. Chrysalises have glistening metallic dots. Compounds in milkweed host plants make these creatures distasteful to predators.

- **Skippers**—broad head and thorax; intricate patterns of brown, black, and white.

  The skipper family is divided into five subfamilies, and identification is aided by studying range maps. More than 200 species of skippers have been seen north of Mexico. There are about 3,600 skipper species worldwide. Caterpillars are usually green or brown, well camouflaged to live among grasses or near the ground. Many are active at night and roll into leaf shelters by day. Most adults are small and have earthy brown wings with indistinct markings, making them a confusing lot to identify.

Species Profiles

On the following pages you will find brief profiles for 40 common North American butterflies. Each profile provides primary host plants for caterpillars and popular sources of nectar for adults. Life-cycle entries describe what to look for as eggs and caterpillars develop on host plants in your garden. Caterpillars are sometimes difficult to identify, so supplemental pictorial guides may help resolve questions about them. The habitat category lists ecological settings where each species is typically found. The backyard section adds tidbits of useful knowledge for butterfly gardeners. Range maps show areas where each species resides in red and areas occupied seasonally in blue. Yellow dots document sightings outside the normal range. Size gives the typical wingspan, measured from outer wingtip to outer wingtip.

Key to Range Maps

Red: summer range

Blue: winter range

Yellow: extra limital appearance of strays

SWALLOWTAILS

Pipevine Swallowtail

Battus philenor   SIZE: 2¾–3½"

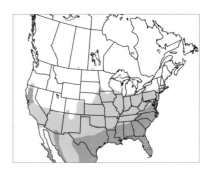

HOST PLANT
Dutchman's pipe, Virginia snakeroot.

NECTAR PLANT
Swamp milkweed, phlox, thistle, honeysuckle, azalea, butterfly bush.

LIFE CYCLE
Eggs are tan, in clusters. Caterpillar is black with black (or red) spines and red warts.

HABITAT
Meadows, fields, canyons, forest edges, pine woods.

BACKYARD
Range is expanding. Frequently seen in gardens, orchards, and near water.

Like all North American swallowtails, the pipevine is a large, graceful creature. Above: black with iridescent blue hindwings and a single row of pale marginal spots. Below: hindwings have bright orange spots amid blue iridescence.

Black Swallowtail

Papilio polyxenes   SIZE: 2¾–3½"

HOST PLANT
Parsley, dill, fennel, carrot, Queen Anne's lace.

NECTAR PLANT
Ironweed, milkweed, mistflower, phlox, thistle, butterfly bush.

LIFE CYCLE
Eggs are yellow. Young caterpillar mimics bird dropping. Mature caterpillar is green or white with yellow spots on black bands.

HABITAT
Old-fields, meadows, farmland, near water.

BACKYARD
Caterpillars frequently dine on parsley or carrot in vegetable and herb gardens.

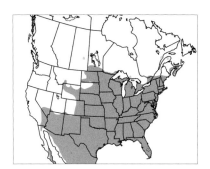

Look for rows of yellow spots on the abdomen; hindwings have an orange eyespot with black pupil. Above: males display two rows of parallel yellow spots on black wings. Females' hindwings have pale marginal spots and large iridescent blue areas. Below: two parallel bands of yellow and orange spots.

Anise Swallowtail

Papilio zelicaon   SIZE: 2½–3"

HOST PLANT
Carrot, cow parsnip, fennel, parsley, citrus.

NECTAR PLANT
Mint, penstemon, zinnia, butterfly bush.

LIFE CYCLE
Eggs are yellow. Caterpillar is green with orange spots in black bands.

HABITAT
From sea level to mountaintops, sagebrush, canyons, but not in dense woods.

BACKYARD
The most common swallowtail west of the Rocky Mountains; frequents gardens and parks.

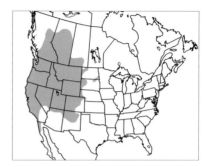

The anise swallowtail's abdomen is black with wide yellow side stripes beneath. Above: wings black with yellow marginal spots and a parallel wide yellow band. Below: wings yellow with prominent black veins, iridescent blue band, and orange spots.

Giant Swallowtail

Papilio cresphontes   SIZE: 3½–5½"

HOST PLANT
Rue, citrus, Hercules' club, hoptree, pricklyash.

NECTAR PLANT
Goldenrod, milkweed, lantana, honeysuckle, azalea, citrus.

LIFE CYCLE
Eggs are dull brown. Caterpillar is splotched brown and buff and resembles bird dropping.

HABITAT
Fields, forest edges, glades, hammocks, river corridors, citrus groves.

BACKYARD
Most common in South, but can fly long distances and strays widely.

Giant swallowtails are indeed large, with a distinctive yellow abdomen. Above: black wings sport eye-catching yellow marginal and horizontal bands that cross near the tips. Below: wings are pale yellow with black edging; hindwing has a blue iridescent band with rusty spots.

Eastern Tiger Swallowtail

Papilio glaucus   SIZE: 3–5½"

HOST PLANT
Tuliptree, ash, cherry, sweet bay.

NECTAR PLANT
Beebalm, red clover, ironweed, milkweed, phlox, thistle, butterfly bush.

LIFE CYCLE
Eggs are yellow-green. Young caterpillar resembles bird dropping. Mature caterpillar is green-brown with crosswise yellow band, large eyespots. Adult males and some females are yellow with black tiger stripes. Dark-phase females are blue-black with only traces of stripes.

HABITAT
Woods, shrubby fields, orchards, roadsides, watercourses.

BACKYARD
Widest ranging of the swallowtails; easily seen in gardens and parks.

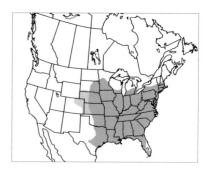

All males and some females are yellow above and below, with black tiger stripes and black margins. Other females are nearly black, but show evidence of tiger stripes in good light. All females have blue iridescence on the hindwings.

Spicebush Swallowtail

Papilio trolius   SIZE: 3½–4½"

HOST PLANT
Spicebush, sassafras.

NECTAR PLANT
Cardinal flower, clover, dogbane, ironweed, jewelweed, joe pye weed, milkweed, phlox, thistle, honeysuckle.

LIFE CYCLE
Green eggs. Tiny caterpillar mimics bird dropping. Humped green adult has large black and yellow eyespots that mimic a snake's head.

HABITAT
Forest edges, pine barrens, meadows, swamps, watercourses, woodlands.

BACKYARD
Visits gardens, especially those rich in native flowers and shrubs.

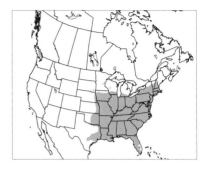

Both sexes are black with pale marginal spots. Above: male hindwings have cloudy greenish blue markings; female markings are bluer. Below: hindwings display blue iridescence with two parallel rows of orange spots.

Zebra Swallowtail

Eurytides marcellus   SIZE: 2¼–3½"

HOST PLANT
Pawpaw.

NECTAR PLANT
Pickerelweed, milkweed, hardy ageratum, joe pye weed, butterfly bush.

LIFE CYCLE
Eggs are pale green. Caterpillar is usually green with tiny black dots, one bold black band, and many yellow and white bands. Less common dark form is mostly black.

HABITAT
Lakeshores, marshes, swamps, watercourses, wooded areas near water.

BACKYARD
Visits gardens that contain, or are located near, pawpaw host plants.

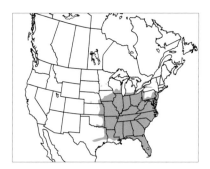

Look for long fragile tails on white wings, bold black stripes, and black margins. Above: hindwings have cherry red spots. Below: hindwings feature a central red band with two red spots at the end.

WHITES AND SULPHURS

Checkered White

Pontia protodice   SIZE: 1¼–2"

HOST PLANT
Shepherd's purse, winter cress, wild peppergrass, cleome, cabbage.

NECTAR PLANT
Aster, dogbane, heliotrope, milkweed, winter cress.

LIFE CYCLE
Eggs are yellow. Caterpillar is downy bluish green with four lengthwise yellow stripes and numerous black spots with tiny hairs.

HABITAT
Weedy fields, vacant lots, disturbed areas, sandy places, primarily in low elevations.

BACKYARD
Most common in southern and western U.S. Frequents roadsides, fields, and urban habitats; huge numbers in some years.

Males are white with a charcoal gray or black forewing cell spot. Females have more extensive marginal markings and are generally darker than males. There is much variation among individuals. The spring generation is smaller and veins below are darker than in summer broods.

Sara Orangetip

Anthocharis sara   SIZE: 1¼–1¾"

HOST PLANT
Rock cress, winter cress, hedge mustard, other mustards (eats flowers, seed pods).

NECTAR PLANT
Dandelion, monkeyflower, strawberry, bitter cherry.

LIFE CYCLE
Egg are yellow to orange. Caterpillar is moss green, stippled with white and dark green.

HABITAT
From seaside to mountains and deserts; canyons, open areas, ridgetops.

BACKYARD
Attracted to sunny habitats, high or open places. Seen in spring to early summer.

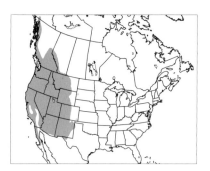

Appearance is regionally variable. Above: white (or pale yellow) with orange tips, bordered in black, on the forewings. Males are darker than females. Below: hindwings have dusky mottling.

Clouded Sulphur

Colias philodice   SIZE: 1½–2"

HOST PLANT
Alfalfa, trefoil, vetch, white clover, white sweetclover.

NECTAR PLANT
Aster, clover, dandelion, dogbane, goldenrod, milkweed, phlox, sedum.

LIFE CYCLE
Eggs are bright green. Green caterpillar has prominent side stripes of white over dark.

HABITAT
Most open areas except deserts. Abundant in clover and alfalfa fields.

BACKYARD
Originally in eastern North America; has spread widely. Interbreeds with orange sulphur.

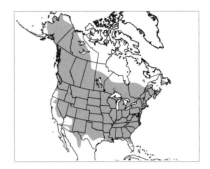

Usually sits with wings closed. Above: male is yellow; female is yellow or greenish white. Both have black wing margins. Below: wings are yellow with prominent red-rimmed (often double) spot in midst of hindwing. Variable dark dots near wing edges.

Orange Sulphur

Colias eurytheme   SIZE: 1½–2½"

HOST PLANT
Alfalfa, vetch, white clover, white sweetclover, wild indigo.

NECTAR PLANT
Alfalfa, aster, clover, coreopsis, heliotrope, thistle, rabbitbrush, redosier dogwood.

LIFE CYCLE
Eggs are white. Caterpillar is green with adjoining white, pink, and dark side stripes and fine hairs.

HABITAT
Open areas, especially agricultural fields with alfalfa or clover.

BACKYARD
Abundant and easy to attract to a wide range of host and nectar plants.

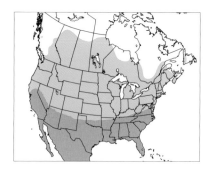

This species hybridizes with the clouded sulphur, making it difficult to distinguish certain individuals. Above: wings show more orange than does clouded sulphur. Below: hind-wing usually has a double cell spot.

Pink-edged Sulphur

Colias interior   SIZE: 1¼–1¾"

HOST PLANT
Blueberry.

NECTAR PLANT
Aster, bristly sarsaparilla.

LIFE CYCLE
Pale yellow egg. Caterpillar is bright yellow-green; has light stripes on back and bluish side stripes edged in red.

HABITAT
Northern bogs, marshes, meadows, clearings, burned areas.

BACKYARD
Males often congregate at moist soil and puddles.

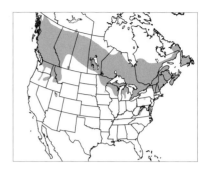

Frequently sits with wings closed, displaying distinct pink-fringed edges on bright yellow wings. Some females are pale yellow-white. Above: males have darker border margins than females. Below: hindwings have a pink-rimmed cell spot.

Southern Dogface

Colias cesonia   SIZE: 1¾–2½"

HOST PLANT
Clover, false indigo, indigobush, leadplant, prairie clover, soybean.

NECTAR PLANT
Alfalfa, aster, butterfly milkweed, coreopsis, thistle, verbena.

LIFE CYCLE
Egg is white and shaped like a tiny football. Caterpillar is green with a variable light lateral stripe. Mature caterpillars have yellow and black bands and black dots.

HABITAT
Diverse; uses open woodlands, scrublands, prairies, deserts.

BACKYARD
With wings closed, resembles other sulphurs. Has a bold black-orange design when wings are open.

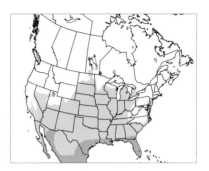

From above or below, the yellow outline on the black fore-wing margin resembles a dog's face, thus the common name. Males have bolder patterns than females.

Cloudless Sulphur

Phoebis sennae   SIZE: 2–2¾"

HOST PLANT
Clover, partridge pea, senna.

NECTAR PLANT
Cardinal flower, hibiscus, lantana, milkweed, morning glory, thistle, firebush.

LIFE CYCLE
Eggs are white, turning orange. Caterpillar is green with a yellow side stripe and black dots.

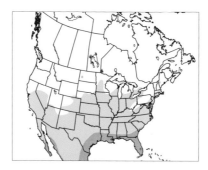

HABITAT
Forest edges, glades, pinelands, roadsides, swamps, thickets, watercourses.

BACKYARD
Some years see huge late-summer and autumn emigrations into North and West.

Large and conspicuous. Males are bright yellow, but females may be yellow, yellow-orange, or greenish white. Above: females have narrow dark wing margins. Below: both sexes display central cell spots on fore- and hindwings.

Sleepy Orange

Eurema nicippe   SIZE: 1¼–2"

HOST PLANT
Clover, senna, other legumes.

NECTAR PLANT
Beggarticks, blue porterweed, sweet alyssum, tickseed sunflower.

LIFE CYCLE
Eggs are yellow. Caterpillar is downy blue-green; darker below with a light side stripe.

HABITAT
Old-fields, wet meadows, woodland edges, open pine forests, scrub.

BACKYARD
Visits herb gardens to nectar on chives, lavender, mint, marigold, and oregano.

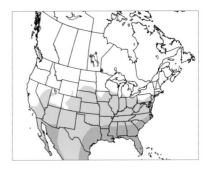

Above: brilliant orange-yellow with wide black wing margins. Below: bright yellow with brownish diagonal markings. In autumn, the underside is often rich orange, as seen here.

GOSSAMER-WINGS

American Copper

Lycaena phlaeas   SIZE: ¾–1¼"

HOST PLANT
Sheep sorrel, mountain sorrel, curly dock.

NECTAR PLANT
Daisy, goldenrod, hardy ageratum, yarrow.

LIFE CYCLE
Eggs are pale green. Caterpillar is downy, sluglike, and green (or yellow-green or reddish).

HABITAT
East: Pastures, old-fields, disturbed land. West: mountain slopes, rock-strewn Arctic areas.

BACKYARD
Sheep sorrel and curly dock are considered weeds but will bring caterpillars to your garden, especially in Northeast. Adult butterflies stay low to the ground.

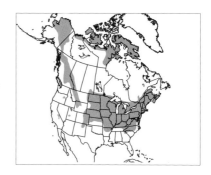

Look for sharply contrasting colors on these black-spotted sprites. Above: forewings are orange with brown margins; hindwings show brown with orange trailing edges. Below: forewings display orange with gray margins; hindwings are gray with narrow orange line.

243

Brown Elfin

Callophrys augustinus   SIZE: ¾–1¼"

HOST PLANT
Blueberry, bearberry, huckleberry, Labrador tea, leatherleaf, madrone, salal.

NECTAR PLANT
Buckwheat, winter cress, heath, bitterbrush, blueberry, wild plum, willow.

LIFE CYCLE
Eggs are greenish. Caterpillar is bright green, with red and yellow bands when mature.

HABITAT
Pine barrens, bogs, forest edges, open woodlands, stream banks.

BACKYARD
Widespread in spring; easy to lure with host plants. Also visits moist ground.

Regionally variable, from tan-brown to dark purple-brown. Usually sits with wings closed. Above: plain rusty brown. Below: subtle scalloped pattern with lighter wing margins.

Gray Hairstreak

Strymon melinus SIZE: 1–1¼"

HOST PLANT
Corn, cotton, hops, various legumes, mints, strawberry, oak.

NECTAR PLANT
Boneset, butterfly milkweed, goldenrod, mint, sedum, yarrow, verbena, wild lilac.

LIFE CYCLE
Eggs are pale green. Caterpillar is slug-shaped; often green (pink, red, or brown) with a slightly darker stripe on back and many short hairs on each segment.

HABITAT
Open spaces, vacant lots, old-fields, roadsides, coastal areas, forest openings.

BACKYARD
Very adaptable and widespread; visits many domestic crop plants and herbs.

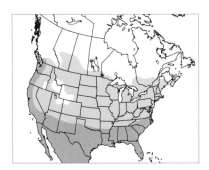

Unlike many other hair-streaks, the gray basks with wings open. Fresh individuals have fragile tails. Above: uniform gray-brown with a distinct orange eye spot on each hindwing. Below: gray with black-on-white dashed line and parallel black dashed line near wing margins.

Eastern Tailed-blue

Everes comyntas   SIZE: ¾–1¼"

HOST PLANT
Beans, clovers, lespedeza, lupine, tick trefoil, vetch, wild pea.

NECTAR PLANT
Lavender, legumes, mints, oregano, yarrow.

LIFE CYCLE
Eggs are green. Caterpillar is tiny with downy hairs. Variable green (pink, rose, purple, or yellow-brown) with a darker stripe on back and lower side.

HABITAT
Open and disturbed areas, such as roadsides, rights of way, old-fields.

BACKYARD
Flies low to the ground. Attracted to weedy patches with wild clover.

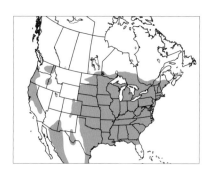

Very small, with distinct tails in freshly hatched adults. Above: male is shimmering blue, female is dull gray-brown. Below: both sexes are pale blue-gray with tiny dashes near wing margins and double orange spots with black centers near tail.

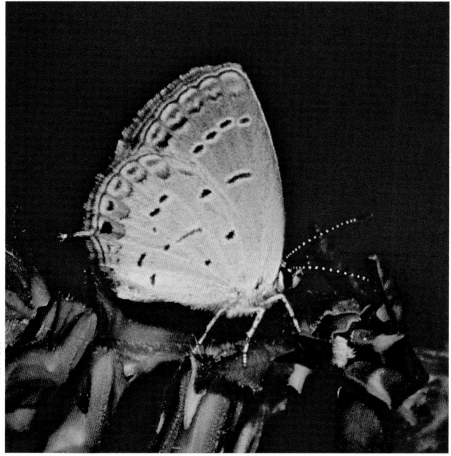

Spring Azure

Celastrina ladon SIZE: ¾–1¼"

HOST PLANT
Black snakeroot, meadowsweet, blueberry, wild lilac, viburnum, flowering dogwood.

NECTAR PLANT
Coltsfoot, dandelion, forget-me-not, rock cress, violet.

LIFE CYCLE
Eggs are green. Caterpillar is flattened and wrinkled. Variable green (pink, cream, or brown) with tiny white hairs.

HABITAT
From shorelines to mountaintops; clearings, brush, open woodlands, glades.

BACKYARD
Visits herb gardens for nectar. Males cluster around damp soil and dung piles.

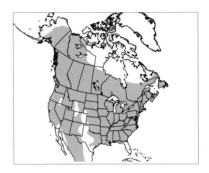

These delicate butterflies demonstrate much regional variability and may actually comprise several species. They are often the first butterfly seen in spring. Above: males are intense silvery blue; females are duller with dark wing borders. Below: pale blue with dark flecks.

METALMARKS

Mormon Metalmark

Apodemia mormo   SIZE: ¾–1¼"

HOST PLANT
Buckwheat.

NECTAR PLANT
Desert marigold, groundsel, mustards, rock cress, rabbitbrush.

LIFE CYCLE
Eggs are pale pink. Tufted caterpillar is gray-purple, darker on back, lighter below.

HABITAT
From sea level to mountains, usually on open dry areas or rocky slopes.

BACKYARD
Flies low to the ground. Attracted to yellow nectar flowers.

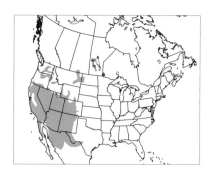

Several distinct regional subspecies are currently included in this complex. In general, watch for small butterflies that open and close their wings with mechanical precision. They display a busy pattern of white spots on two-toned orange-and-brown wings with dark upper margins.

SNOUTS

American Snout

Libytheana carinenta   SIZE: 1½–2"

HOST PLANT
Hackberry, sugarberry.

NECTAR PLANT
Mountainmint, verbena, zinnia, butterfly bush, rabbitbrush, dogwood.

LIFE CYCLE
Eggs are pale green, laid in clusters. Caterpillar is humped, variably colored, with two black tubercles behind head. Most are green with tiny pale spots and a pale side stripe; there is also a dark-phase caterpillar.

HABITAT
Watercourses, forest edges, thickets, hardwood forests with hackberry trees.

BACKYARD
Can be lured to yards with patches of damp soil. Adults resemble dead leaves when perched.

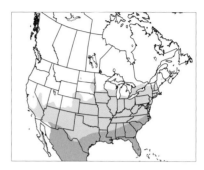

When perched with wings closed, the conical shape of the snout's head is distinctive. With wings open, this creature presents an angular outline. Above: orange blotches and white spots on dark background. Below: hindwings are cryptically patterned to mimic dead leaves.

BRUSH-FOOTS

Gulf Fritillary

Agraulis vanillae   SIZE: 2½–3"

HOST PLANT
Passionflower.

NECTAR PLANT
Beggarticks, lantana, passionflower, thistle, Mexican sunflower.

LIFE CYCLE
Eggs are yellow. Caterpillar is marked with black (or purple) and bright red-orange lengthwise stripes. Body is shiny, with many sharp black spines.

HABITAT
Old-fields, pastures, thickets, hammocks, forest edges.

BACKYARD
Fairly easy to lure to sunny gardens with passionflower.

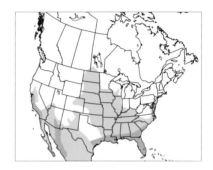

Wings are long and slender, giving these butterflies a graceful appearance. Above: rich orange with black markings and a few dainty white spots. Below: large, silvery white spots on orange-and-brown wings.

Great Spangled Fritillary

Speyeria cybele   SIZE: 2–3"

HOST PLANT
Violet. Caterpillars feed at night.

NECTAR PLANT
Blackeyed Susan, milkweed, purple coneflower, thistle, verbena.

LIFE CYCLE
Eggs are pale brown. Caterpillar is dark; has black branching spines with orange bases. Head is orange and black.

HABITAT
Meadows, pastures, open woodlands, clearings near conifer forests.

BACKYARD
Tiny caterpillars overwinter near violets. Shelter them with leaf litter.

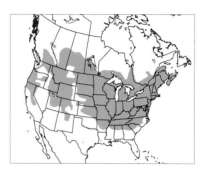

Large, conspicuous, and regionally variable. Above: orange with black markings, lighter at margins and darker near body. Below: diagnostic light marginal band and silver spots on hindwings.

Pearl Crescent

Phyciodes tharos   SIZE: 1–1½"

HOST PLANT
Aster. Caterpillars feed in small groups.

NECTAR PLANT
Aster, beggarticks, daisy, fleabane, goldenrod, purple coneflower, thistle.

LIFE CYCLE
Eggs are yellow, in clusters. Caterpillar is dark brown with light speckles; light lines on sides; branched spines emerge from bulbous brown warts. Head is shiny black with white marks.

HABITAT
Open areas, old-fields, roadsides, damp meadows, stream banks.

BACKYARD
Widespread; easy to lure with asters. Males puddle at moist areas and defend perches.

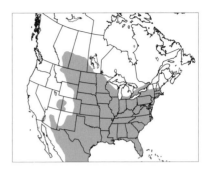

These small creatures often bask with wings spread. Above: intricate black markings on bright orange. Below: bright and pale orange, with brown markings; crescent-shaped spot on hindwings.

Question Mark

Polygonia interrogationis   SIZE: 2¼–2¾"

HOST PLANT
Nettle, hops, elm, hackberry.

NECTAR PLANT
Carrion, dung, rotting fruit, tree sap.

LIFE CYCLE
Eggs are green, laid in rows or stacks; may be near, rather than on, host. Caterpillar is black with tiny white speckles; has black spines on head, orange spines and lines on back.

HABITAT
Open woods, glades, roadsides, stream banks.

BACKYARD
Common near orchards and in suburbs where rotting fruits are available. Especially drawn to rotting crab apples. May become drunk after eating fermented fruit juices.

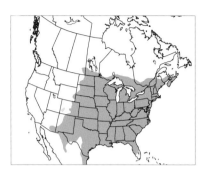

Distinguish these from closely related commas by longer tails and a silver ? on the hindwings below. Above: dark hindwings identify a summer-hatched adult. Orange hindwings indicate the overwintering generation.

Mourning Cloak

Nymphalis antiopa   SIZE: 2¾–3½"

HOST PLANT
Birch, cottonwood, elm, hackberry, poplar, willow.

NECTAR PLANT
Aphid honeydew, carrion, dung, rotting fruit, tree sap.

LIFE CYCLE
Eggs are in clusters; olive when laid, turning black. Caterpillar is shiny black with tiny white speckles, red markings in center of back, red legs, and black spines.

HABITAT
Forest edges, glades, woodland clearings, watercourses.

BACKYARD
Caterpillars feed within a web when small; remain in a group until nearly mature. If frightened, they thrash back and forth in unison. Adults overwinter and are often the first spring butterfly in a garden.

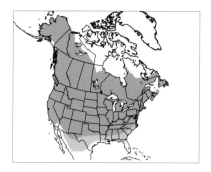

Distinctive from all other North American species. Above: rich purple–brown with golden wing margins and iridescent blue spots. Below: cryptically patterned dark brown wings with pale margins.

Milbert's Tortoiseshell

Nymphalis milberti   SIZE: 1¾–2"

HOST PLANT
Nettle.

NECTAR PLANT
Tree sap, wide variety of wildflowers.

LIFE CYCLE
Eggs are pale green, in clusters. Caterpillar is black with light speckles; has yellow-green markings on back and sides, black branched spines, and stiff white hairs.

HABITAT
Widely varied, from beaches to mountain slopes and rocky alpine areas; meadows, roadsides, watercourses, weedy places.

BACKYARD
Tiny caterpillars gather in silken webs; groups defoliate host plants. Older caterpillars are solitary and rest in folded leaves. They are well adapted to cold climates; overwintering adults may bask on warm winter days.

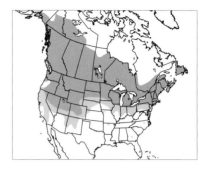

Look for two owlish eyes staring from the open wings of this butterfly. Above: the dark "face" is surrounded by a bright orange band, trimmed by a narrow dark margin. Below: wings close and the butterfly disappears into dull brown shades that mimic tree bark.

Painted Lady

Vanessa cardui   SIZE: 2–2¼"

HOST PLANT
Thistle. Also borage, burdock, groundsel, hollyhock, knapweed, mallow, pearly everlasting, wormwood.

NECTAR PLANT
Aster, blazing star, joe pye weed, ironweed, tickseed sunflower, verbena, zinnia, rabbitbrush, chaste tree.

LIFE CYCLE
Eggs are pale green. Caterpillar is variable (black, green, yellow, pink, or gray-brown) but always has a black head, fine white hairs, and short branched spines (black, yellow, orange, or buff) with black tips on back. Usually has a dark line flanked by pale stripes on the back and pale side stripes.

HABITAT
Visits most sunny habitats from deserts and meadows to mountains and suburbs.

BACKYARD
Known as the thistle butterfly because of its favorite host. Similar-looking and closely related West Coast lady is common in West, and American lady is common in East.

A medium-sized butterfly with white-tipped antennae. Above: forewings are bright orange with black margins and white-spotted black wingtips. Four blue dots grace each orange hindwing. Below: four blue eye-spots decorate each cryptic hindwing.

Red Admiral

Vanessa atalanta   SIZE: 1¾–2¼"

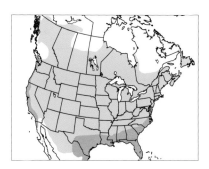

HOST PLANT
Stinging nettle, false nettle, wood nettle, hops.

NECTAR PLANT
Rotting fruit, tree sap. Aster, beggarticks, blazing star, goldenrod, milkweed, red clover, thistle, butterfly bush.

LIFE CYCLE
Eggs are green. Caterpillar is variable, usually black (white or yellow-green) with white flecks. Pale splotches or a pale line on lower side, stiff pale spines on the back; head is black.

HABITAT
Meadows, fields, forest edges, glades, roadsides, swamps, watercourses, barnyards.

BACKYARD
Caterpillars make shelters at leaf tips or by folding a leaf over themselves. Adults allow close approach; they commonly land on humans.

When its wings spread, this butterfly is easily identified by bold orange slashes on forewings and wide orange hindwing margins. When the wings close, the intricately patterned brown hindwings mimic tree bark.

Common Buckeye

Junonia coenia SIZE: 2–2½"

HOST PLANT
Plantain, gerardia, Mexican petunia, monkeyflower, snapdragon, toadflax, vervain.

NECTAR PLANT
Aster, boneset, dogbane, goldenrod, ironweed, milkweed, mistflower, peppermint, sedum, wild buckwheat.

LIFE CYCLE
Eggs are dark green. Caterpillar is dark with a pale back stripe and white or orange side markings. Blue-black spines on back; side spines have warty orange bases. Head and prolegs are orange.

HABITAT
Fields, marshes, meadows, shorelines, swamps, roadsides.

BACKYARD
Caterpillars consume lawn weed plantain. Adults often bask on warm bare ground.

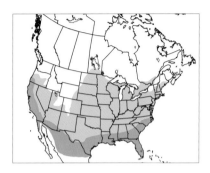

Large, dark eyespots set in golden rims decorate the open chestnut brown wings of common buckeyes. Look also for red-orange bars on both surfaces of the forewings. Hindwings below are dull brown in spring and rusty in fall generations.

Red-spotted Admiral

Limenitis arthemis   SIZE: 3–3½"

Until recently, both butterflies below were considered separate species. Since they interbreed where their ranges overlap, they are now regarded as one species, but are usually described by their distinctive characteristics.

Red-spotted Purple

Limenitis arthemis astyanax

White Admiral

Limenitis arthemis arthemis

HOST PLANT
Apple, aspen, black cherry, hornbeam, and oak for red-spotted purple. Birch, hawthorn, poplar, and willow for white admiral.

NECTAR PLANT
Aphid honeydew, carrion, dung, rotting fruit, tree sap, spiraea, viburnum.

LIFE CYCLE
Eggs are green. Humped caterpillar resembles bird droppings. Brown with creamy saddle marking and a side stripe; has a pair of branched horns behind head.

HABITAT
Forest edges, meadows, open deciduous woods, shorelines, and watercourses for red-spotted purple. Boreal and mixed hardwood forests and scrubby mountain slopes for white admiral.

BACKYARD
Adult red-spotted purples (southern form) and white admirals (northern form) are distinct color races of the same species. Their caterpillars look alike.

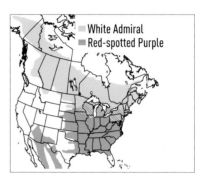

The red-spotted purple is iridescent blue-black above and dark below, with orange spots near the base and margins of each hindwing.

The white admiral sports a wide white band on dark upper and lower surfaces of the fore- and hindwings.

Viceroy

Limenitis archippus   **SIZE: 2½–3"**

HOST PLANT
Apple, aspen, cherry, plum, poplar, willow.

HABITAT
Marshes, meadows, moist open areas, watercourses.

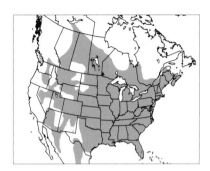

NECTAR PLANT
Aphid honeydew, carrion, dung, rotting fruit, aster, beggarticks, joe pye weed, ironweed, milkweed, thistle, butterfly bush.

BACKYARD
Caterpillars hibernate in shredded leaves attached to small branches of host plant. In southern and western areas where monarchs are scarce, viceroys mimic queens.

LIFE CYCLE
Eggs are greenish. Caterpillar mimics bird droppings. Brown with creamy saddle marking and side stripe; humped, with a pair of branched horns behind head, spines on back and side of head.

Have you ever noticed a monarch with extra stripes? Look again and see a viceroy mimicking the distasteful milkweed-munchers. Viceroys have an extra black band crossing the hindwing above and below. They also have paired white spots above on the forewing.

Lorquin's Admiral

Limenitis lorquini   SIZE: 2¼–3"

HOST PLANT
Aspen, chokecherry, cottonwood, willow.

NECTAR PLANT
Bird droppings, dung, fernbush, yerba santa, California buckeye.

LIFE CYCLE
Eggs are pale green. Tiny caterpillar is dark with a white saddle. Mature caterpillar is mottled olive and brown-buff, with a light side stripe and saddle, and bristly horns. It overwinters in a rolled leaf.

HABITAT
Widespread from lowlands to mountains. Forest edges, watercourses, damp places.

BACKYARD
Pugnacious; will "attack" passing dragonflies, butterflies, birds, and mammals.

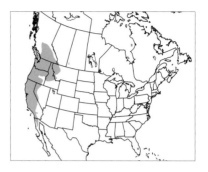

Above: rich brown–black with a broad white band and orange wingtips. Below: a broad white band decorates brown (or gray) fore- and hindwings.

SATYRS

Common Wood-nymph

Cercyonis pegala   SIZE: 2-3"

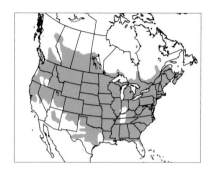

HOST PLANT
Beardgrass, bluegrass, bluestem grasses, oatgrass, purpletop grass, redtop grass.

NECTAR PLANT
Rotting fruit, tree sap, alfalfa, spiraea.

LIFE CYCLE
Eggs are yellow. Caterpillar is green or yellow-green with short fuzzy hairs, a darker green stripe on back, and yellow-green side stripes. Tail end has two reddish pink tips.

HABITAT
Fields, grasslands, meadows, open oak and pine woods, utility rights of way.

BACKYARD
Adult appearance varies regionally, but all are beautifully camouflaged. Look for them sitting quietly on tree bark or branches, where they drink sap.

Patterns on these dark brown creatures vary geographically, with large orange forewing patches in some regions and orange-rimmed eyespots elsewhere. Below: hindwings may or may not have eyespots but are always cryptically patterned.

MILKWEED BUTTERFLIES

Monarch

Danaus plexippus   **SIZE: 3½–4"**

HOST PLANT
Milkweed.

NECTAR PLANT
Milkweed, beggarticks, blazing star, blue mistflower, goldenrod, ironweed, lantana, Mexican sunflower, zinnia, butterfly bush.

LIFE CYCLE
Eggs are pale yellow. Caterpillar is boldly marked with alternating black, white, and yellow bands; it has a pair of black filaments at each end.

HABITAT
Weedy fields, meadows, marshes, roadsides, watercourses.

BACKYARD
The most recognizable butterfly in North America. During migration, may be seen from seashores to mountains, in rural areas and suburbs.

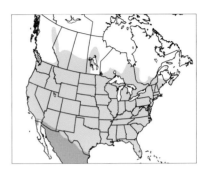

Not all large orange butterflies are monarchs—but this is, and it's a male, identified by paired glands on the hindwing. Recognize monarchs by pumpkin-colored wings overlaid with netlike black vein markings. Also note that black wingtips and margins contain tiny white dots. Below: the monarch's body is black with white spots. The hindwings are pale orange with dark vein patterns.

Queen

Danaus gilippus   SIZE: 3–3¼"

HOST PLANT
Milkweed, white vine.

NECTAR PLANT
Aster, beggarticks, blue mistflower, butterfly milkweed, fogfruit, heliotrope, ironweed, Mexican sunflower, verbena, zinnia.

LIFE CYCLE
Eggs are pale. Caterpillar resembles a monarch but with wider black or reddish brown bands. It has paired long black filaments behind head; shorter pairs on back and at rear.

HABITAT
Coastal areas, fields, glades, hammocks, pine woods, thickets, salt marshes, roadsides in the Southeast; open areas, brushlands, roadsides in the Southwest.

BACKYARD
Queen caterpillars absorb distasteful milkweed toxins and are usually avoided by predators.

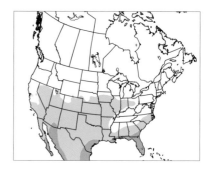

Recognize queens by rich cinnamon color on both surfaces, with black wing margins and bright white spots. Below: hindwings have black netlike vein patterns similar to monarchs. Males have paired black glands on hindwings. Queens in the Southwest have pale edging along hindwing veins.

SKIPPERS

Silver-spotted Skipper

Epargyreus clarus   SIZE: 1¾–2½"

HOST PLANT
Beans, beggarticks, cassia, false indigo, locust, ticktrefoil.

NECTAR PLANT
Bird droppings, aster, ironweed, mistflower, verbena, blue mist shrub, chastetree.

LIFE CYCLE
Eggs are green. Caterpillar is yellow-green with vertical lines of dark green speckles. Reddish brown head is large, bulbous, on a tiny neck.

HABITAT
Canyons, hillsides, meadows, forest clearings, woodlands, barnyards.

BACKYARD
Common in suburban gardens. Look for chewed leaves rolled with silk that hide tiny caterpillars, or larger caterpillars hiding between folded leaves bound with silk.

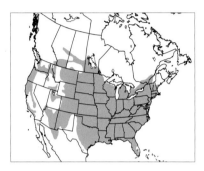

Big, dark eyes and a stocky body help identify this as a skipper. Above and below: dull brown with an orange band across the forewings. Below: prominent silver-white blotch on the hindwing.

Common Checkered-skipper

Pyrgus communis   SIZE: 1–2"

HOST PLANT
Cheeseweed, globe mallow, hibiscus, hollyhock, poppy mallow, wild mallows.

NECTAR PLANT
Aster, beggarticks, coneflower, fleabane, fogfruit, ironweed, mistflower, blue mist shrub.

LIFE CYCLE
Eggs are green, fading to pale. Caterpillar is green to pinkish, with many white speckles and short hairs. Head is bulbous, reddish brown.

HABITAT
Beaches, dry open areas, grasslands, roadsides, weedy places, watercourses.

BACKYARD
One of the most common skippers of cities and developed areas. Small, but males aggressively defend territories.

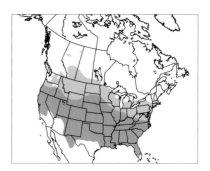

Look for a slight blue-gray tint on the body hair to distinguish the male. Otherwise, both sexes are dark above with neat rows of white checkered banding. Below: hindwings are pale with tan (or olive) markings.

Tawny-edged Skipper

Polites themistocles SIZE: ½–1"

HOST PLANT
Various grasses, including bluegrass and panic grass.

NECTAR PLANT
Alfalfa, bluets, chickory, dogbane, purple coneflower, red clover, thistle.

LIFE CYCLE
Eggs are green. Caterpillar is reddish or tan, with dark speckles and a dark stripe on back.

HABITAT
Bogs, eastern grasslands, moist meadows; forest edges and mountains in West.

BACKYARD
Reproduces on common lawn grasses, making this little creature one of the most common skippers in suburban gardens.

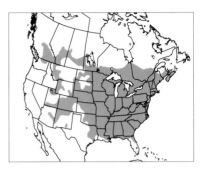

A tiny creature with short antennae and prominent dark eyes. Above: dull orange leading edges on brown forewings. Below: wings are pale brown, forewing has contrasting tawny leading edge.

Appendix 1: Photographing Hummingbirds

PHOTOGRAPHING HUMMINGBIRDS is equal parts skill, knowledge, and luck. Being in the right place at the right time to capture an acceptable shot of a hummer is something even professional photographers struggle to accomplish.

And did I mention luck?

There are many experts who specialize in hummingbird photography (and many of the photographs in this book are theirs), and they have devoted years to honing their craft. If you are bitten by the hummer photo bug, you may want to look for additional advice from these pros either online or as part of a field workshop.

Here are some of my basic tips for photographing hummingbirds.

A MALE ruby-throated hummingbird perches on a feeder.

1. WATCH AND LEARN THE HABITS OF YOUR TARGET BIRDS. Hummingbirds are creatures of habit. By watching them at your feeders or in your garden, you can learn which food sources they regularly visit and when and which perches they favor. When feeding, a hummingbird will drink, move away to hover, return to drink, hover away, etc. Knowing this in advance gives you an advantage in planning your shots.

2. GET IN POSITION. Once you know where to position yourself, you'll need to consider other factors: direction of light (to catch those gorget colors just right), objects in the background (nothing more disappointing that an ugly object cluttering the background), and concealment.

3. USE A BLIND. My best hummer shots have been taken either from inside my portable photo blind (mine is called a "Doghouse" blind and is available at most sporting goods stores) or from behind a curtained but open window adjacent to the feeders. The blind works like a charm because hiding your movements is necessary to catch an extremely wary hummingbird unawares. Some experts suggest setting the blind up well in advance of shooting so the birds will get used to its presence.

4. NATURAL SETTINGS ARE BEST. As a magazine editor, I vastly prefer using images of hummingbirds at flowers or on natural perches to shots of birds at feeders or on clotheslines. One trick is to place a natural-looking perch near your feeders or flowers in perfect light. Then wait. Some photographers will replace feeders with hanging baskets of flowers to improve the "naturalness" of their images.

5. TAKE LOTS OF IMAGES. Digital cameras give us instant feedback and the ability to take numerous shots at little or no expense. When photographing hummingbirds, I put a large memory card in my camera, set the camera on "burst" (multiple images per button click), and let the shutter fly. Sure, I toss out hundreds for every decent handful of "keepers," but not every shot I take is going to be worth saving.

SHOOTING FROM a blind.

6. KNOW YOUR CAMERA. I'm still learning all the things my Canon 30D can do, but I do know a few things that help when photographing hummingbirds. Having the camera on "burst," as mentioned above, is key. Using continuous focus and auto focus is crucial. One very successful hummer photographer I know suggests starting this way. Set up in direct sunlight (early and late in the day offer the best, most pleasing light) with your camera on the following settings (without flash): ISO 400, shutter 1/500 sec, at f/16. This should give you decent results. If you want to get more technical, using single or multiple flash units to freeze the wing motion, shooting in high-resolution formats such as RAW, and so on, I suggest you consult some of the expert resources available online.

7. USE A TRIPOD. A tripod (or a monopod) will help you get sharper images than if you are hand-holding your camera.

8. BE STILL. Hummingbirds respond to motion and noise by fleeing. Even if you are using a blind, keep your movements and sounds to a minimum.

9. BLURRY WINGS ARE OKAY. Freezing the motion of a hummingbird's wings takes lots of fancy flash equipment, perfect camera settings, a cooperative bird, and the aforementioned luck. It's okay if the wings look blurry in your best hummer shots. After all, the wings are moving at something like 80 beats per second!

10. BE PATIENT. Sitting there quietly waiting and watching can be hard to do—for me it's nearly impossible. But when I know the reward is a sweet shot of a male hummingbird in nice light, gorget glowing brightly, I find the inner strength to be still. —BT

Appendix 2: Photographing Butterflies

AS YOU ATTRACT BUTTERFLIES to your backyard, you may discover that photography assists in their identification or enables you to share their beauty with others. Patience and willingness to experiment can result in stunning butterfly images. To master butterfly photography, you'll need reliable equipment and you'll want to perfect techniques that ensure great photos.

Simple Equipment

Excellent digital "point-and-shoot" cameras are currently available at very reasonable prices. What are now standard features would have been unimaginable to professional photographers only a decade ago. A versatile digital model in the $250 to $500 price range should fulfill the needs of most casual butterfly photographers. Digital cameras record their images on small memory cards that are ultimately downloaded into computers for editing and printing. If you plan to travel widely as you photograph, you may need an extra memory card or a portable storage device to hold large numbers of images until you can process them.

To photograph adult butterflies successfully, choose a camera that includes an integral lens with magnifying power equal to or greater than 8x binoculars (equivalent to a 400-mm telephoto lens). Image stabilization is essential if you take pictures without a tripod. For photos of butterfly eggs, small caterpillars, or extreme flower close-ups, select a camera that also includes a "super-macro" feature—the capacity to focus as close as 1 inch. To render sharp prints, the camera should capture 10- to 12-MB images.

All major camera manufacturers currently offer models with self-contained lenses that meet these requirements. To select the brand that best meets your needs, visit a camera store where you can compare several models side by side. Test each model by photographing a butterfly-sized subject as close as it's possible to focus and by aiming a few feet away at something the size of a butterfly. Compare how well each camera performs these tasks by magnifying the images on the viewing screen and scrutinizing how sharp they are. Also note how each model feels in your hands and how intuitive it is to operate.

FOR VERSATILITY, serious butterfly photographers often choose DSLR cameras with the capacity to accept interchangeable lenses.

Bigger Equipment

Highly motivated amateur and professional butterfly photographers select digital single lens reflex (DSLR) equipment. This means the camera body will accept interchangeable lenses keyed to various tasks, such as macro, portrait, wide angle, and telephoto. DSLR equipment is more complicated, weighs more, and costs more than point-and-shoot models. To capture tack-sharp images, you will need a tripod to stabilize the camera and lens. Camera manufacturers offer a bewildering array of such equipment, so visit online nature photography tutorials or peruse nature photography books and magazines before making a major purchase. Another excellent source is the North American Nature Photography Association (www.nanpa. org), which hosts a comprehensive annual instructional summit and trade show.

A DSLR camera body enables the capture of images by regulating the speed at which the photograph is taken, the amount of light that enters through the lens opening, and variables such as exposure compensation and automated bracketing. As a camera body manages more complex tasks, it becomes heavier and more confusing. Full-time professional photographers need top-of-the-line bodies, but most of us do very well with entry- or mid-level DSLR models. They accomplish all necessary functions expertly without the extra bells, whistles, and confusion. Do make certain the body you choose has a large viewing screen, easy-to-use controls, and feels comfortable in your hands.

Invest the dollars you save on the DSLR body in the best lenses you can afford. Premium glass and optical coatings add incredible sharpness and pizzazz to your images. If you are serious about butterfly photography, you will need a macro lens that allows life size (1:1) reproduction. Short telephoto (100 mm or greater) macros allow approach from greater distances and thus are less likely to startle your quarry. Zoom macro-telephotos allow reasonable approach plus the capacity to tweak composition with subtle framing adjustments. For dedicated macro users, they are worth the extra expense.

Technique

Good photographs are not easy to obtain. In many situations, you will need to stalk your subject, select the correct camera settings, compose a pleasing image that shows your subject in a complimentary background, focus sharply, and trip the shutter without vibrating the rest of the camera—all before the butterfly flutters away. In order to achieve this, you will need to practice with your equipment and understand how it works before going into the field.

Begin by reading the camera's manual and repeatedly doing the processes or functions you require until they become second nature. You don't have to photograph a live butterfly. Make a paper cutout, or practice by photographing a colorful flower about the same size as a butterfly. Look carefully at your results to see if the image is sharp. Can you improve the composition or find a more pleasing background? Do you understand how to use features such as exposure compensation? Once you have mastered the camera, delete the practice images and head outside!

Start by trying to photograph butterflies as they bask quietly with wings spread to absorb warmth. You'll find them most easily during overcast weather or on cool mornings. Approach slowly and quietly, taking care that your shadow does not fall across the butterfly. If you find a cooperative subject, try vertical and horizontal compositions.

For the best overall sharpness of entire wing surfaces, position yourself so the subject's wings are parallel to the front of the lens. If there is enough natural light, select a high f-number (f-22 or f-32) for best depth of field. You can also adjust the ISO setting to a higher number (ISO 200, 400, 800), which allows the camera's sensor to capture the scene with less light input. There will be a point of diminishing returns, however, when the dim light will create distractingly grainy images. Check your photos on the viewing screen, and if they aren't good quality, readjust the ISO downward until the graininess disappears.

It's a good idea to photograph butterflies as they nectar on flowers. On sunny days, venture into the backyard or seek places in the wild where butterflies feed and rest. Be aware that warm butterflies move faster than chilly ones, and good in-flight images are exceedingly hard to obtain. That shouldn't stop you from trying a few flight shots, but you will be more successful if you find a flower with abundant nectar where a butterfly lingers to feed. For sharp side views of butterflies that hold their wings upright, stoop down and compose so the wing surface is parallel to the front of the lens.

Photos using natural light are ideal for rendering the best color of butterfly wing scales and including background habitats. But if you are employing heavy DSLR equipment, you'll do best with a tripod (or monopod) to steady the weight. If trying to hand-hold a telephoto lens, set your shutter speed equal to or faster than the fraction made by putting 1/focal length of the lens. (Example: minimum shutter speed for a 400-mm lens is 1/400 second.)

Another method for hand-holding big macro or telephoto lenses is using fill flash to add supplemental illumination. Many pros mount two small flash units with adjustable power settings on a slim bracket that attaches to the bottom of the camera, or they connect a ring flash in front of the lens. The goal is to allow ambient light to expose the background properly, then adjust flash settings for just enough pop to add crisp detail to the butterfly subject. If your photos with a rig like this show the butterfly in garish light and a black background, the flash is overpowering natural light. Decrease the flash output, and if necessary, adjust the ISO upward. Experiment with various setting ratios to achieve the correct balance.

You might also become interested in documenting butterfly life stages, such as eggs, hatching caterpillars, or pupation. This is easiest if you make a screened box in which to raise caterpillars while they roam potted host plants. Basic photo equipment will include a tripod, macro lens, and flash units. To adequately document very tiny subjects, you will need specialized close-up attachments or bellows, which can increase image sizes as much as 10 times life size. To master flash and extreme close-up techniques, consult books on insect and macro photography, visit on-line photography tutorials, or enroll in a photo workshop that specializes in insect imagery.

The desire to photograph butterflies may lead you to diverse habitats near your home or to worldwide travels in quest of unusual species. You can also photograph exotic beauties in butterfly aviaries, which offer additional opportunities to practice techniques and occasionally capture behavioral photos—such as butterfly pairs mating or females laying eggs—that are difficult to see in the wild.

Whether you photograph solely in your backyard or roam the world in search of new species, remember to edit your images ruthlessly and learn from your best shots so you can continue improving your skills. —*CT*

FOR ENTIRE wing-surface sharpness, stoop low and compose so the upright wings of butterflies such as this great spangled fritillary are parallel to the front of the lens. This exposure was made with a combination of natural light illuminating the sky in the background and minimal fill flash highlighting the flower and butterfly.

Resources

BOOKS: Hummingbirds

Day, Susan, Ron Rovansek, and Jack Griggs. *The Wildlife Gardener's Guide to Hummingbirds and Songbirds from the Tropics.* New York: HarperCollins, 2003.

Donnelly, David B. *Creating Your Backyard Bird Garden.* Marietta, OH: Bird Watcher's Digest, 2008.

McKinley, Michael. *All about Attracting Hummingbirds and Butterflies.* Des Moines, IA: Meredith Books, 2001.

Newfield, Nancy L., and Barbara Nielsen. *Hummingbird Gardens.* Shelburne, VT: Chapters Publishing, 1996.

Peterson, Roger Tory. *Peterson Field Guide to the Birds of North America.* Boston: Houghton Mifflin, 2008.

Schneck, Marcus. *Your Backyard Wildlife Garden.* Emmaus, PA: Rodale Press, 1992.

Stokes, Donald, and Lillian Stokes. *The Hummingbird Book.* New York: Little, Brown, 1987.

Toops, Connie. *Hummingbirds: Jewels in Flight.* Stillwater, MN: Voyageur Press, 1992.

Williamson, Sheri L. *Hummingbirds of North America.* Boston: Houghton Mifflin, 2001.

Zickefoose, Julie, and Bird Watcher's Digest. *Natural Gardening for Birds.* Emmaus, PA: Rodale Press, 2001.

BOOKS: Butterflies

Allen, Thomas J., Jim P. Brock, and Jeffrey Glassberg. *Caterpillars in the Field and Garden.* New York: Oxford University Press, 2005.

Brock, Jim P., and Kenn Kaufman. *Butterflies of North America.* Boston: Houghton Mifflin, 2003.

Cech, Rick, and Guy Tudor. *Butterflies of the East Coast.* Princeton, NJ: Princeton University Press, 2005.

Daniels, Jaret C. *Your Florida Guide to Butterfly Gardening.* Gainesville: University Press of Florida, 2000.

Feltwell, John. *The Natural History of Butterflies.* New York: Facts on File, 1986.

Glassberg, Jeffrey. *Butterflies Through Binoculars: The East.* New York: Oxford University Press, 1999.

———. *Butterflies Through Binoculars: The West.* New York: Oxford University Press, 2001.

———. *Enjoying Butterflies More.* Marietta, OH: Bird Watcher's Digest, 1995.

Haggard, Peter, and Judy Haggard. *Insects of the Pacific Northwest.* Portland, OR: Timber Press, 2006.

Mitchell, Robert T., and Herbert S. Zim. *Butterflies and Moths.* New York: Golden Press, 1964.

Mizejewski, David. *National Wildlife Federation: Attracting Birds, Butterflies and Other Backyard Wildlife.* Upper Saddle River, NJ: Creative Homeowner, 2004.

Opler, Paul A., and Vichai Malikul. *A Field Guide to Eastern Butterflies.* Boston: Houghton Mifflin, 1998.

Opler, Paul A., and Amy Bartlett Wright. *A Field Guide to Western Butterflies.* Boston: Houghton Mifflin, 1999.

Pyle, Robert Michael. *The Audubon Society Field Guide to North American Butterflies.* New York: Alfred A. Knopf, 1981.

Roth, Sally. *Attracting Butterflies and Hummingbirds to Your Backyard.* Emmaus, PA: Rodale Press, 2001.

Schneck, Marcus. *Butterflies: How to Identify and Attract Them to Your Garden.* Emmaus, PA: Rodale Press, 1990.

Sutton, Patricia Taylor, and Clay Sutton. *How to Spot Butterflies.* Boston: Houghton Mifflin, 1999.

Tekulsky, Mathew. *The Butterfly Garden.* Boston: Harvard Common Press, 1985.

Wagner, David L. *Caterpillars of Eastern North America.* Princeton, NJ: Princeton University Press, 2005.

Wildlife Viewing Program, Environment Yukon. "Yukon Butterflies." Whitehorse: Government of Yukon, 2005.

Wright, Amy Bartlett. *Peterson First Guide to Caterpillars of North America.* Boston: Houghton Mifflin, 1993.

Xerces Society, the. *Butterfly Gardening.* San Francisco: Sierra Club Books, 1990.

BOOKS: Plant References

Brenzel, Kathleen Norris, ed. *Sunset Western Garden Book.* Menlo Park, CA: Sunset Publishing, 2001.

Brockman, C. Frank. *Trees of North America.* New York: Golden Press, 1986.

Craighead, John J., Frank C. Craighead, Jr., and Ray J. Davis. *A Field Guide to Rocky Mountain Wildflowers*. Boston: Houghton Mifflin, 1963.

Halpin, Anne, ed. *Sunset Northeastern Garden Book*. Menlo Park, CA: Sunset Publishing, 2001.

Loughmiller, Campbell, and Lynn Loughmiller. *Texas Wildflowers*. Austin: University of Texas Press, 1984.

Niehaus, Theodore F., and Charles L. Ripper. *A Field Guide to Pacific States Wildflowers*. Boston: Houghton Mifflin, 1976.

Niehaus, Theodore F., Charles L. Ripper, and Virginia Savage. *A Field Guide to Southwestern and Texas Wildflowers*. Boston: Houghton Mifflin, 1984.

Peterson, Roger Tory, and Margaret McKenny. *A Field Guide to Wildflowers of Northeastern and North-central North America*. Boston: Houghton Mifflin, 1968.

Petrides, George A. *A Field Guide to Trees and Shrubs*. Boston: Houghton Mifflin, 1972.

Tallamy, Douglas W. *Bringing Nature Home*. Portland, OR: Timber Press, 2007.

Websites

http://butterfly.ucdavis.edu

Professor Arthur Shapiro, butterfly research, University of California, Davis

http://plants.usda.gov

USDA, Natural Resources Conservation Service, Plant Database

http://www.calflora.org

Calflora—Wild California Plants for Conservation

http://www.floridata.com

Florida Plant Database

http://www.flowervisitors.info/index.htm

Insect Visitors of Illinois Wildflowers, website by John Hilty

http://www.hummingbirds.net/

Operated by hummingbird enthusiast Lanny Chambers, this site has a volume of basic hummingbird information, including videos, migration arrival maps, and answers to frequently asked questions.

http://www.hummingbirdsociety.org

    The Hummingbird Society is an organization for people who love hummingbirds. It also sponsors hummingbird research and conservation efforts.

http://www.hummingbirdsplus.org/

    Operated by the Hummer/Bird Study Group founded by hummer researchers Bob and Martha Sargent, this site shares the insights and discoveries from the organization's banding and research activities.

http://www.invasive.org

    Center for Invasive Species and Ecosystem Health, University of Georgia

http://www.monarchwatch.org

    Monarch Watch, the Kansas Biological Survey, University of Kansas

http://www.naba.org

    North American Butterfly Association; "Publications" tab includes a checklist of North American butterflies

http://www.njaudubon.org/sectionBackyardHabitat/welcome.aspx

    New Jersey Audubon, hummingbird and butterfly gardening

http://www.sabo.org

    The Southeastern Arizona Bird Observatory site is hosted by hummingbird experts Sheri Williamson and Tom Wood. Great hummingbird information and advice, plus tips for where to watch hummingbirds in southeastern Arizona.

http://www.texasento.net/leps.htm

    Texas Butterflies and Moths

http://www.usna.usda.gov/Hardzone/ushzmap.html

    U.S. National Arboretum, USDA Plant Hardiness Zone Map

http://www.wildflower.org

    Native Plant Information Network, Lady Bird Johnson Wildflower Center, University of Texas, Austin

Humnet Listserv

    This is an automated listserv for hummingbird enthusiasts and researchers to share information. To subscribe, send an email message to listserv@listserv.LSU.edu with "subscribe HUMNET-L YOUR NAME" as the body of the message.

Photography and Illustration Credits

Glenn Bartley 107 left

Jim Berry v

Bill Bouton 227 bottom right, 236, 240, 248

Richard Day / Daybreak Imagery 24, 90, 93, 194, 249

Larry Ditto 1, 20, 21, 104 left, 111 top, 114, 119, 141, 142, 224 bottom, 227 top left, 245, 272

Jim Gallion 217

Phyllis Greenberg 131

Maslowski Wildlife Productions 3, 7, 8, 23, 30, 36 bottom, 37 top, 91, 104 right, 116 bottom

Robert McCaw 32 bottom, 103 center left, 109 right, 163 bottom, 209, 213 bottom, 225 center, 230, 260, 262

Charles Melton 4, 5, 6, 10, 13 bottom, 14, 17, 22, 29, 103 top left, 103 center right, 103 bottom right, 105 top, 105 bottom, 107 right, 108 top, 108 bottom, 110, 111 bottom, 112 right, 115 top, 115 bottom, 116 top, 117 top, 117 bottom, 118 top, 118 bottom, 122 bottom, 223 bottom, 224 second down, 235, 255, 266

Claire Mullen 9, 37 bottom

Rachel Pennington 132 bottom

Jeff Pippen 128, 215, 224 top, 242, 243, 244

Kevin Pope 13 top

Mike Reese 239

Bjorn Rorslett 162 top, 162 bottom

Hugh P. Smith 18, 19, 25 bottom, 45, 50 bottom, 56, 60 top, 70, 103 bottom left, 106 top, 109 left, 113, 170, 185

Bill Thompson III 27, 31, 32 top, 33, 35, 36 top, 38, 268, 269

Connie Toops 16, 25 top, 40, 41, 42, 43, 44, 46, 47, 50 top, 51, 54, 55, 57, 58, 60 bottom, 62, 63, 64, 65, 66, 68, 72, 74, 76, 78, 80, 82, 84, 86, 88, 106 bottom, 112 left, 121 top, 121 bottom, 122 top, 123, 124 top, 124 bottom left, 124 bottom right, 125 left, 125 right, 127, 129, 130, 132 top, 134, 135, 136, 137, 139 top, 139 bottom, 143, 144 top, 144 center, 144 bottom, 145 top, 145 bottom, 146, 147, 148, 149, 150, 151 top, 151 bottom, 152, 153 top, 153 bottom, 154, 155, 156, 158, 160, 161, 163 top, 165, 167, 168, 171, 172, 173, 174 top, 174 bottom, 176, 177, 180, 181, 188, 191, 195, 199, 202, 206, 207, 208, 211, 212, 213 top, 214, 218, 221, 222, 223 top, 224 third down, 225 top, 225 bottom, 227 center left, 227 center right, 227 bottom left, 228, 229, 231, 232, 233, 234, 237, 238, 241, 246, 247, 250, 251, 252, 253, 254, 256, 257, 258, 259 left, 259 right, 261, 263, 264, 265, 267, 275

Julie Zickefoose 28, 34, 94

Index